BLACK AMERICA SERIES

FAYETTEVILLE
NORTH CAROLINA

BLACK AMERICA SERIES

FAYETTEVILLE
NORTH CAROLINA

Fred Whitted

ARCADIA
PUBLISHING

ISBN 978-0-7385-0593-0

Published by Arcadia Publishing
Charleston, South Carolina

Printed in the United States of America

Library of Congress Catalog Card Number: 00-104867

For all general information contact Arcadia Publishing at:
Telephone 843-853-2070
Fax 843-853-0044
E-Mail sales@arcadiapublishing.com
For customer service and orders:
Toll-Free 1-888-313-2665

Visit us on the Internet at www.arcadiapublishing.com

Contents

Acknowledgments

No publication of this magnitude is accomplished by an individual. This was not only a labor of love but was also the result of the labor of a number of individuals and institutions. What is important is that connections were made and the end result is that, finally, there is published documentation of the history of blacks in Fayetteville and Cumberland County.

First, there are those who contributed photographs of themselves, family members, and friends. This group is too numerous to name individually, but my heart-felt gratitude goes out to each of you. The same applies to those who provided biographical and historical information on those featured herein.

There is a second group of people who made significant contributions in the form of pictures and information on several individuals. Special thanks go to the following: Fayetteville State University archivist Paul Baker, Marion Crowe and "La-La" Bland of the Fayetteville State Sports Information Office, Adrian Ferguson of the Winston-Salem State Sports Information Office, Kyle Serber of the North Carolina Central Sports Information Office, the University of North Carolina Sports Information Office, the Minnesota Vikings, the New York Jets, the Kansas City Chiefs, the Green Bay Packers, the San Diego Chargers, Mrs. Daisy Maxwell and Charles Broadwell of the *Fayetteville Observer*, Mr. Ike Walker, the North Carolina Archives, Betty Rucker of the 82nd Airborne Museum, the crew from the North Carolina Room of the Cumberland County Public Library—Wanda Hunter, Arletha Campbell, Rhonda Williams, and Joyce Codrington. All of you helped to make this book happen.

INTRODUCTION

Fayetteville grew out of two villages, Campbellton and Cross Creek, into a thriving city on the banks of the Cape Fear River. Over the past half century, the greatest industry has been the military presence that was built up during World War II. Prior to that, agriculture was the largest employer, with a sprinkling of light industry. The military presence has created a situation that makes Fayetteville and Cumberland County one of the most racially mixed cities on the East Coast. There are people here from nearly every ethnic group in the world.

The black community grew out of a mixture of freemen and slaves who populated the area prior to the Civil War. There was a significant population of free blacks prior to the war. The Lomax, Harris, Chesnutt, and Learey families played a significant role in the daily life of the city, before and after the Civil War. Most of them left for a time in the 1850s to get away from the systematic oppression that was so prevalent in the South. A number of them would return after the war and become part of the power structure of the city and the state.

Still, their contributions to the community have been great. They were divinely positioned to help make Fayetteville what it is today. It was a black man, Henry Evans, who built the first church in the city (it was used by both races). He preached the gospel to a town that was being built on the backs of slaves. On the surface, he was just passing through town, but actually, he was sent to the city. Evans brought the gospel to both blacks and whites, and was subsequently run out of town on several occasions, but withstood the threats and continued to preach in the woods. His efforts are memorialized in Evans Metropolitan AME Zion Church.

During Reconstruction, blacks represented Fayetteville in the state assembly and on the county commission. As a race, they withstood the ravages of the post-Reconstruction era, in which they were disenfranchised by Jim Crow laws and racism. Fayetteville was and remains a city of great diversity, and a city of great separation. Because of the military influence, many neighborhoods are mixed. There are also a number of areas that are easily recognized as black neighborhoods. The original black areas were along Wilmington Road and Campbell Avenue, stretching to Gillespie Street. There was also another area along North Street. The section around Fayetteville State University is known as the College Heights community, which grew after the university was built on what was once farmland during the early twentieth century. Until the late 1960s, this area was the black center of town. The university, in its 133 years, has become a beacon for knowledge to the city, to the state, and to the nation. It provided education at a time when the city and county refused to provide education for blacks or whites. At one point, Fayetteville State Normal School was working so well that there were more blacks who could write their names than whites. This led to the development of the local school system for whites.

The local black population has been an important part of the success of Fayetteville. For years, they labored in the background because of legal restrictions. This population was a sleeping giant that would later deliver the city from its own bigotry and open doors that had once been shut. Until this occurred, Fayetteville did not grow.

Fayetteville is now the fifth largest metropolitan area in North Carolina. It boasts a black population of roughly 40 percent. Overall, there is racial harmony in the community, although there have been a number of incidents that have interrupted the general peace. Most notable, in 1995, three white supremacists murdered two black citizens as part of their initiation into a white supremacist group; all three were convicted. Also, there are ongoing problems with local law enforcement and the black community—primarily concerning the lack of black officers and the treatment of black officers on the force by ranking officers who tend to be white. Most recently, there were a number of threatening letters sent to historically black colleges and universities (HBCUs) that originated in Fayetteville.

Historically, proper respect has not been given to a people who lack knowledge of themselves. To date, the history of Fayetteville's black community has been compiled like patches for a quilt, but never put together. This book is an effort to begin bringing these varied pieces together. There are many more people, places, and events than this work could hope to contain, and it is my hope that this book will get things rolling so that a more complete history will be compiled and published.

This book offers a pictorial sample of Fayetteville's rich black history. The discussion of Fayetteville's black history could go back as far as the late 1600s. Unfortunately, there is little visual record of that era. There were no cameras, only paintings and drawings; most of that was destroyed in the fire of 1831. We can only imagine how Henry Evans actually looked.

Antebellum history has direct ties to Evans Chapel. Following the war, things sprang forth from Evans Metropolitan AME Zion Church. Before the Howard School building was constructed, classes were held in the basement of the church. Once the Howard School was established, it quickly became part of the center of life for the greater Cumberland County area, making it the center of education for the southeastern seaboard of North Carolina. It remained the center of education for the black community even into the twentieth century.

Once Fayetteville State moved to its present location, the school actually extended the boundaries of the city. At one time, the College Heights area, to include the grounds of the university, was all farmland. Fueled by the university, the area would become the new center of black life. Eventually, the addition of the military base would also help to expand the economic base for the black community.

In this visual history, you will meet many of the people who have helped to make Fayetteville and Cumberland County the great places that they are today. Although not perfect, by any stretch of the imagination, it is a great place to live and grow.

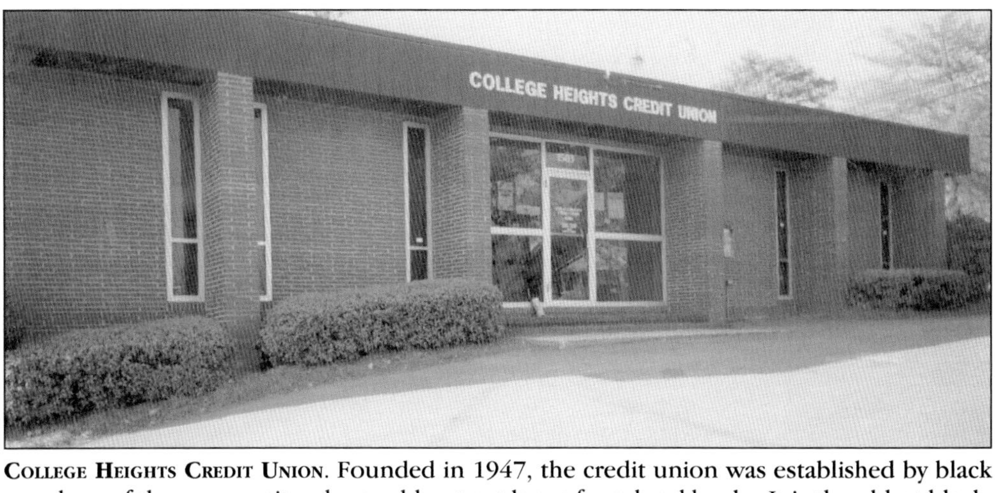

College Heights Credit Union. Founded in 1947, the credit union was established by black members of the community who could not get loans from local banks. It is the oldest black-owned financial institution in Eastern North Carolina.

One

Early Years

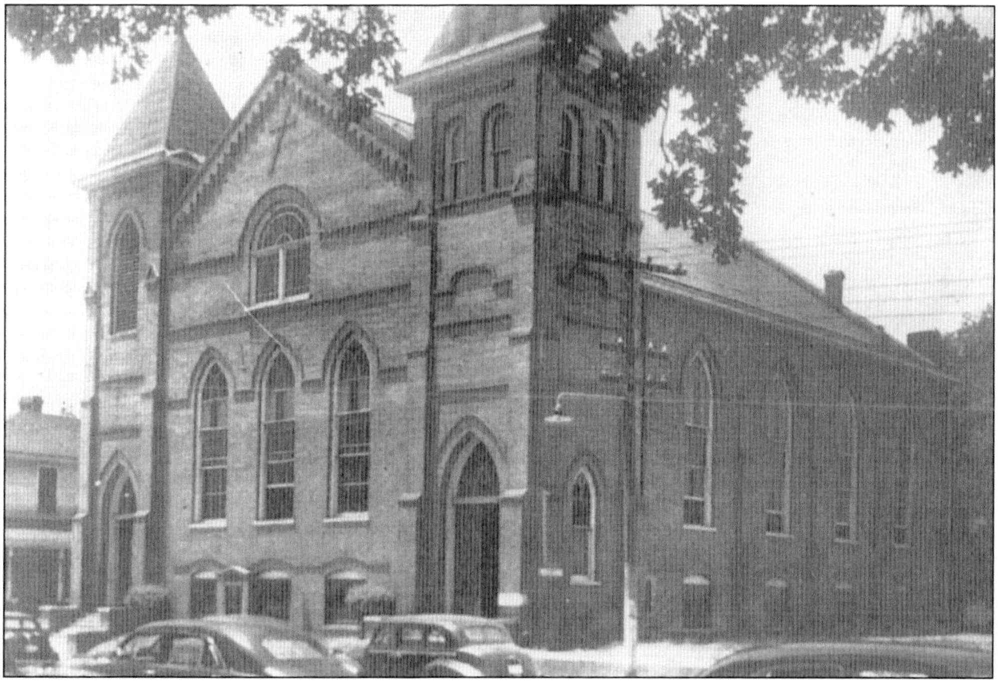

Evans Metropolitan AME Zion Church. Evans Metropolitan AME Zion Church is the oldest institution in Fayetteville related to the black community. Founded by Henry Evans in 1796 as the African Chapel, it was the first church established in the city by either race. At one point, the African Chapel served both blacks and whites. The original structure burned and was rebuilt by Evans. The second building was destroyed in the fire of 1831 and was rebuilt by the congregation. In 1864, J.W. Hood was named pastor. After the Civil War, the church became affiliated with the AME Zion Church, of which Hood would later be named bishop. The church housed a school for blacks before the Howard School was founded. One of its pastors, Cicero Harris, would later found Livingstone College in Salisbury, North Carolina.

Evans remains one of the outstanding churches in Zion, and it thrives today under the leadership of Dr. L.A. Miller. With a congregation containing a rich mixture of maturity and youth, it continues to play a major role in the ministry of the Fayetteville community and seeks to meet the needs of its people. As a member of the Zion church, it also has an international reach through its missionary department.

Presently, Evans is in a year of bicentennial celebration. Few churches in America can boast two centuries of delivering the Word of God and serving people.

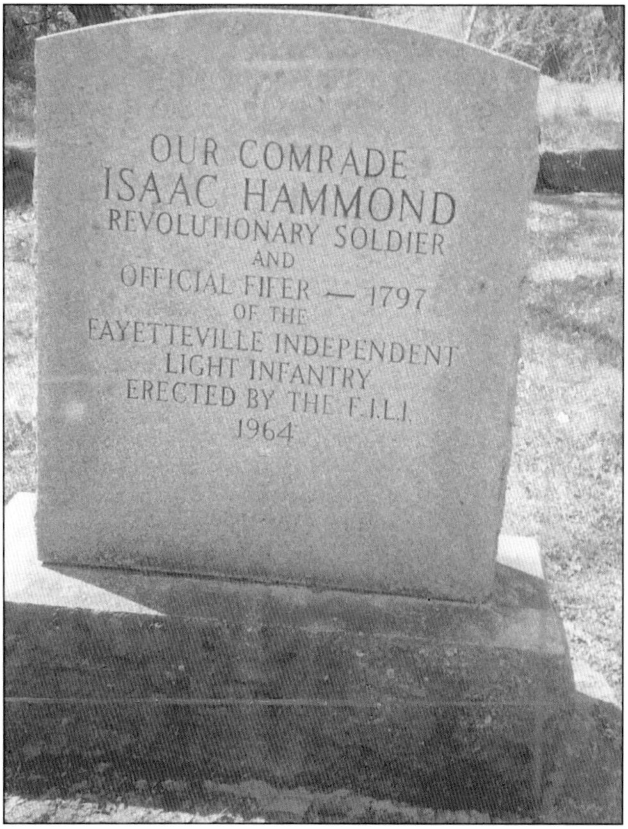

Isaac Hammond's Memorial. Hammond was a well-known and well-respected free man of color in Fayetteville. He became a member of the Fayetteville Independent Light Infantry at its beginning in 1793, when he was just a teenager. Hammond served as a fifer for the militia for nearly 40 years. Hammond was also a highly respected member of the community. It was thought that he had so much clout with the black population that whites feared that he was influencing local elections unfairly. The truth was that Hammond was a great leader, one who had the best interests of the greater community at heart. During the visit of the Marques de LaFayette, Hammond was one of several veterans who greeted him.

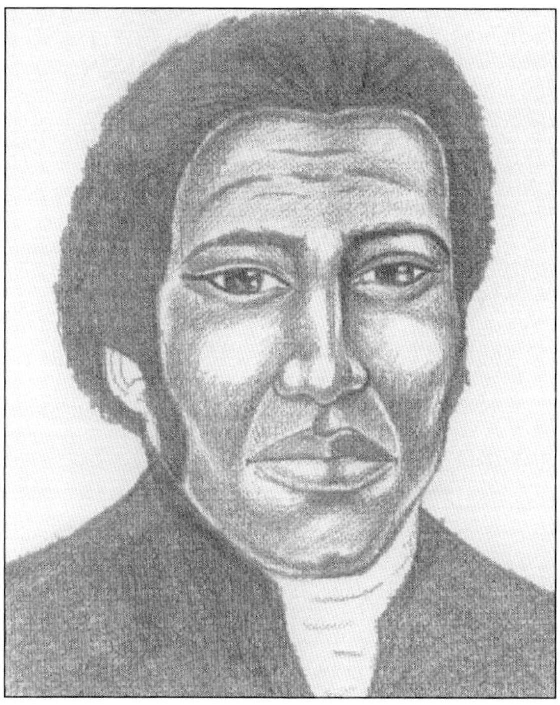

Henry Evans. Henry Evans was a preacher and shoemaker who was passing through Fayetteville on his way to South Carolina. Seeing the condition of blacks, he began holding church services and eventually built the first church, which was called the African Chapel. So dedicated to the cause of God, Evans swam the Cape Fear River to bring boards to build the chapel. Evans died in 1810.

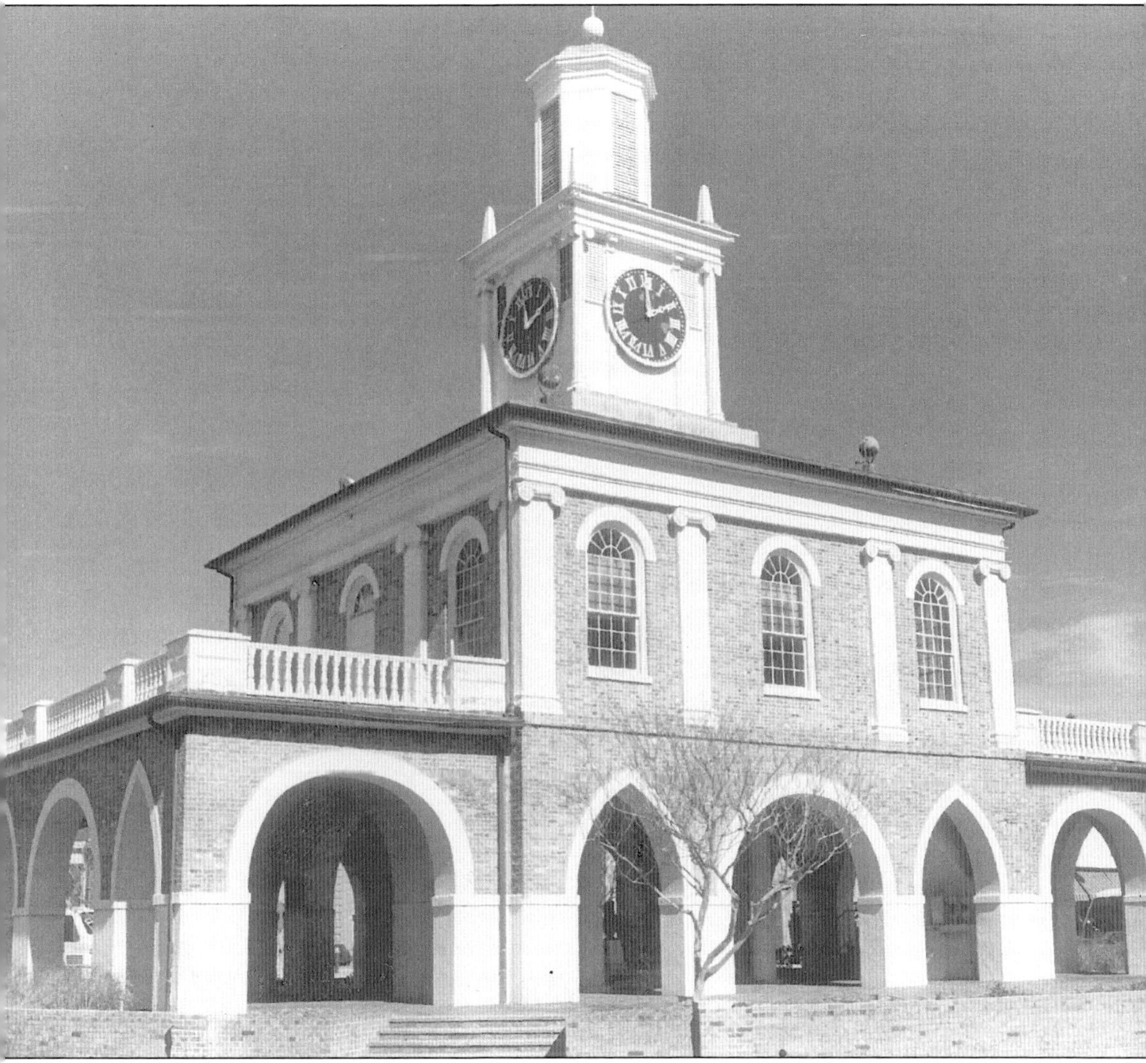

Market House. The Market House is the best-known building in the city of Fayetteville. It serves as the symbol of the city, but it has had a very checkered past since its construction in the late 1700s. In truth, it has served as the town hall, state house, courthouse, and town market. It is in the role of the town market where the controversy lies. There has been an ongoing argument as to whether this was a slave market. In essence, it was a matter of semantics. Some have called it the city market, or the produce market, and say that slaves were sold only as part of estates sales. Others have called it the slave market because slaves were sold, for whatever reason.

As the town market, it was used to sell all manner of "merchandise" of the day. Among that "merchandise" were slaves owned by various citizens of the town and county. Slaves, or "chattel," were sold as part of estate sales and on the general market at the Market House on a number of occasions. There are advertisements in the *Fayetteville Observer* that announce slaves for sale—there is no mention of estates, as in other advertisements.

The present building was constructed in 1831, and it was most likely built by slaves, who made up the majority of the masons and carpenters at the time. It did serve in the selling of slaves in Fayetteville, although it was not the primary location for the slave trade.

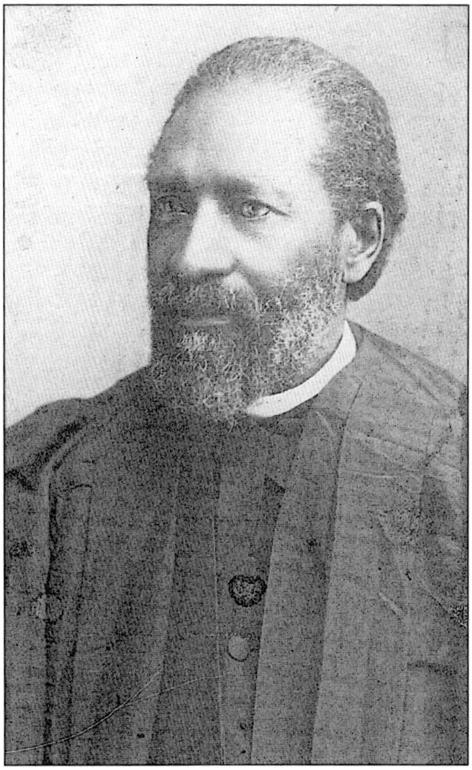

Right Reverend James W. Hood. Bishop Hood was born in Kennett Township, Chester County, Pennsylvania. He was self-educated, although his mother did teach him grammar and to speak publicly. He delivered his first anti-slavery speech at the age of 15, speaking eloquently and prophetically against the Dred Scott decision, the Fugitive Slave law, and the Missouri Compromise. He served the Episcopacy for 46 years.

Bishop Hood had great concern for the education of young blacks. He served on the committee, along with James N. Lee and George C. Scurlock, that petitioned the Peabody Fund for aid for the Howard School in 1875 that enabled the school to supply free books and other materials and helped to defray the costs of student travel. Hood Hall, Hood Memorial AME Zion Church, and Hood Street are all named in his honor.

Hiram Rhodes Revels. Born in Fayetteville, North Carolina, to a black Baptist minister and a Scottish mother, Revels was destined to make history. Unable to receive an education in North Carolina because of his race, Revels began preaching as a teenager but was not ordained until 1845. He met opposition and was imprisoned in 1854 for preaching to blacks. During the Civil War, he helped organize the first two Maryland regiments for the United States Army. He helped the Freedmen's Bureau establish schools, served as chaplain, and was assistant to the provost marshal in Vicksburg. In 1868, he was elected alderman in Natchez. During Reconstruction, he was the first free black to be seated in the United States Senate when he was elected to complete the term that had been initiated by Jefferson Davis.

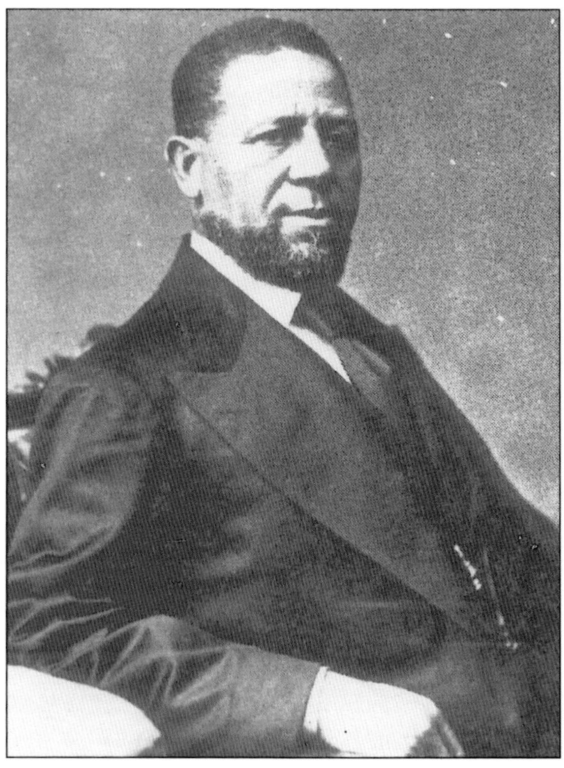

William Hooper Councill. Born of slave parents in Fayetteville, North Carolina, in 1848, Councill would spend most of his life in Alabama. During the Civil War, he befriended a chaplain in the Union Army who taught him to read and write. In 1868, he passed the Alabama State Teachers' Examination and later founded the first school for blacks in Jackson and Madison Counties. Councill was the founder and principal of Huntsville State Normal School, which became a land-grant institution in 1890. Councill was the first black president of a college in the State of Alabama and held that position for 35 years. Councill died in 1909 from medical complications of his diabetes.

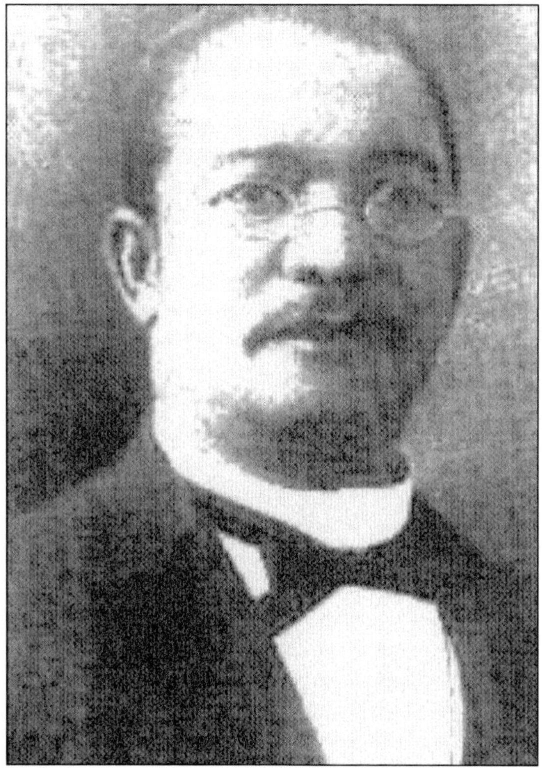

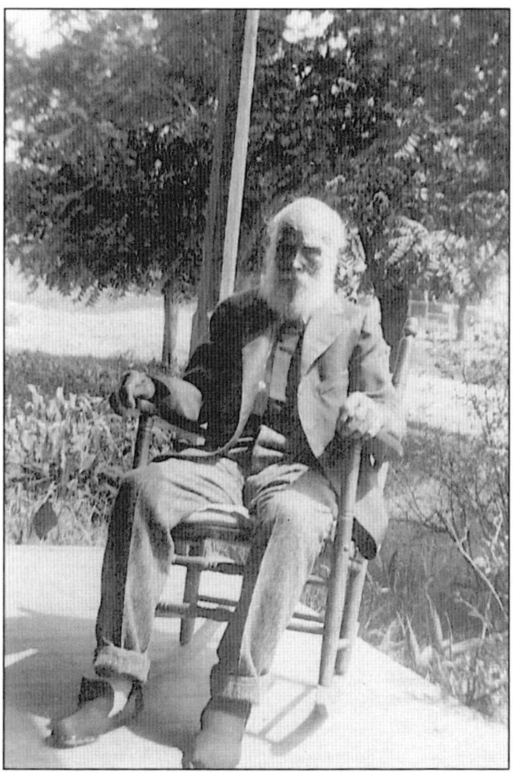

Andrew Jackson Chesnutt. Chesnutt spent the early portion of his life in Fayetteville before migrating to Ohio along with other free blacks from the area. During his time in Ohio, he married and had a son in 1858 named Charles Waddell, who would become one of the first prominent blacks writers in literature. Chesnutt returned to Fayetteville around 1866, opening and operating a store, a transfer business, and a farm. Chesnutt became one of several blacks in the Fayetteville area of means during the Reconstruction days, for he was one of the men who put up the $140 to purchase the land for the Howard School. Chesnutt died in 1920. Two of his daughters, Anne and Sarah, rose to prominence in education as teachers. A school was named for Anne, who served as superintendent of schools.

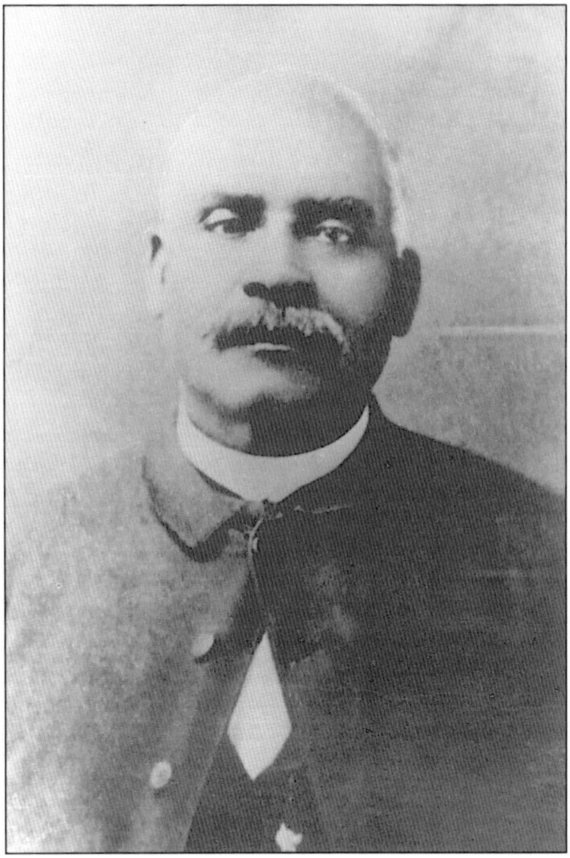

Reverend Robert Simmons. Reverend Simmons, a preacher and operator of a grocery store, was a local leader, one of six who helped to raise the $140 that was used to buy the property on which the Howard School was built. Reverend Simmons also served on the board that was set up to maintain the school.

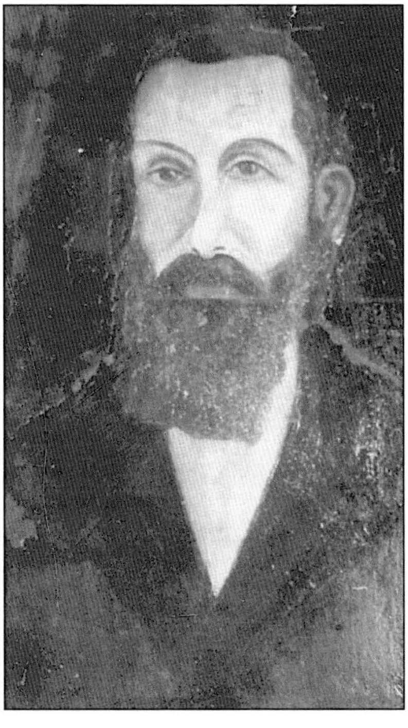

Robert Harris. Robert Harris is possibly the most vital component in the success of the Howard School and the founding of Fayetteville State Normal School. Born in 1839, he moved to Ohio in 1848. In 1864, Harris moved to Virginia, and in November 1866, he came back to Fayetteville to take charge of the fledgling school for blacks. Upon his return, Harris found struggling schools that could barely keep their doors open. He saw the need to put the school under one roof and led the move to acquire Freedmen's Bureau financial support for the building of the new school. Harris and others were able to convince the state to designate the Howard School as the state's first state-supported normal school for blacks in 1877. Harris was named principal and served until his death in 1880.

Right Reverend Cicero R. Harris. Cicero was the younger brother of Robert Harris. In 1866, he and his brother returned to Fayetteville, where they founded the Harris School in the basement of the Evans Chapel (Metropolitan) Church. The school was recognized for the quality of its students. After the Howard School was established, Harris continued to serve as a teacher and was licensed to preach in 1872. He was awarded a doctor of divinity degree by Howard University in 1891. Bishop Harris served the Episcopacy for 29 years, retiring in 1916. He died in 1917.

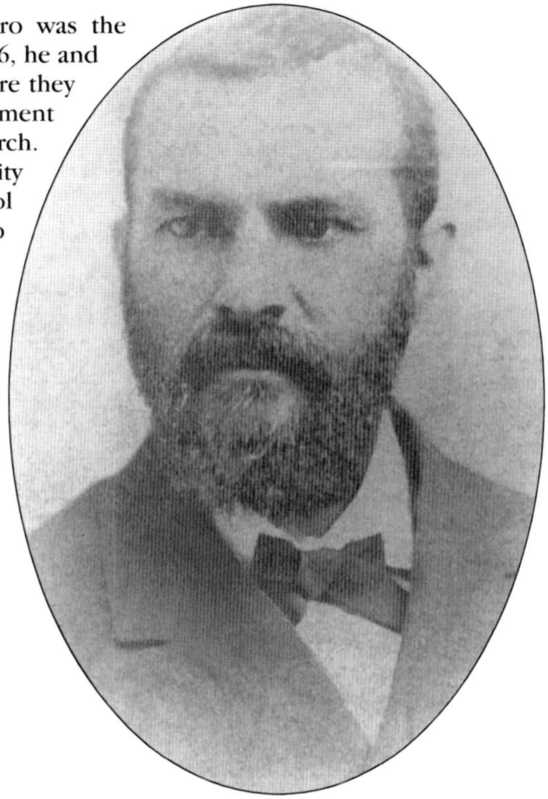

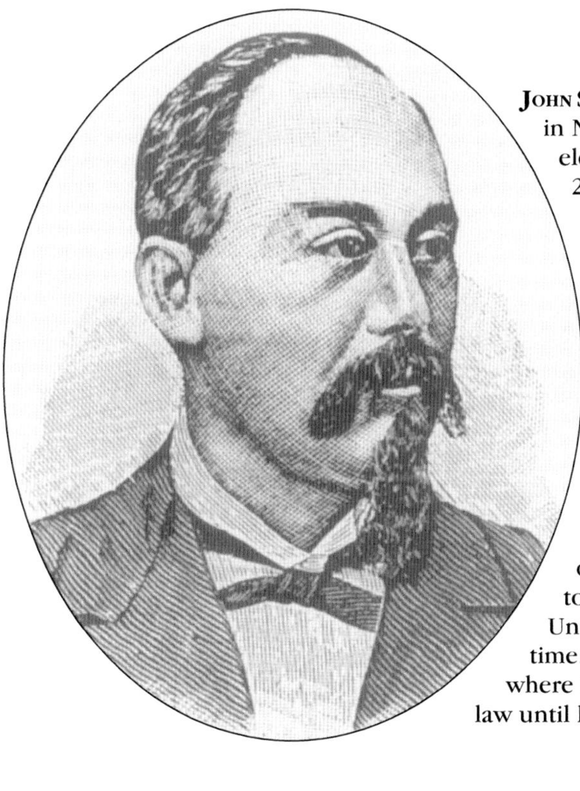

John S. Leary. One of the youngest legislators in North Carolina history, John Leary was elected to the state legislature at age 24. He was also one of the first blacks elected to represent Cumberland County in Raleigh. The son of Cumberland County's first black county commissioner, Matthew Leary, John Leary attended Howard University and was one of the early blacks to be admitted to the North Carolina Bar after the Civil War. He was Fayetteville's first black lawyer. Leary, along with Isham Swett, were elected to the general assembly at a time when they were at the forefront of the Republican Party. Leary helped to establish the law school at Shaw University and served as its dean for a time. In 1892, Leary moved to Charlotte, where he devoted his time to the practice of law until his death in 1904.

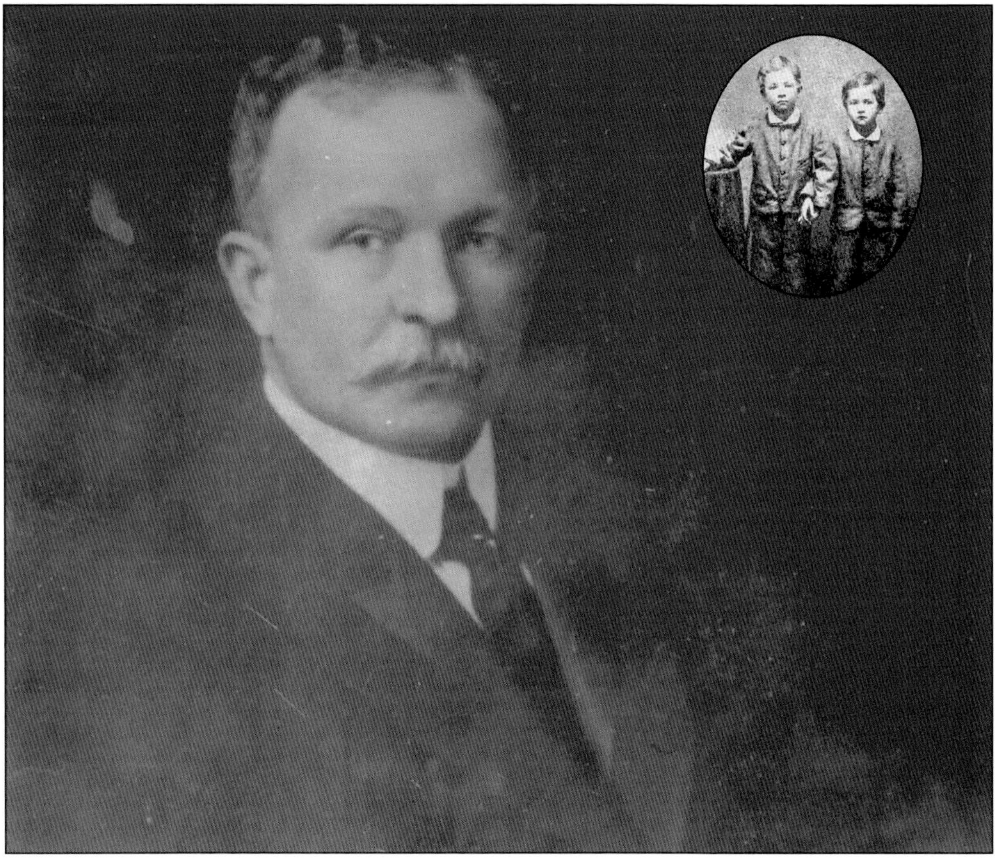

CHARLES WADDELL CHESNUTT. (*Inset*: **CHARLES AND LEWIS CHESNUTT, 1864.**) Dr. Chesnutt was born in Cleveland, Ohio, on June 20, 1858. His parents, Ann Maria and Andrew Jackson Chesnutt, were free African Americans in Cumberland County before the Civil War, and they had moved to Ohio. They returned to Fayetteville in 1866, when Charles was eight years old. Charles attended the Howard School and studied under Robert Harris, showing a natural brilliance and a thirst for knowledge. He read widely to gain knowledge in the classics, including French and German. At the age of 19, he served as the assistant principal to Principal Harris, and after Harris's death in 1880, Chesnutt became the second principal. Chesnutt became an inspirational educational leader in his three years at the helm. He resigned in 1883 and moved to New York City, and later, back to Ohio. He worked as a stenographer and court reporter while studying law. He passed the Ohio Bar Exam in 1887. Chesnutt's real ambition was to become a great writer. A large portion of his time was devoted to writing essays, poems, short stories, and sketches. He had a strong urge to create, and his work began to be published in newspapers and magazines and by book publishers in 1885. His work was well received, and by 1899, he gave up his law practice and set up a literary office in his home. He retained his job as a court reporter, since writing could not yet support his family. His first book, *The Conjure Woman*, a collection of his stories, appeared in 1889. Other publications were as follows: *The Wife of His Youth*, *Other Stories of the Color Line* (1889), *The Life of Frederick Douglass* (1889), *The House Behind the Cedars* (1900), *The Marrow of Tradition* (1901), and *The Colonel's Dream* (1905). Chesnutt was awarded the NAACP Spingarn Medal in 1928. His last book, *Post-Bellum-Pre-Harlem,* was published in 1931, the year before his death. Chesnutt is recognized as North Carolina's first literary giant.

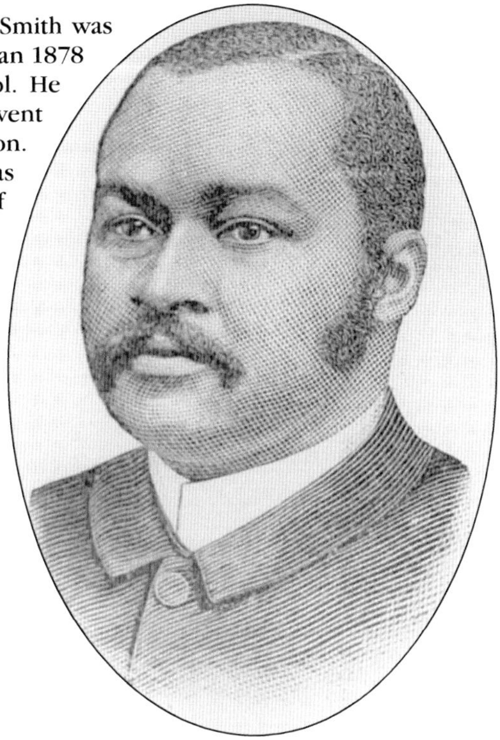

RIGHT REVEREND JOHN WESLEY SMITH. John W. Smith was born in Fayetteville, North Carolina, and was an 1878 graduate of Fayetteville State Normal School. He was a pupil of Robert and Cicero Harris and went on to pursue private courses in higher education. In 1880, he was ordained as a minister and was admitted to the North Carolina Conference of the AME Zion Church in 1881. He pastored churches in Hartford, Connecticut; Little Rock, Arkansas; Washington, D.C.; Louisville, Kentucky; Harrisburg and Carlisle, Pennsylvania. In 1896, Reverend Smith was appointed editor of the *Star of Zion*. He became a bishop in the AME Zion Church in 1904.

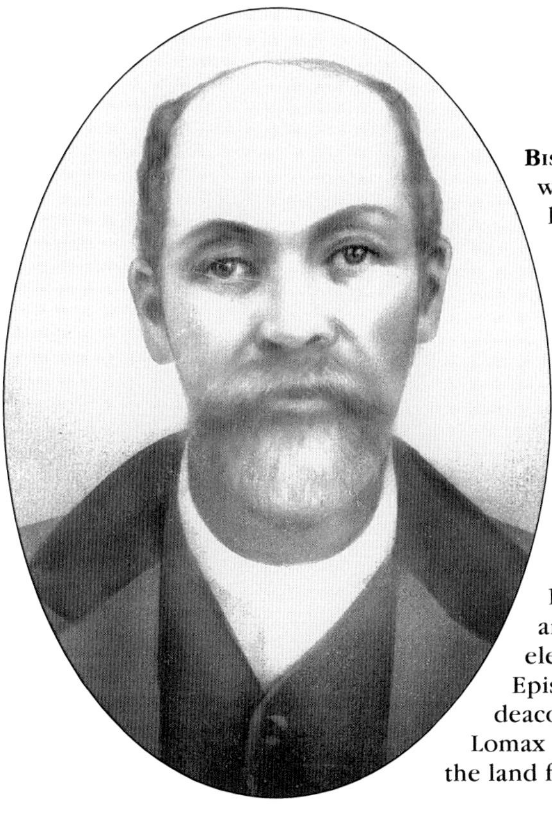

BISHOP THOMAS H. LOMAX. Bishop Lomax was born in Cumberland County and learned to read and write in night school. He was brought up on stories about Henry Evans because one of Evans's preaching locations was at the home of Dicey Hammons, Lomax's grandmother. The Lomax family believed strongly in education. After serving in the Revolutionary War, Bishop Lomax's grandfather and his brothers hired a private teacher to instruct them. Bishop Lomax was licensed to preach in 1864 by Bishop J.W. Hood, ordained a deacon by Bishop J.J. Clinton, and appointed an elder by Bishop J.J. Moore. He was elected bishop in 1876 and served the Episcopacy for 32 years. While still a deacon of the Fayetteville District, Bishop Lomax contributed funds for the purchase of the land for the Howard School in 1867.

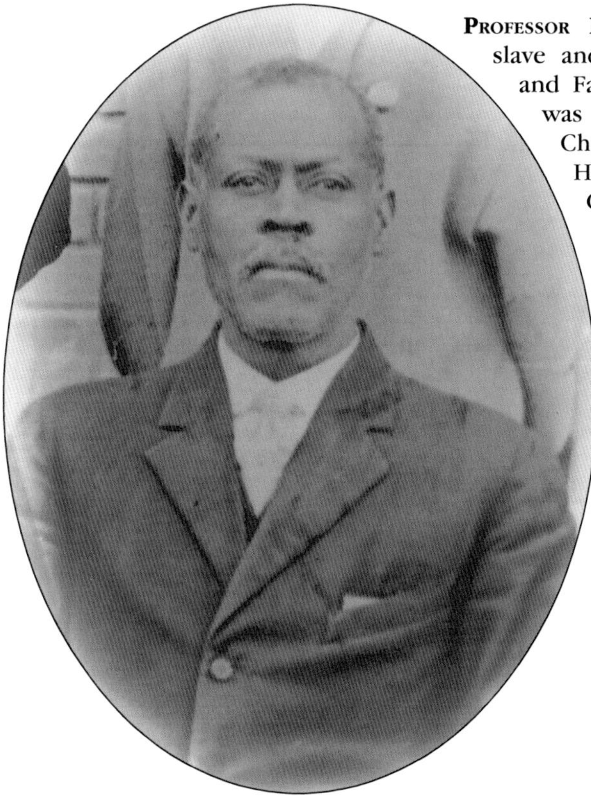

Professor Edward Evans. Evans was born a slave and educated at the Howard School and Fayetteville State Normal School. He was taught by Professor Robert Harris, Charles Chesnutt, and Dr. E.E. Smith. He became a teacher in 1883 at the Godwin Graded School, where he taught for one year. Next, he moved to Fayetteville Elementary School, where he served from 1884 to 1896. He returned to Fayetteville State Normal School in 1896 as an instructor and served for six years. In 1903, Evans was appointed principal of Fayetteville Graded School and held that position for 35 years. Evans was also active in Evans Metropolitan Church and was the Sunday school superintendent for 42 years.

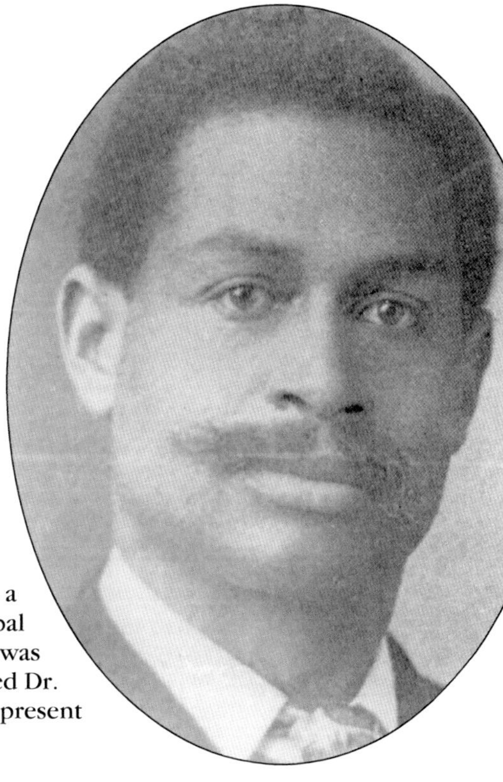

Reverend J.G. Smith. Reverend Smith was a local minister and served as vice-principal at Fayetteville State Normal School. He was one of the signers of the note that allowed Dr. E.E. Smith to purchase the land for the present site of Fayetteville State University.

Two

The Quest for Advancement through Education

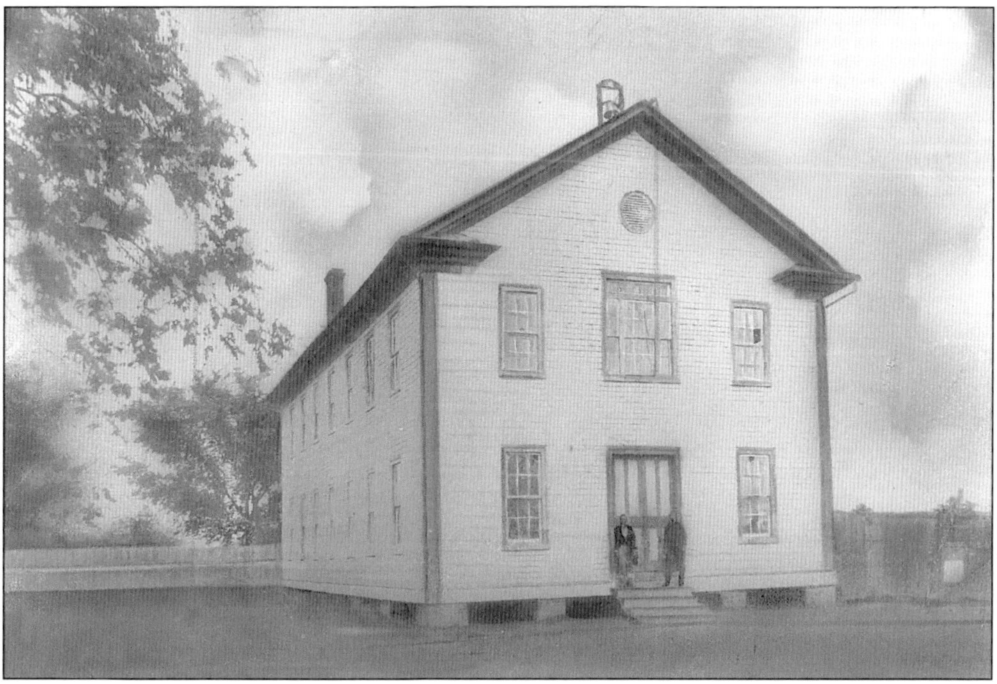

The Howard School. Fayetteville's black population had to defy state laws to seek education prior to the Civil War. A number of Sunday schools were held in churches, but local officials sought to prohibit them in order to prevent slaves from learning to read and write. Eventually, free blacks had to send their children away to obtain education. Many settled in Ohio, around Oberlin and Cleveland; a few returned after the war and played major roles during Reconstruction. One of the first moves of those returning was to establish a school, the Howard School, which would later become Fayetteville State University.

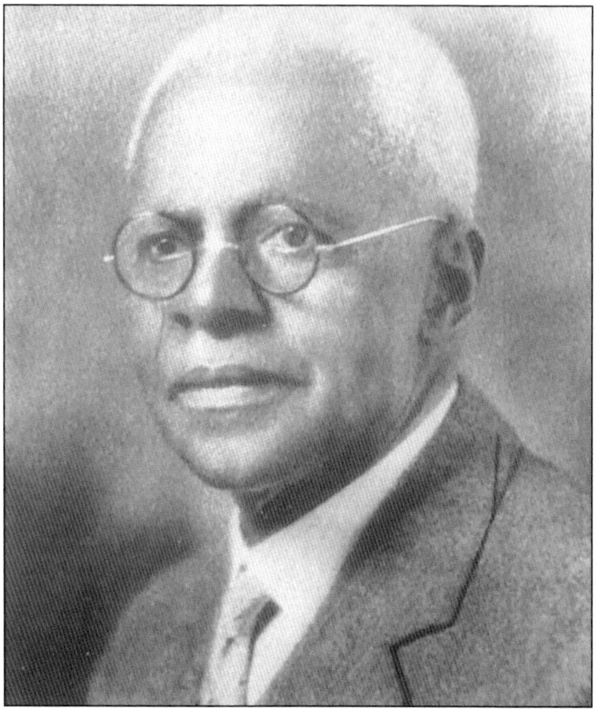

DR. EZEKIEL EZRA SMITH. When Dr. Smith was born in Duplin County in 1852, there were no schools for African-American students in North Carolina. Teaching African Americans to read, write, and count was strictly forbidden by law. Smith, like other free African Americans of that day, learned bits and pieces from playing games and working with whites.

Smith got his first paying job making barrel staves for the turpentine plant for which he was paid 25¢ per day. Even with the low wages, he soon had saved enough to enter Shaw Collegiate Institute, known as Shaw University. Shaw proved to be an encouraging and rewarding educational experience for him.

In 1880, he was ordained into the ministry and served as a pastor at the First Baptist Church for six years. He joined the National Guard in 1880 and was appointed major. In 1883, Smith was chosen to replace Charles Chesnutt as the principal at Fayetteville State Normal School. In 1888, Grover Cleveland appointed Dr. Smith the resident minister and consul general to Liberia. Smith settled into the job, but his wife could not deal with the climate, so he resigned.

Smith's own unceasing quest for knowledge was passed on to his students. His efforts were bringing good results at Fayetteville State Normal School when, in 1898, he was called up with his regiment to serve in the Spanish-American War, during which he was an adjutant.

More than anything, Smith wanted progress for his people, and he knew that education was the key. He understood that for the students to grow, the school had to grow, so he moved from Gillespie Street to Ashley Heights, and then to Worth Street. Smith took it upon himself to build up the school. In 1907, 50 acres was purchased as a permanent home for the school. The first building was constructed in 1908.

In order to pay for the land, several African-American men endorsed a note for $3,000. The other endorsers were F.D. Williston, E.N. Williams, J.G. Smith, and Dr. P.N. Melchor. The note was renewed several times when several endorsers dropped out, until the final payment was made by Dr. Smith alone. A dedicated educator, Dr. Smith served Fayetteville State for nearly 50 years.

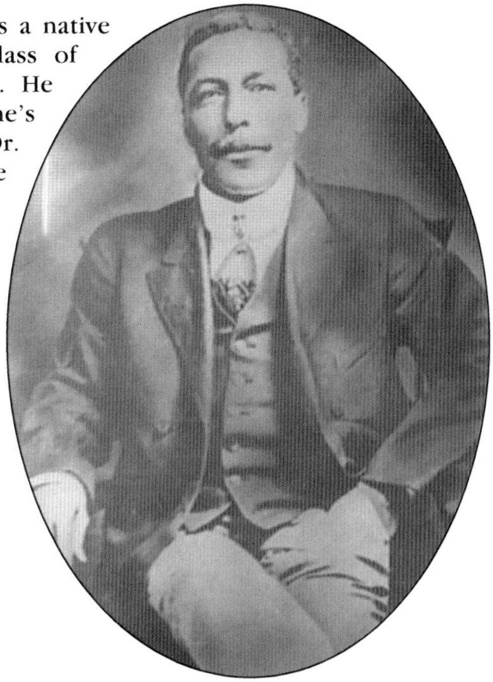

George H. Williams. Professor Williams was a native of Fayetteville and a graduate of the Class of 1879 at Fayetteville State Normal School. He continued his education at St. Augustine's College, completing his degree in 1882. Dr. Williams began his career at Fayetteville State Normal School, first as a teacher, and later as principal during the absence of Dr. E.E. Smith from 1888 to 1895. Professor Williams was later a principal in New Bern, Long Creek, and Asheville, all in North Carolina. He returned to Fayetteville and worked as a mail carrier for the postal service for 26 years.

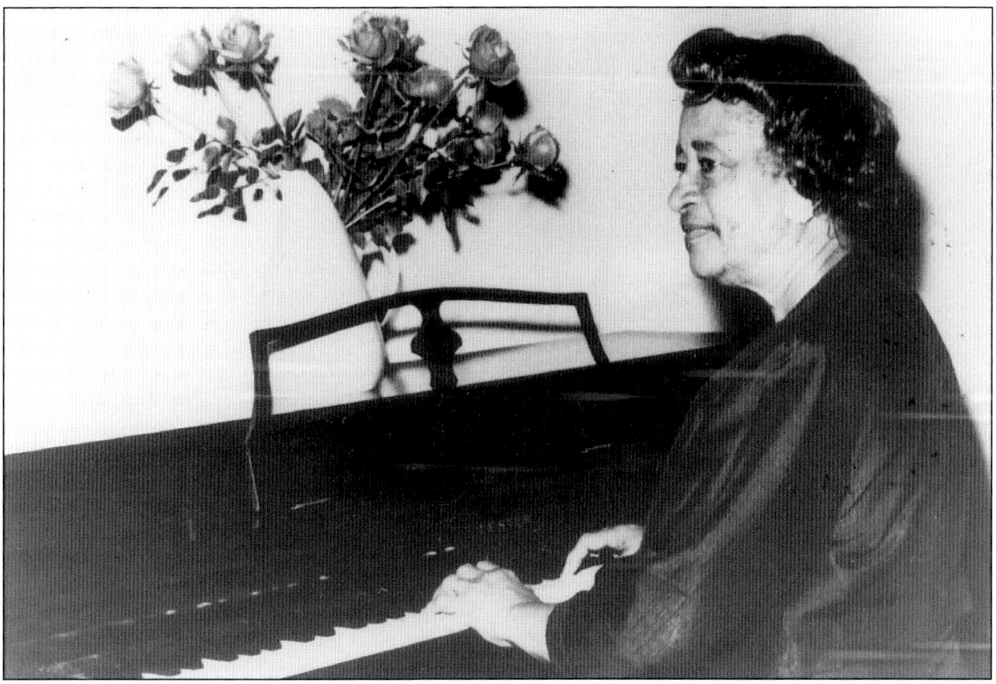

Alberta Simmons Simms. The daughter of Robert Simmons, Alberta Simms was a member of the Class of 1904 at Fayetteville State Normal School. She furthered her education at Oberlin College and later taught music there. Mrs. Simms also worked as a teacher at Tuskegee Institute (University) and was assistant director and organist for the Institute Choir. Mrs. Simms owned and operated a music studio.

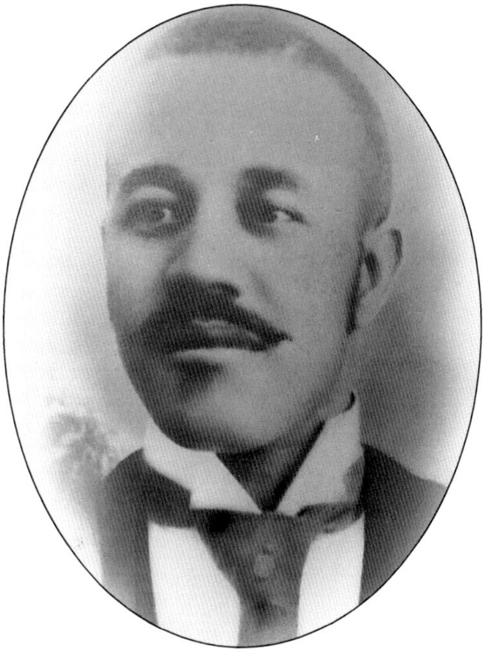 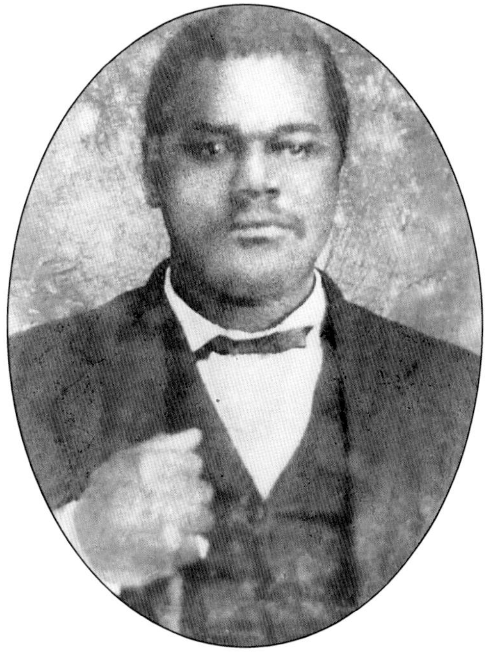

Left: **Charles Williams**. A member of the Class of 1883, Mr. Williams served as the bookkeeper at the Ashley-Bailey Silk Mill. *Right*: **Owen Monk**. A member of the Class of 1885, Monk taught school in the Sampson County school system.

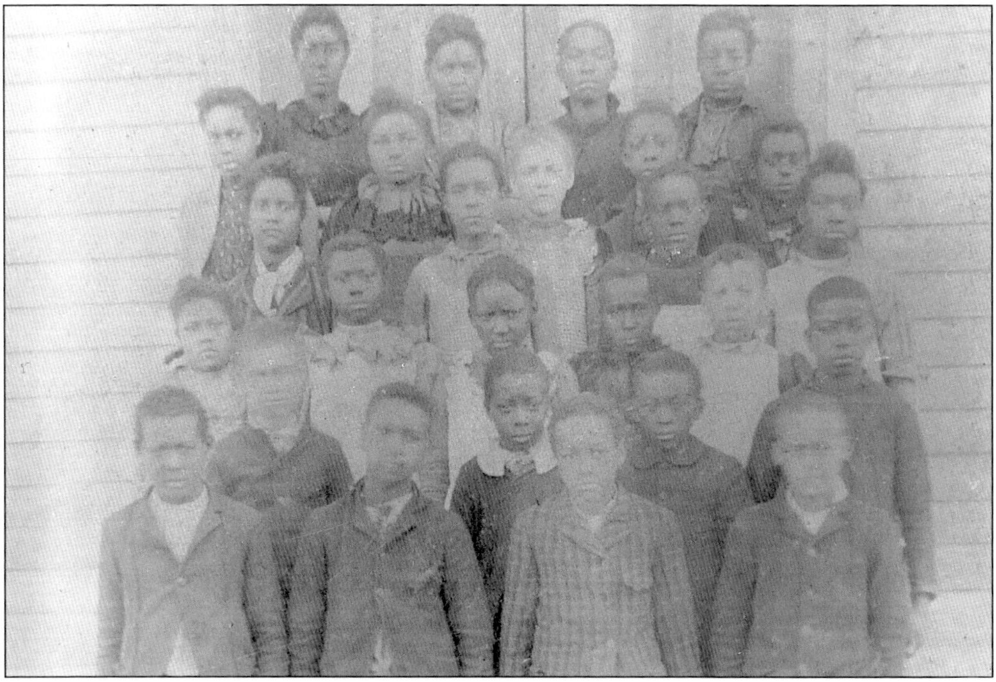

Howard School Students. This photograph is a portrait of Howard School students in 1892. Included in the image are Jane C. Williams, Maggie Evans, Christine Pierce, and William Webb.

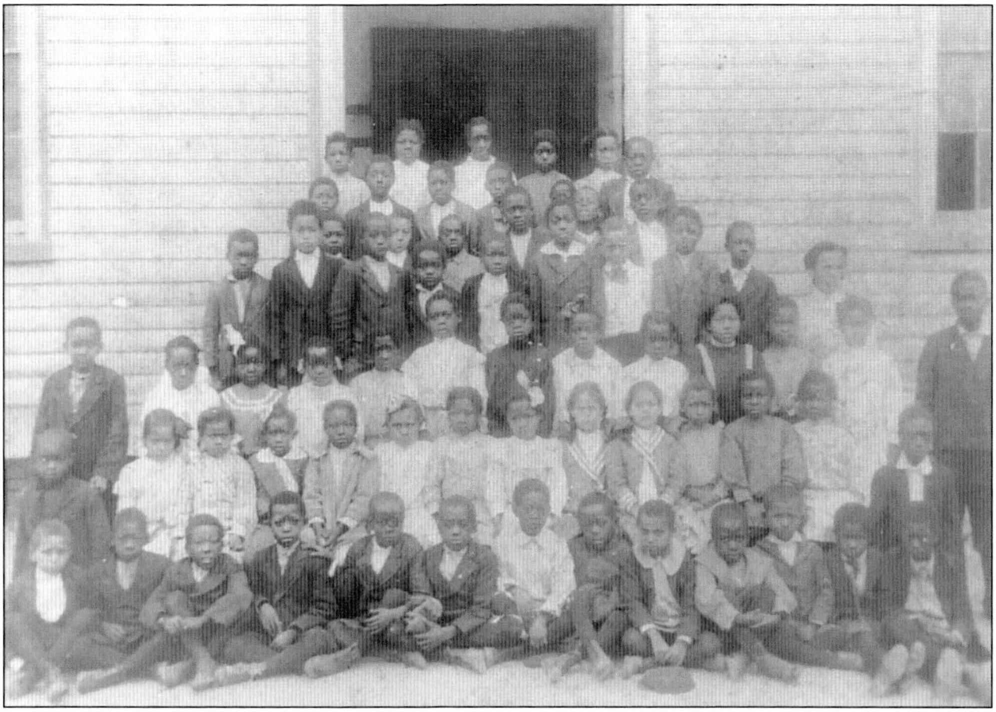

Howard School Students. This is another portrait of Howard School students in the 1890s.

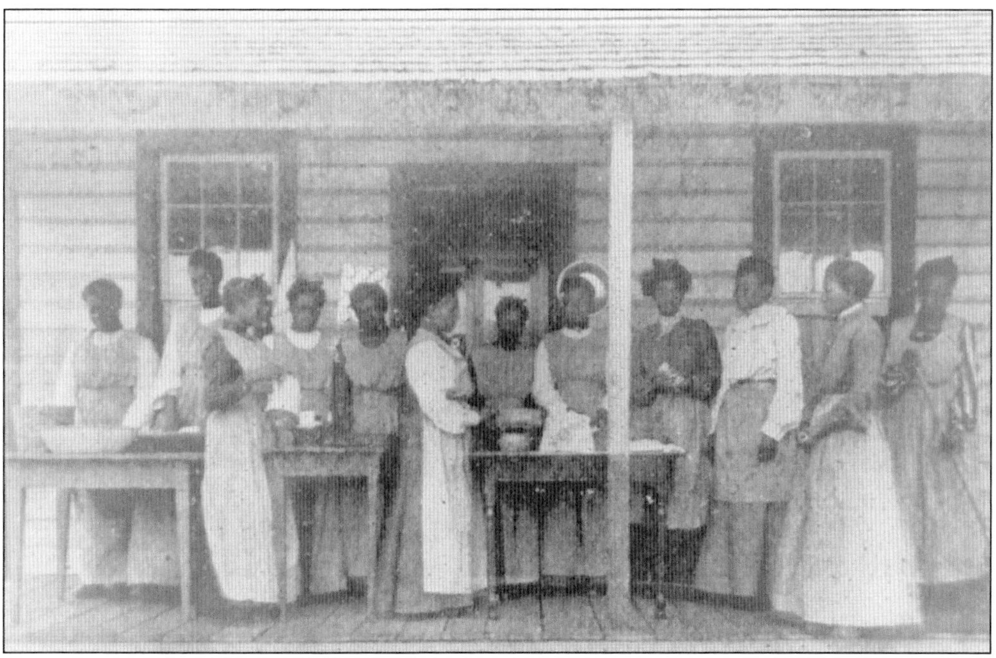

Howard School Cooking Class. This photograph shows Ms. Emma Courent's cooking class in 1903.

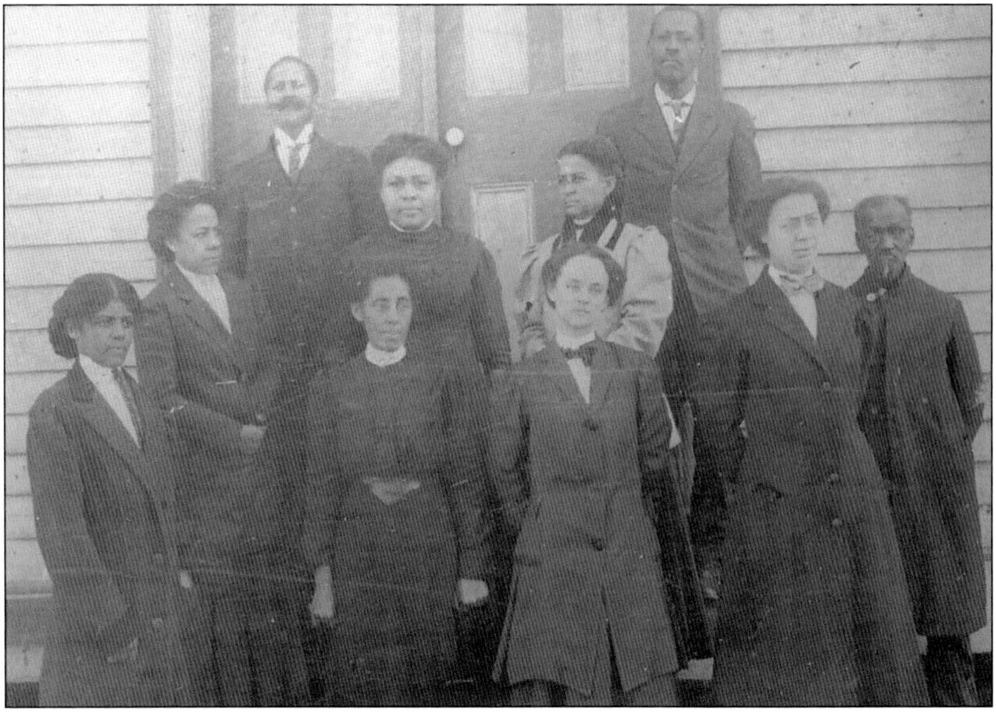

Howard School Faculty, 1904.

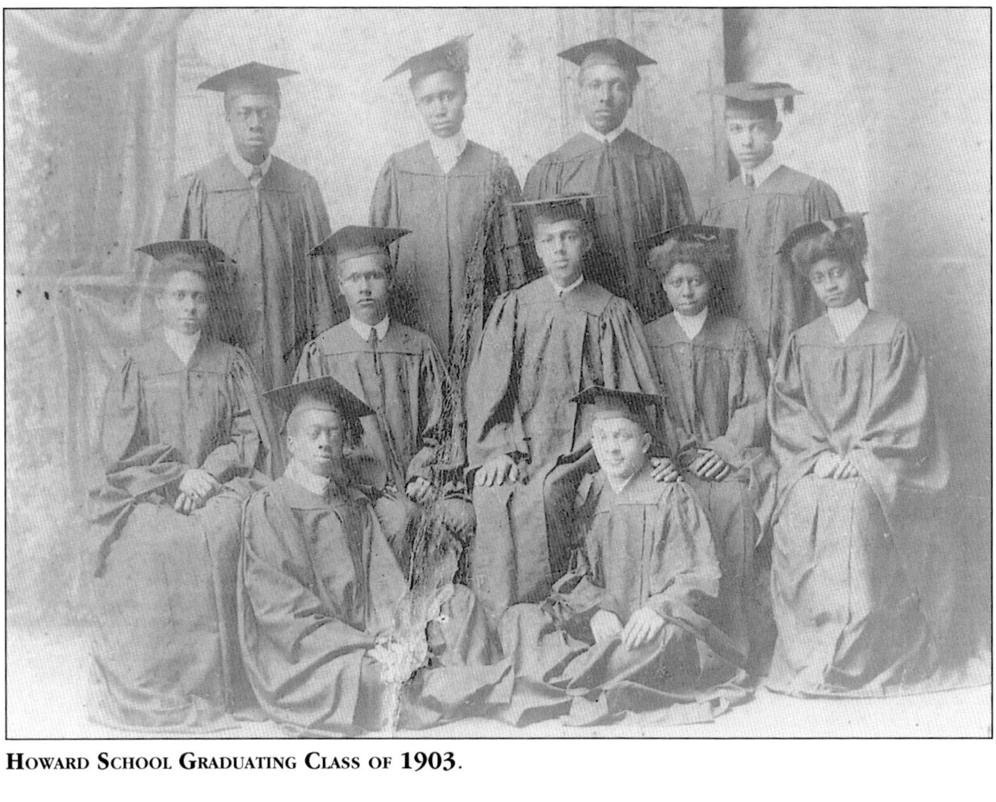

Howard School Graduating Class of 1903.

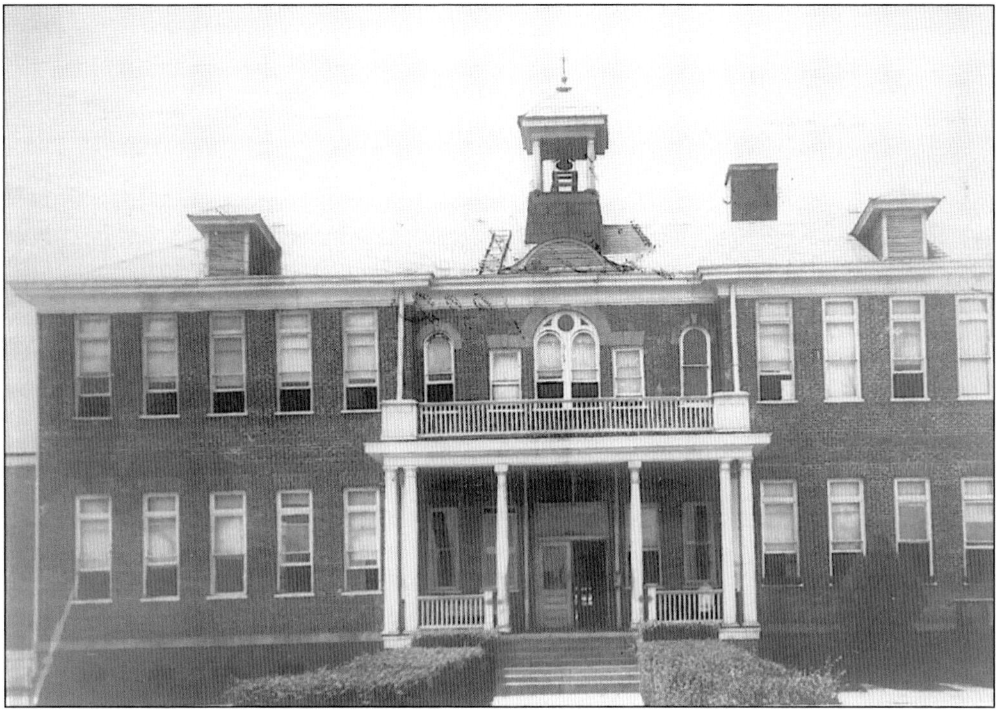

Aycock Building. This was the first building on the present campus as seen in 1909.

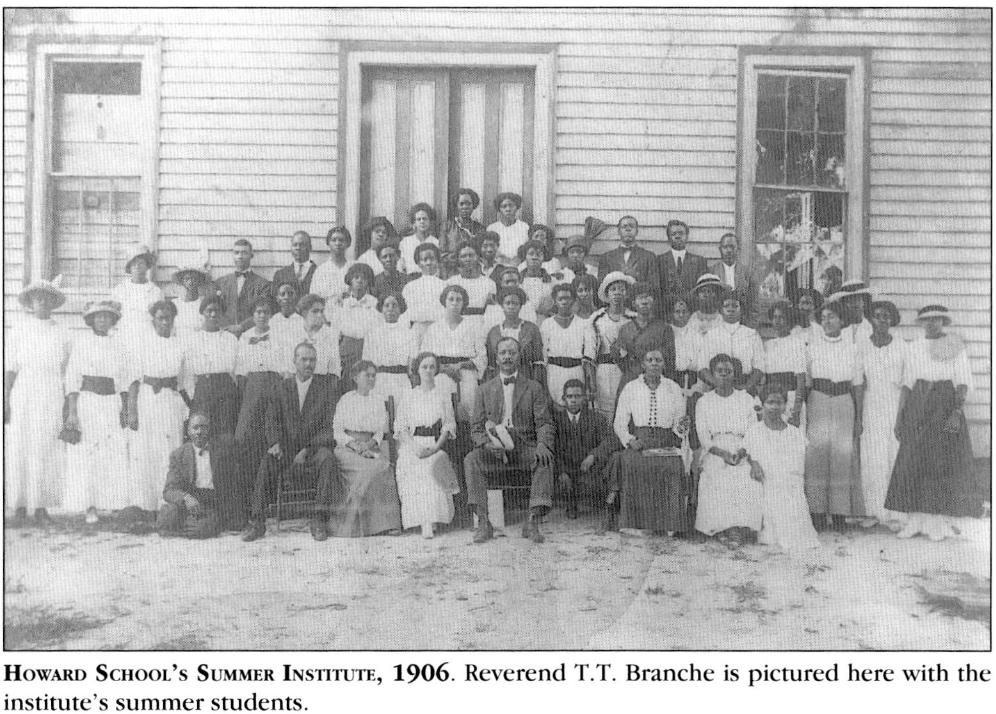

Howard School's Summer Institute, 1906. Reverend T.T. Branche is pictured here with the institute's summer students.

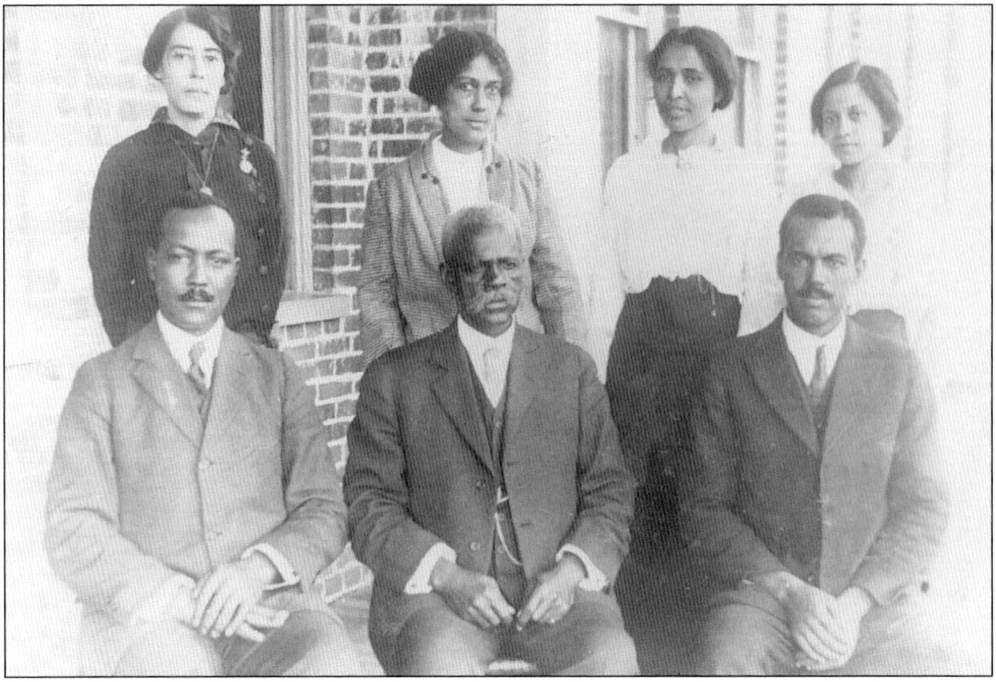

State Normal School Faculty, 1910. The faculty members are identified, from left to right, as follows: (front row) Reverend T.T. Branche, Dr. E.E. Smith, and Professor John W. Mitchell; (back row) Miss Mattie J. Chavis, Mrs. Nannie L. Smith, Florence S. McNeill, and Goldie P. Scruggs.

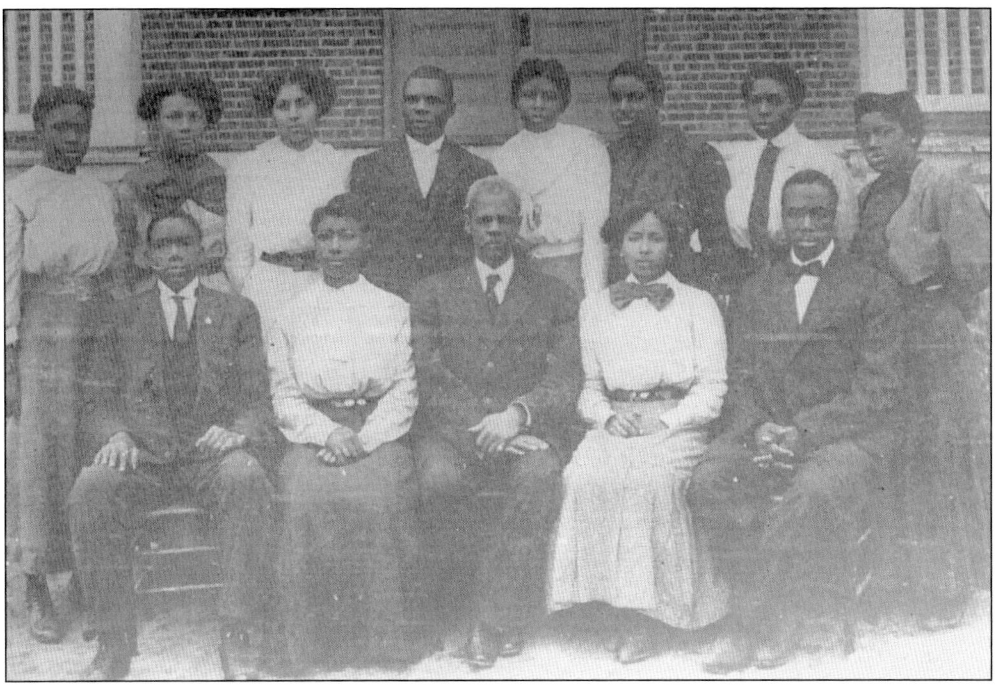

Dr. E.E. Smith with Fourth-Year Students, 1910.

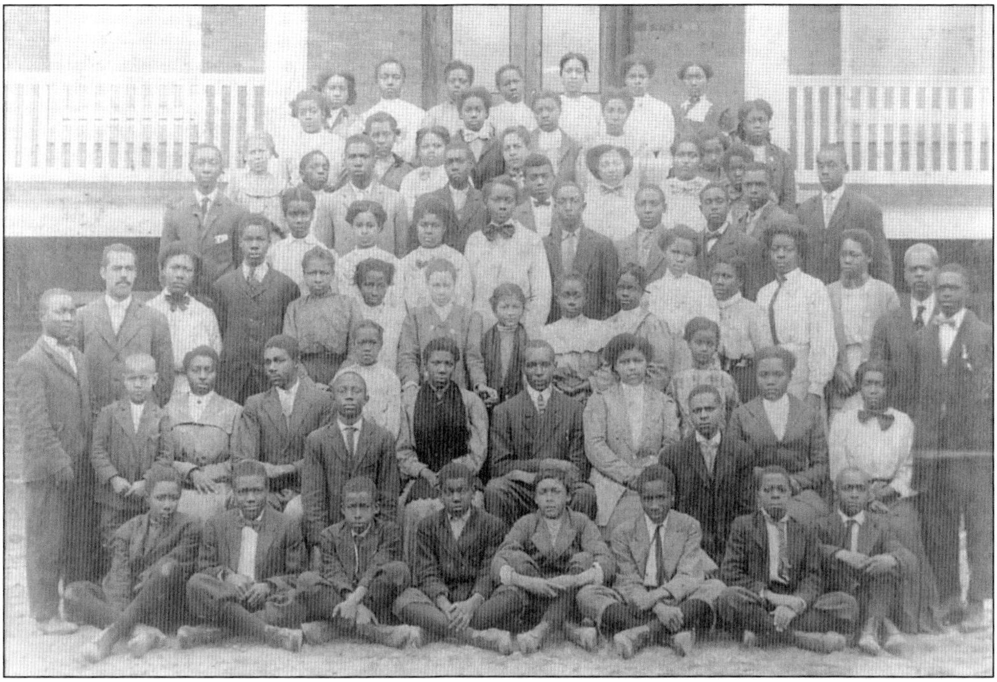

PREPARATORY CLASS, 1910. Also included in the image are Dr. E.E. Smith and Professor John W. Mitchell.

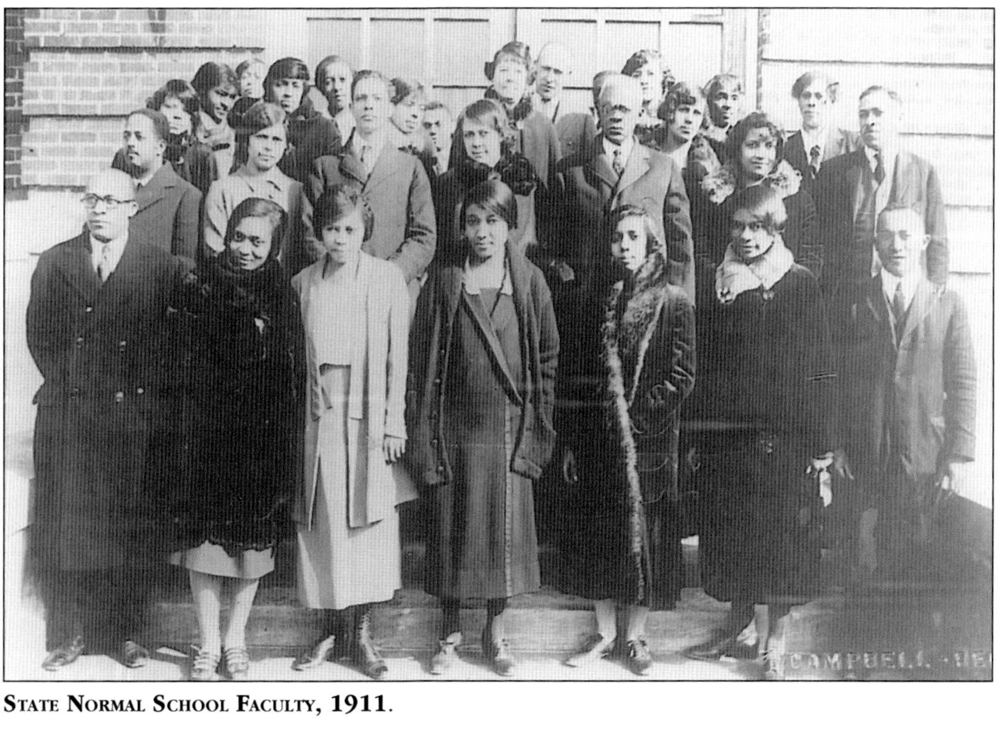

STATE NORMAL SCHOOL FACULTY, 1911.

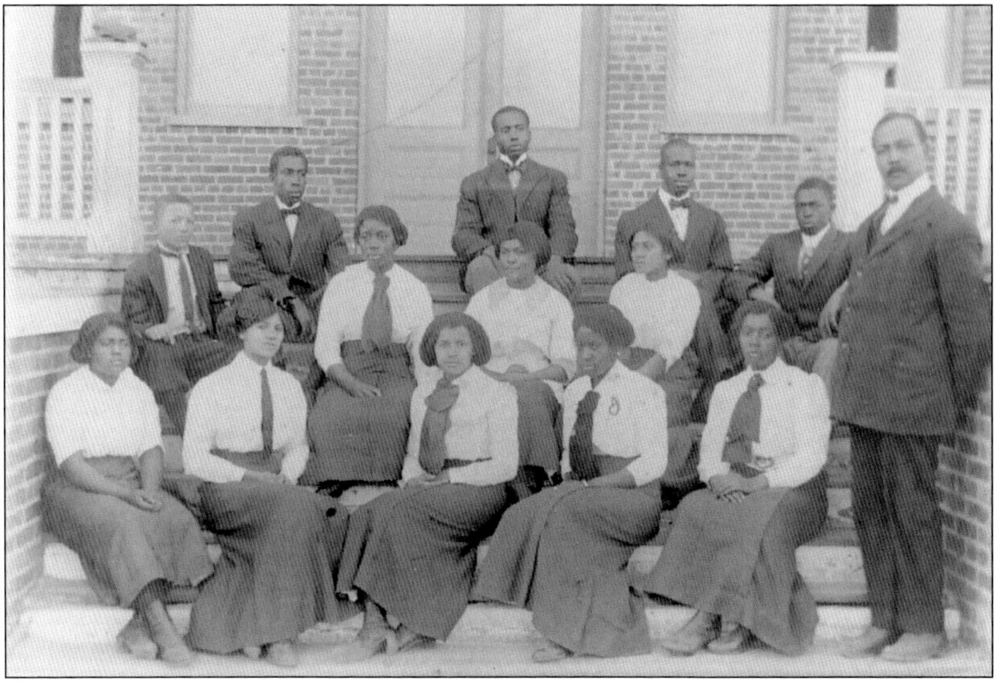

REVEREND T.T. BRANCHE AND FIRST-YEAR STUDENTS, 1911.

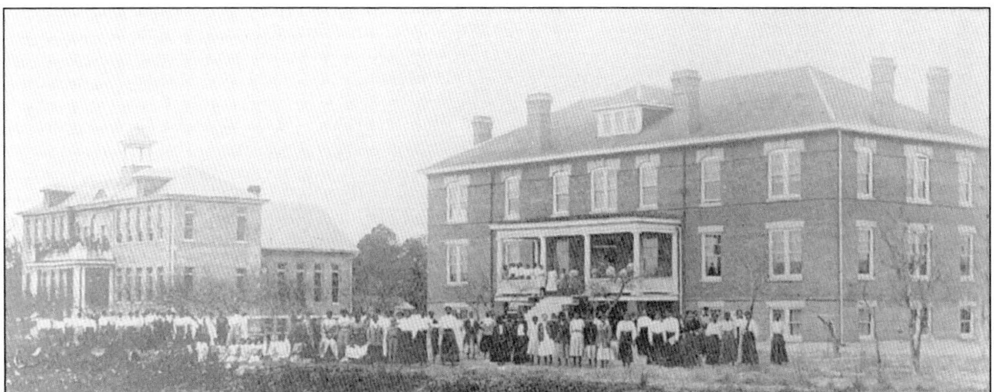

AYCOCK BUILDING AND DORMITORY, 1911.

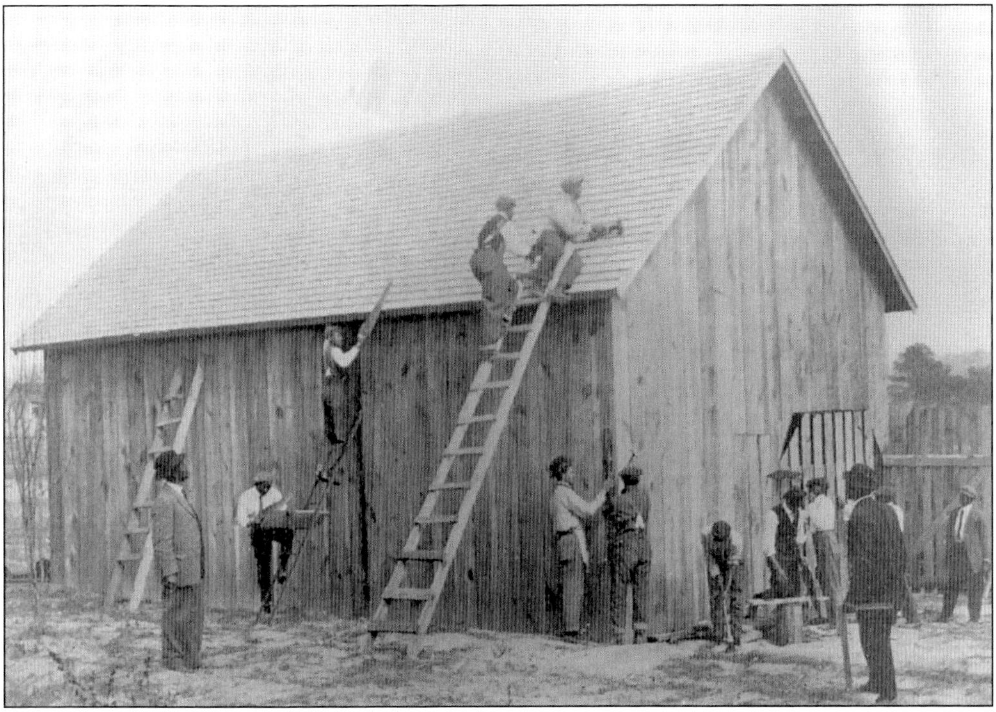

Carpentry Class as They Build a Barn, 1916.

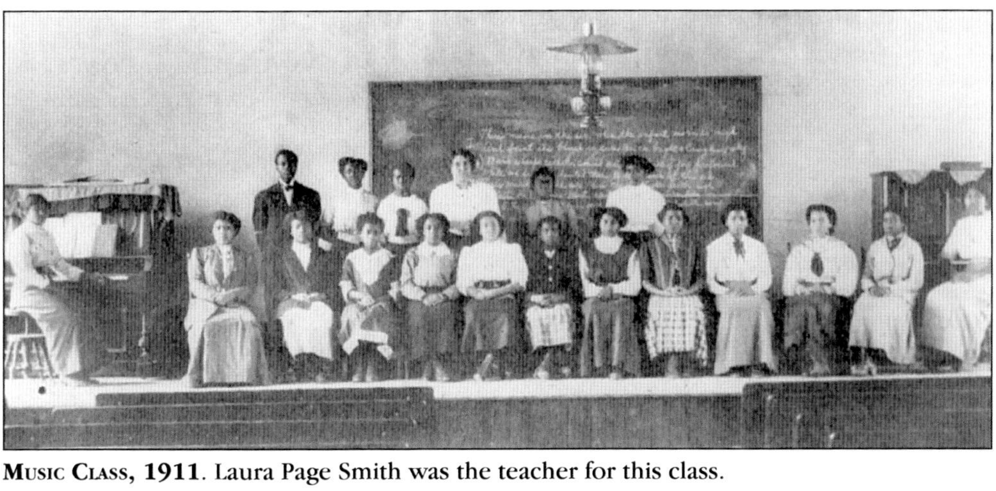

Music Class, 1911. Laura Page Smith was the teacher for this class.

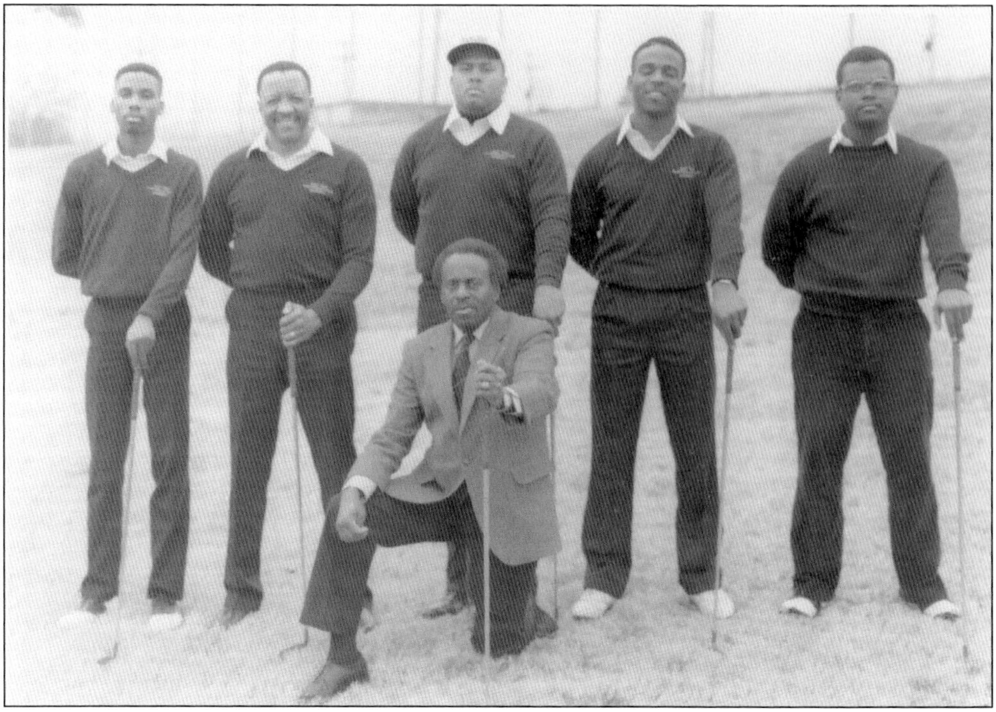

CHAIR CANING CLASS, 1918.

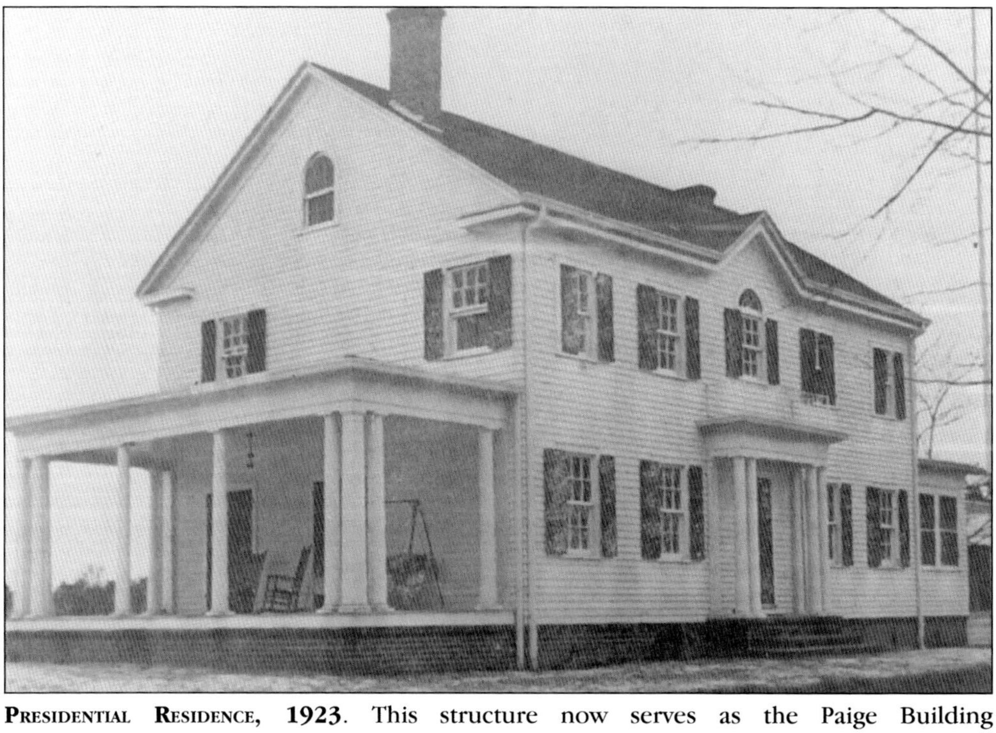

PRESIDENTIAL RESIDENCE, 1923. This structure now serves as the Paige Building and Commons.

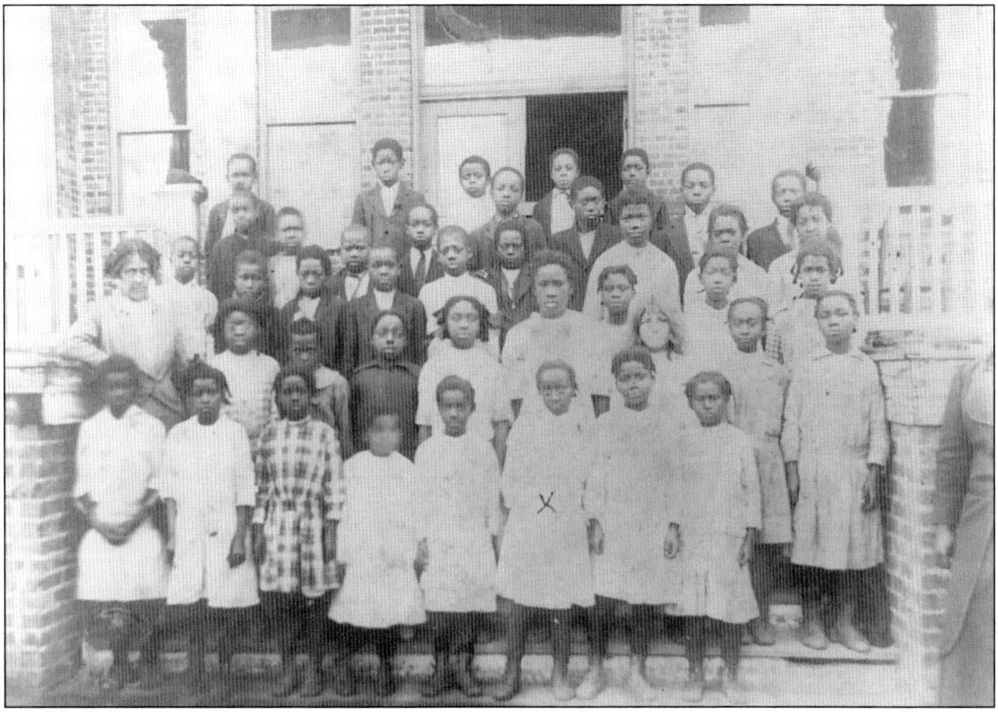

Model School, 1917. Mrs. Hannah Smith was the teacher for this classroom of children.

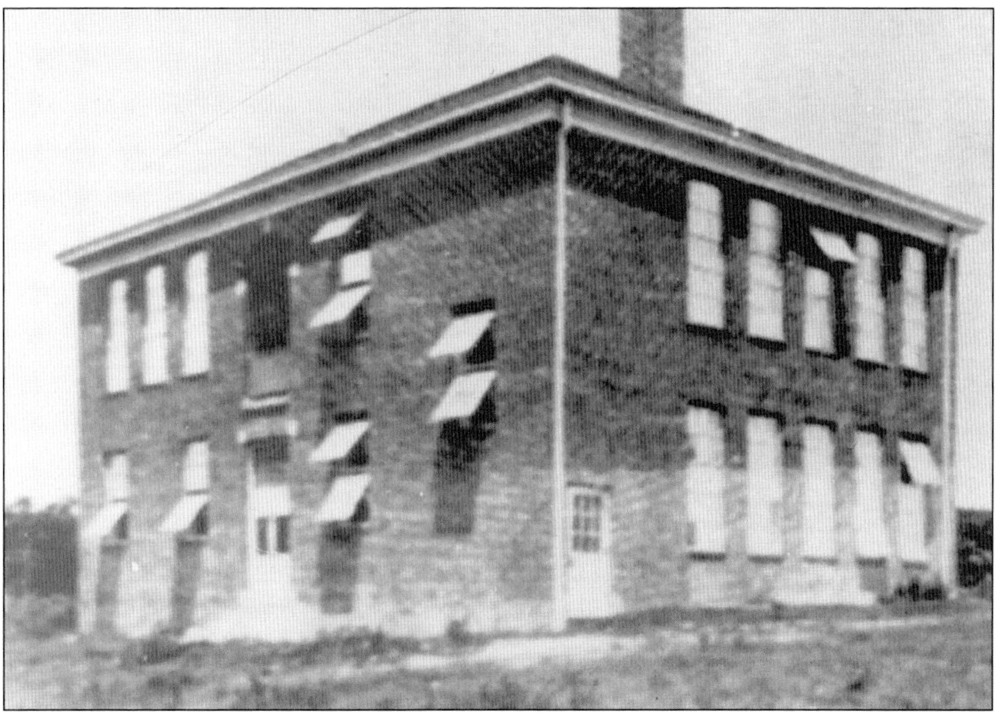

Mitchell Industrial Arts Building, 1923.

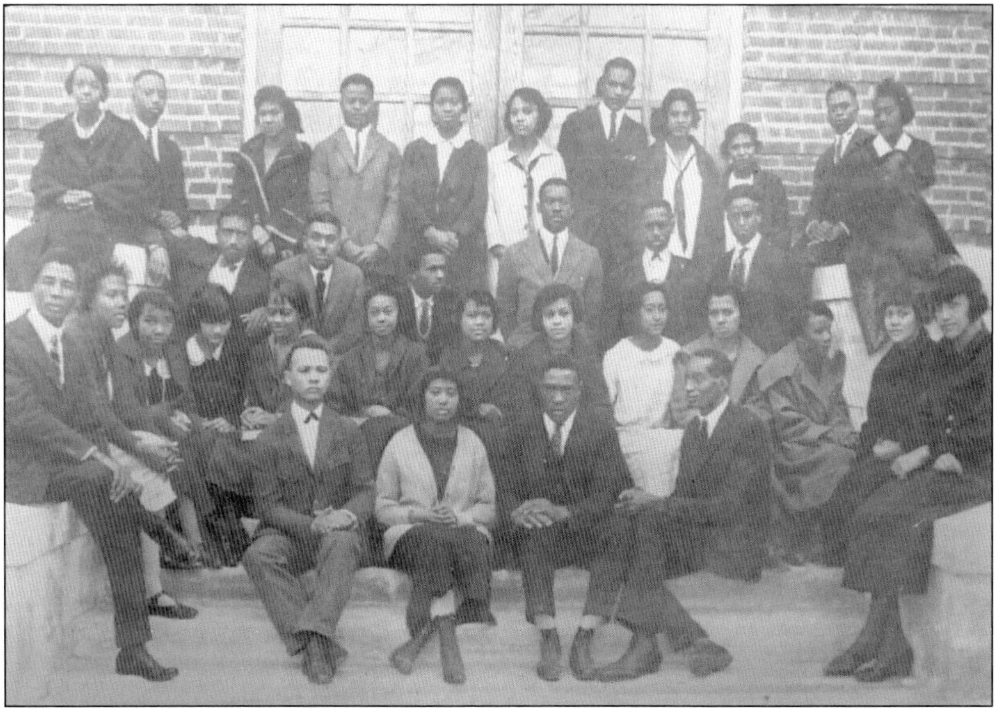

CROWN AND SCEPTER CLUB, 1924.

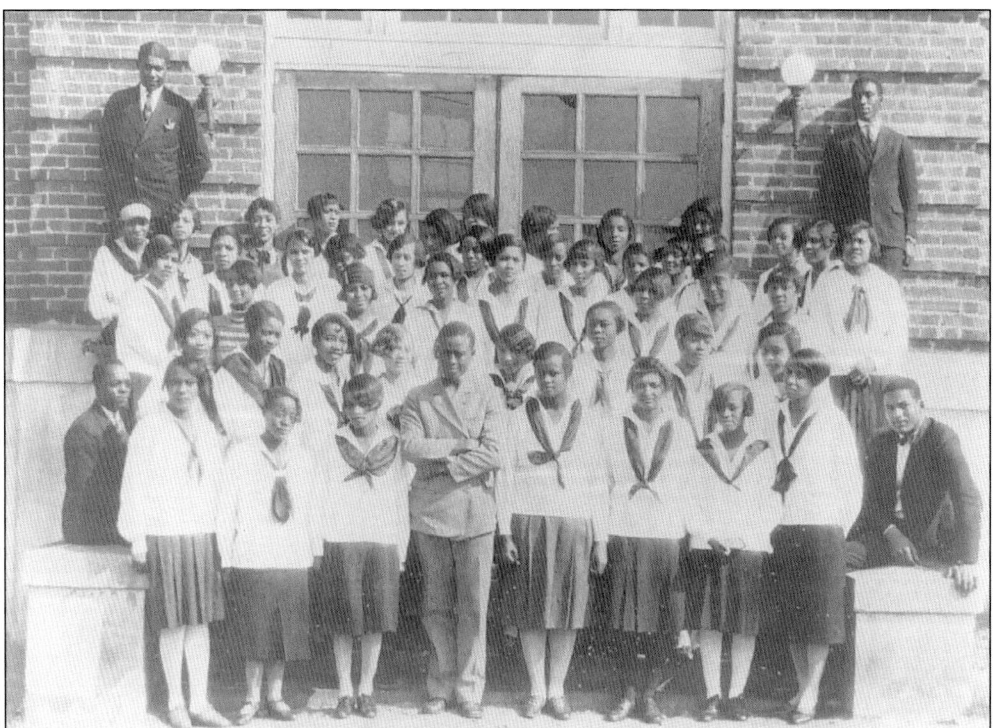

JUNIOR NORMAL CLASS, 1926.

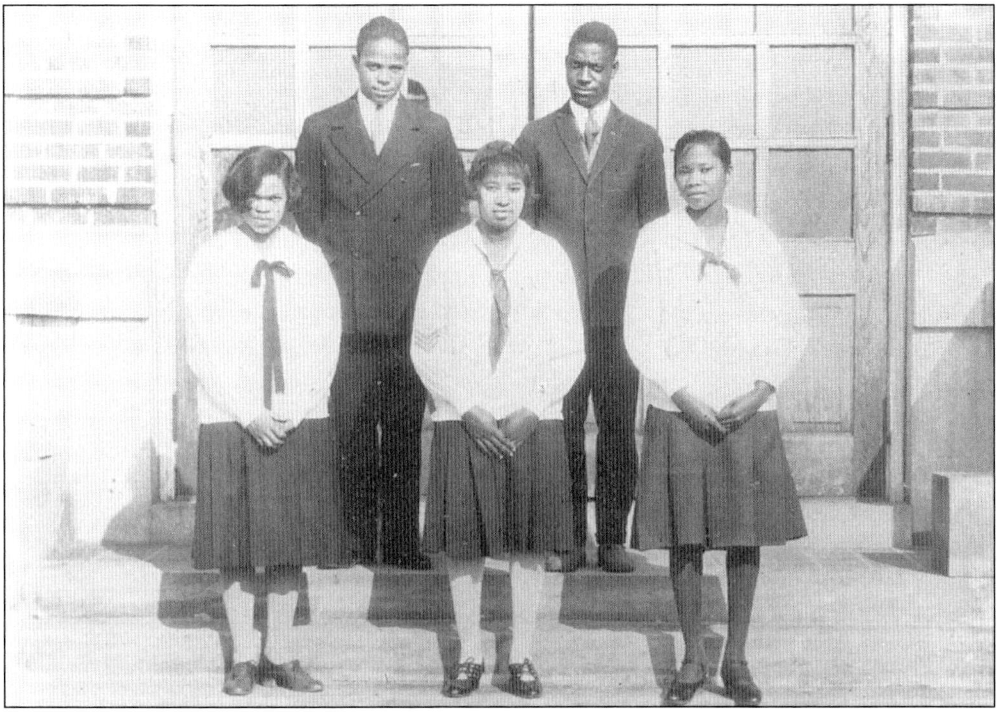

Debating Team, 1927. The team is identified, from left to right, as follows: (front row) Helen Singletary, Novella Pearsoll, and Annie Street; (second row) Richard Lankford and Tolar Vance William.

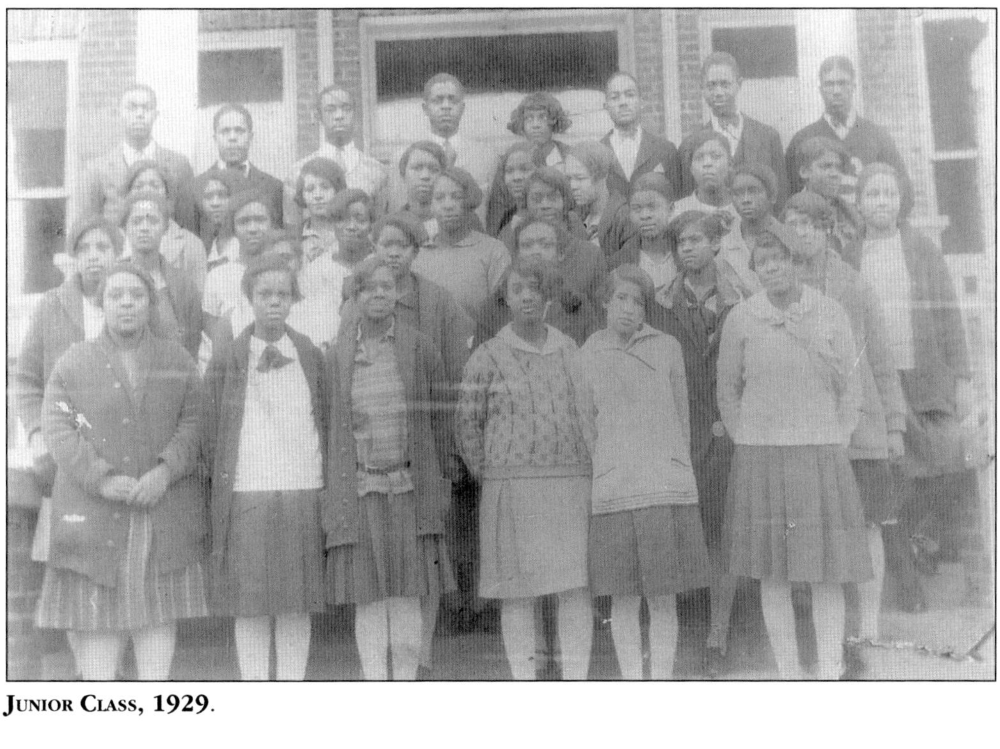

Junior Class, 1929.

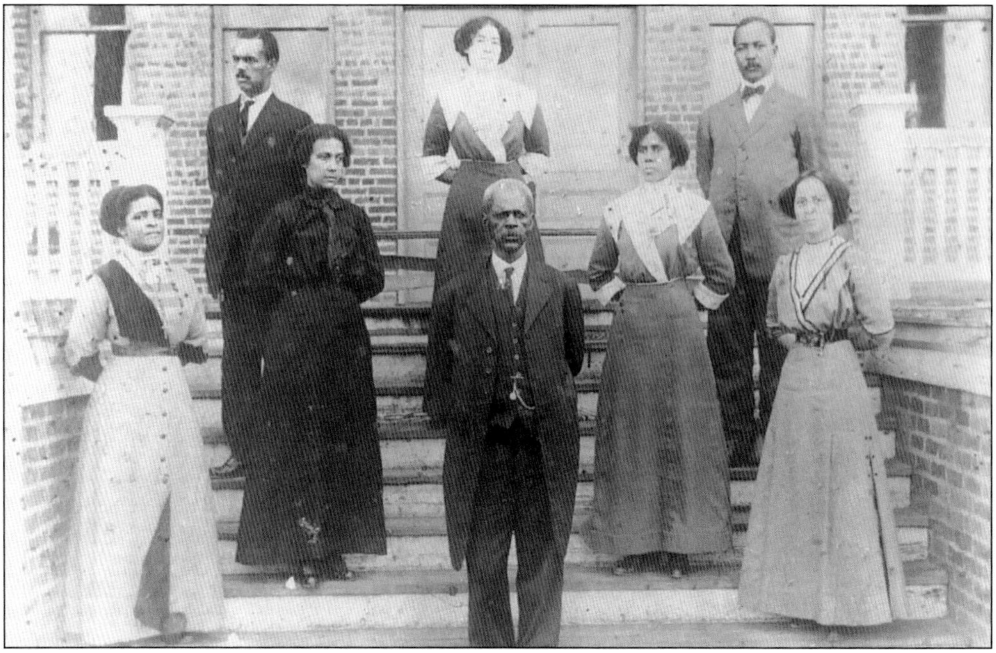

Dr. E.E. Smith with the State Normal School Faculty, 1919. The following faculty members are pictured here: Dr. E.E. Smith, Mrs. Nannie L. Smith, Miss Lassiter, Miss Stewart, Professor John W. Mitchell, Miss Mattie J. Chavis, and Reverend T.T. Branche.

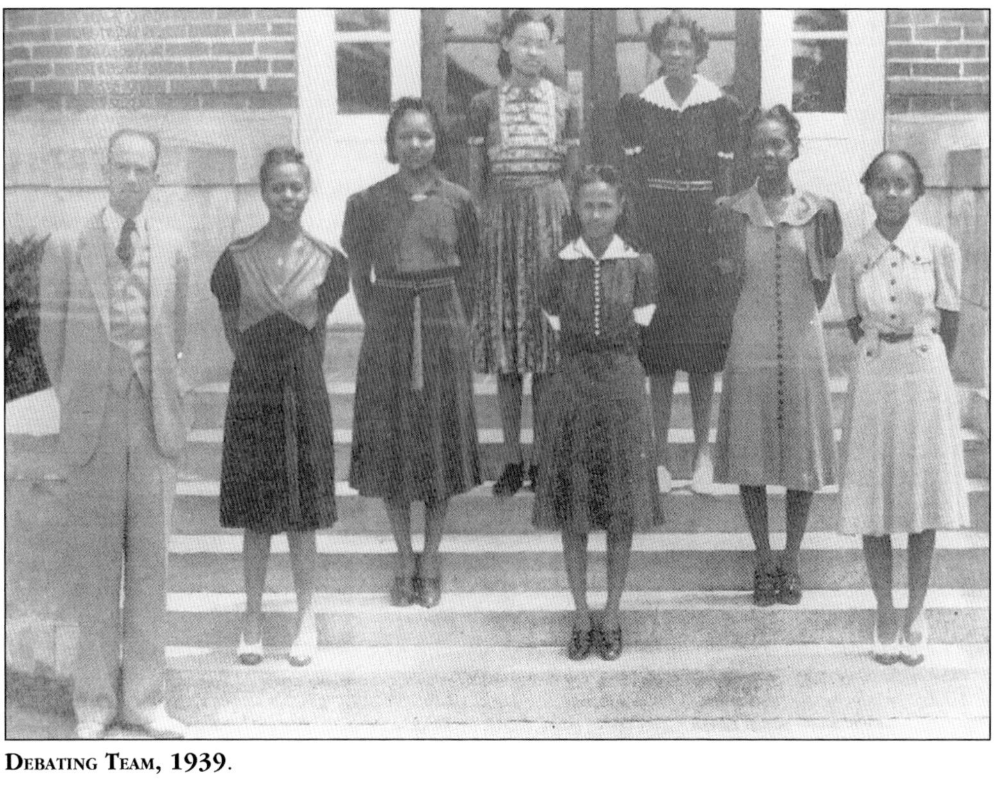

Debating Team, 1939.

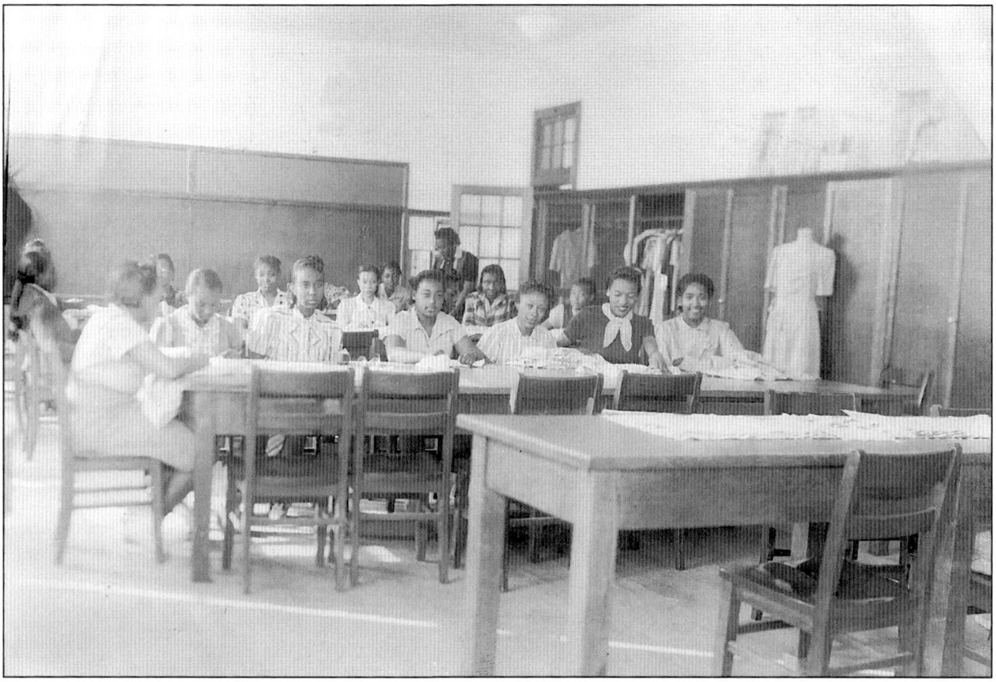

Home Economics Class, 1941.

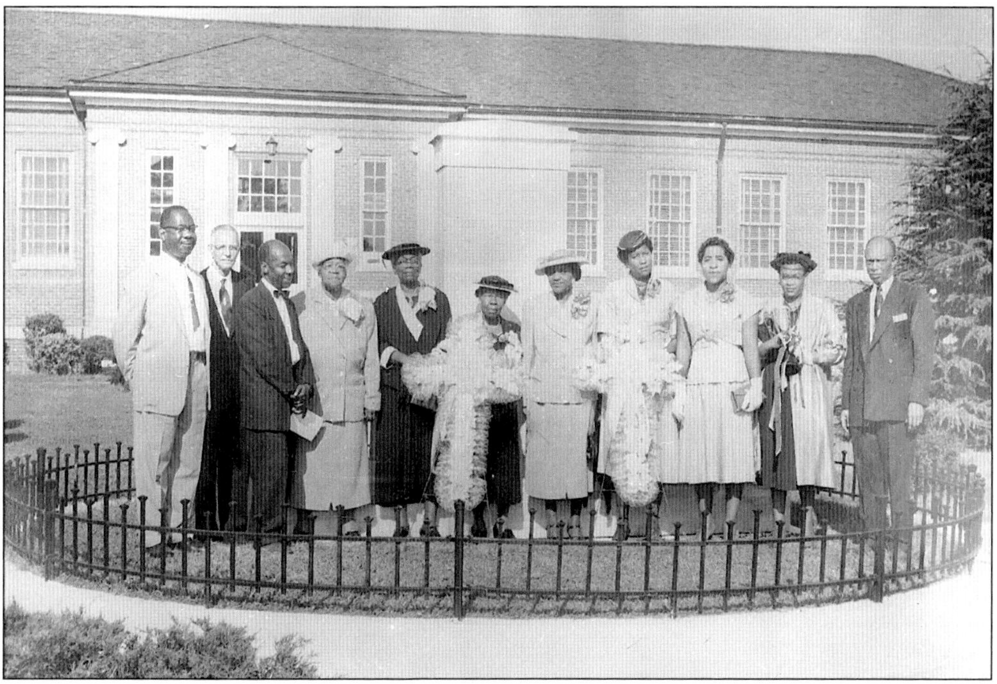

Founders' Day, 1955. These men and women are identified, from left to right, as follows: William E. Smith (alumni president), Dr. Seabrook, Alexander Barnes, Rachel W. Simpson, Lula Gilmore, Emma Crump, Julia Ferguson, Annie D. Drame, Eunice M. Ferguson, Lucille P. Phillips, and Louis Austin (speaker).

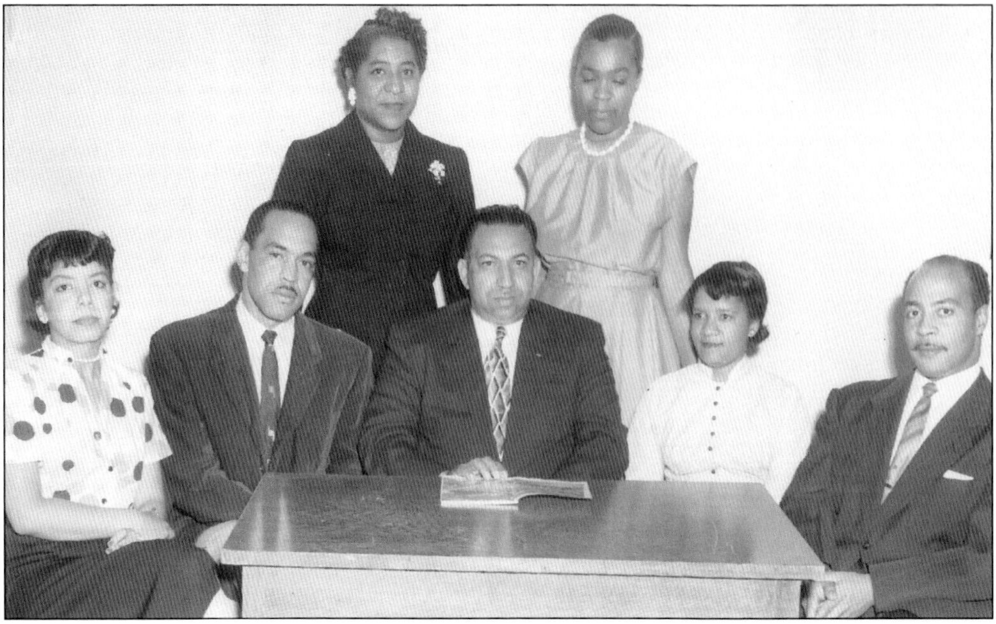

President Jones with New Faculty, 1958. The following members are included: Carolyn McDow, Joseph Kunckles, Odoll Uzzell, President Rudolph Jones, Eunice M. Ferguson, and Alice B. Brown.

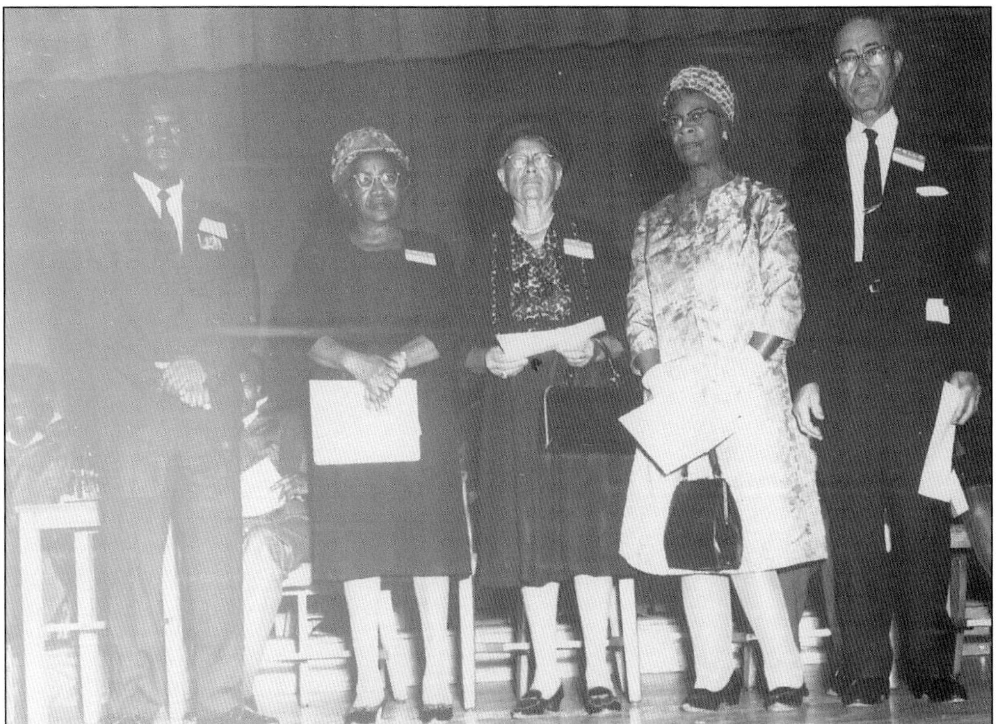

Certification of the Class of 1916 on Their 50th Anniversary. Milton Yarboro presented these class members with their gold certificates on Alumni Day in 1966.

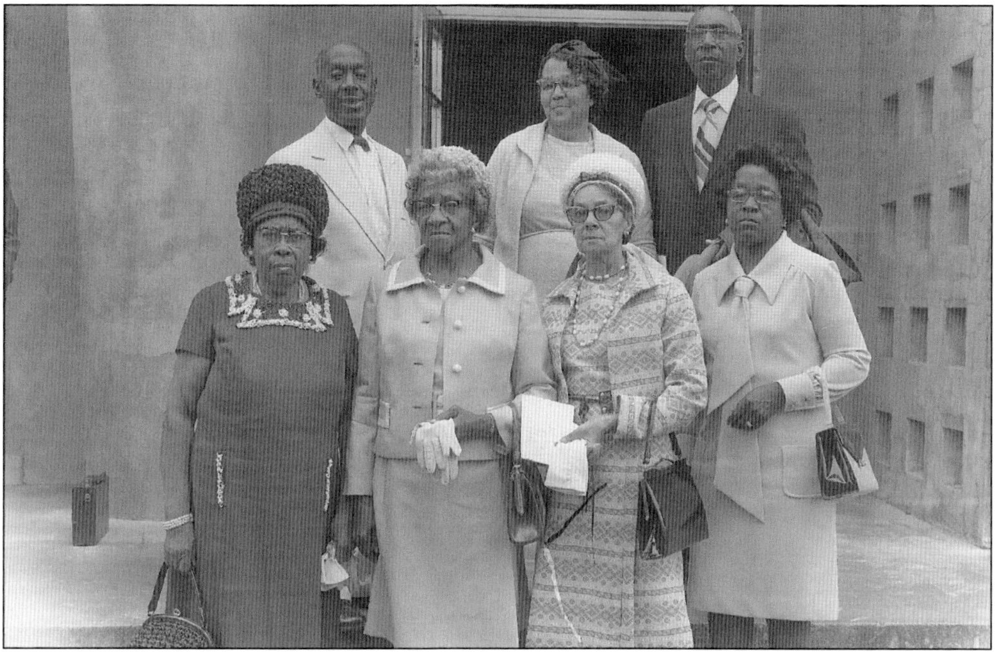

Reunion of the Class of 1921 on Their 50th Anniversary. These members of the Class of 1921 were photographed on May 15, 1971, and include Irene Mitchell Hill, Estelle Torrey McNeill, Mary Watson, and Alexander Barnes.

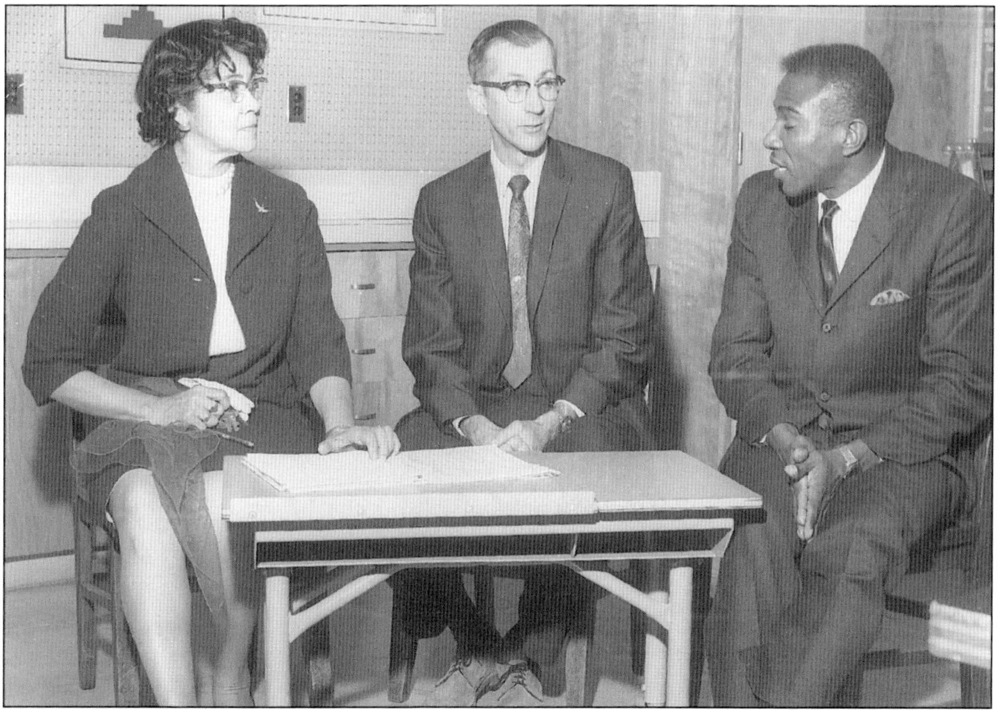

Art Department. Professors Helen Chick and Harvey Jenkins (right) of the Art Department are photographed here with a visiting professor (center).

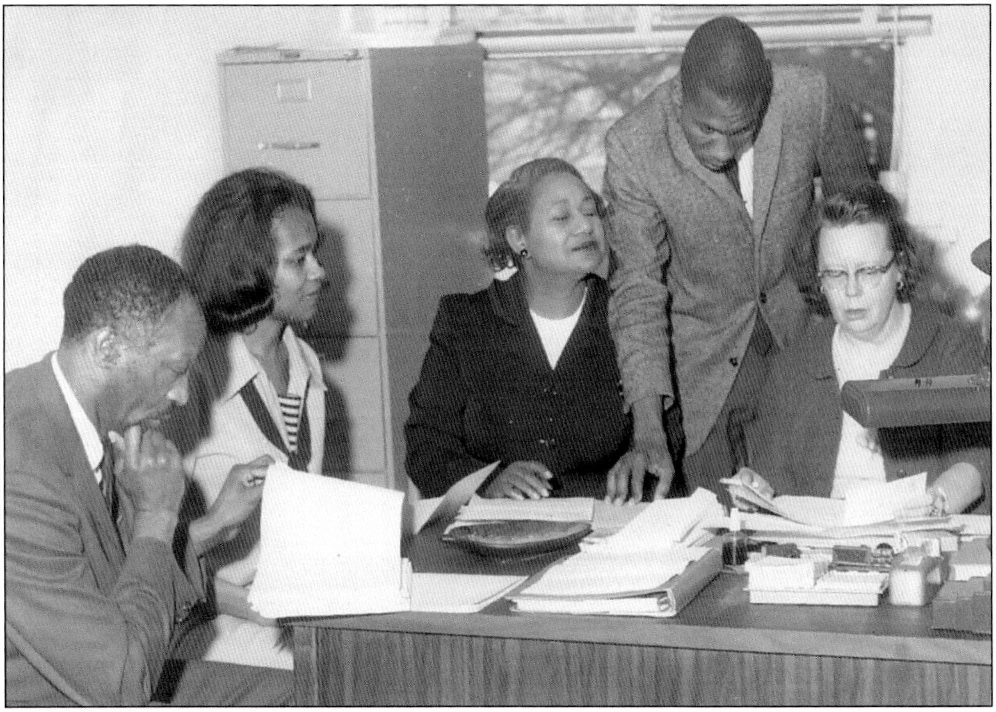

English Department, 1966. These members of the English Department are identified, from left to right, as follows: Ollie Cox, Elaine Newsome, Lois Turner, Edwin Clark, and Joan Corbett.

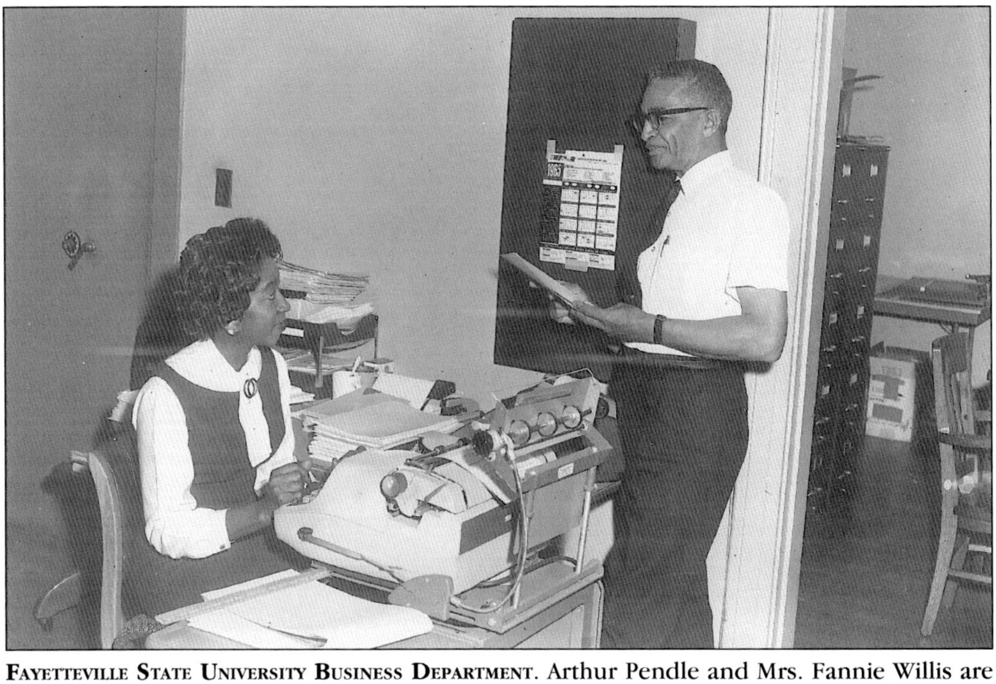

Fayetteville State University Business Department. Arthur Pendle and Mrs. Fannie Willis are pictured here.

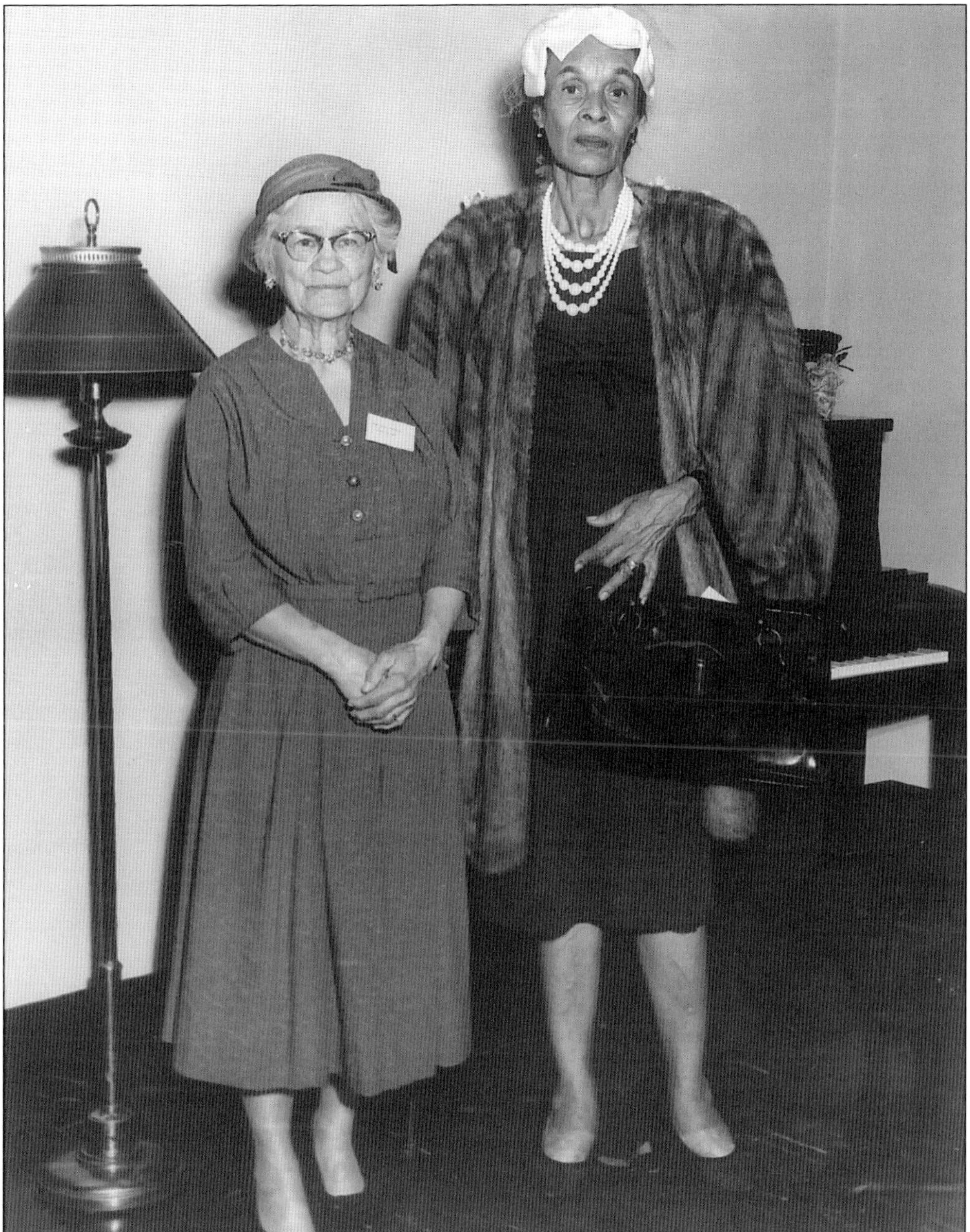

Miss Sarah Chesnutt and Mrs. Bonnie O'Daniel. Both women are descendants of original trustees A.J. Chesnutt and Thomas Lomax.

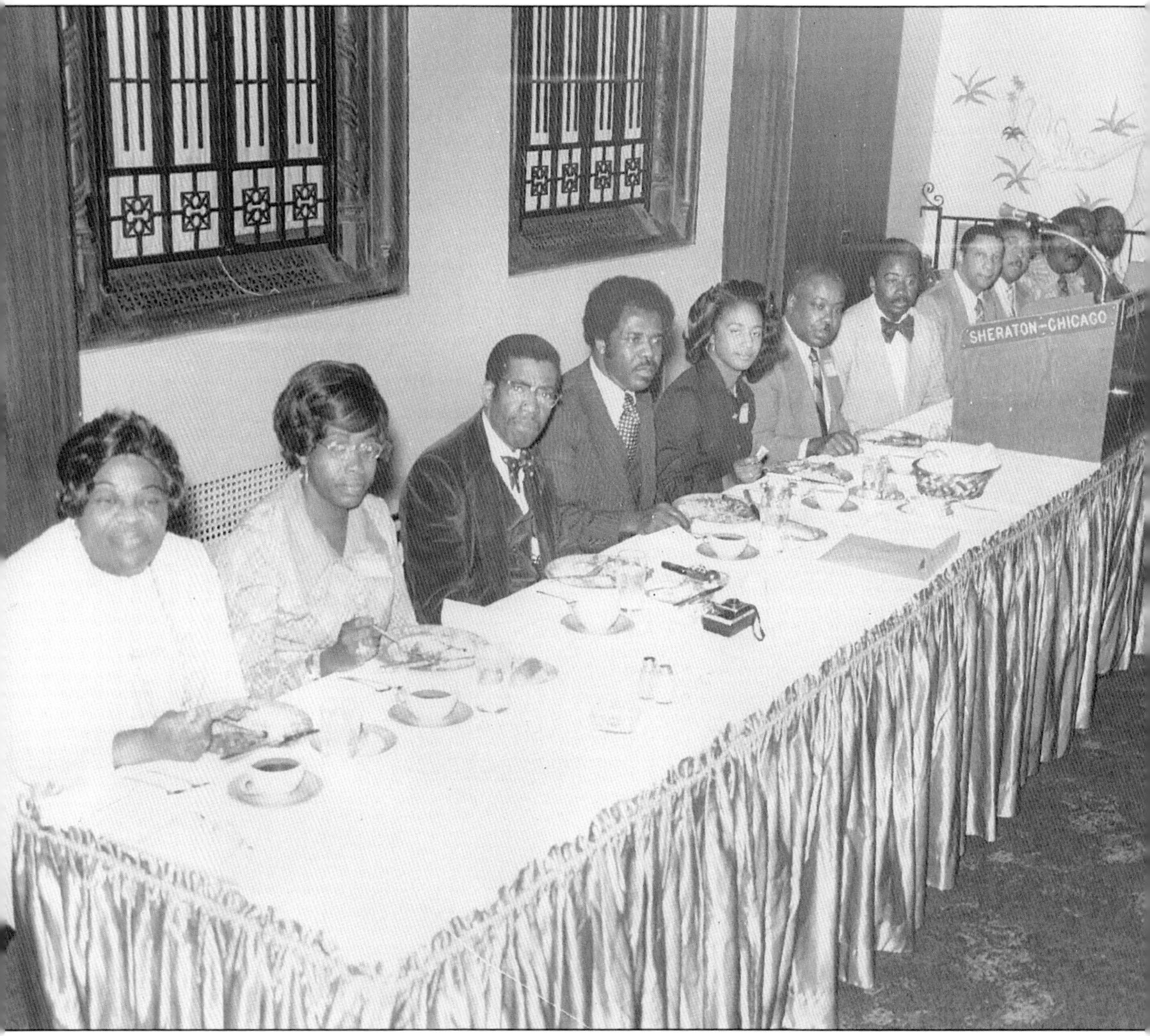

DR. LYONS AND FAYETTEVILLE STATE UNIVERSITY ALUMNI, CHICAGO, 1975.

Three

Modern Leaders

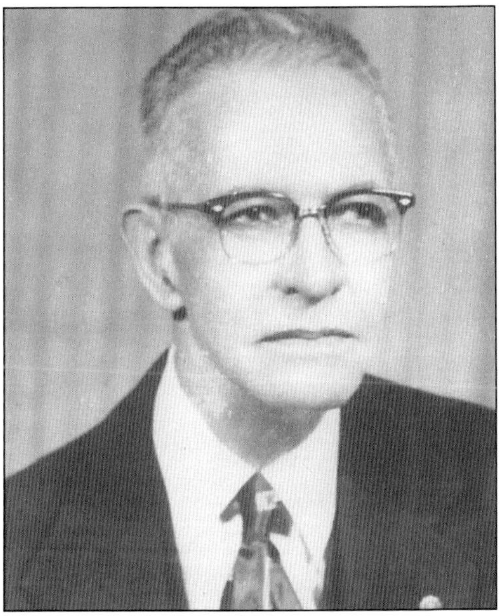

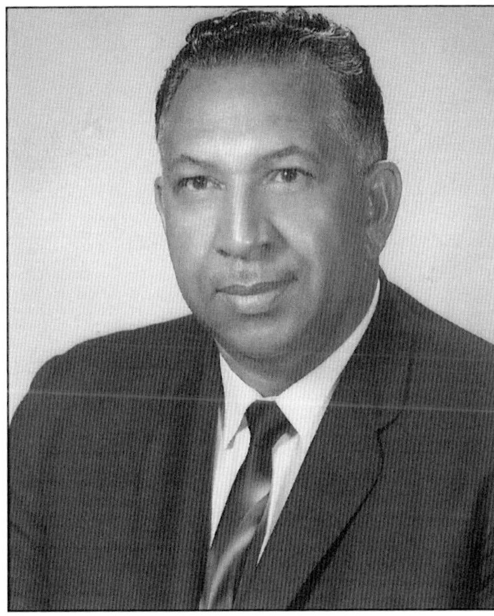

Left: **Dr. James W. Seabrook.** Dr. Seabrook came to Fayetteville State in 1922 as principal of the high school department. A graduate of Johnson C. Smith University, he had a 34-year affiliation with Fayetteville State—as a dean and later as president. He succeeded Dr. Smith when he retired in 1933. During his tenure, the college became a four-year institution and the name was changed to Fayetteville State Teachers College. It also received state and regional accreditation and became a member of the American Association of College for Teacher Education. Eight buildings were added to the campus. Dr. Seabrook was an avid Broncos supporter, but he believed in keeping athletics in its proper place. After ending his 47-year career in education, he earned his stockbroker's license and became active in politics, participating in many state and national Republican events. He stayed close to the university as long as he was in Fayetteville.

Right: **Dr. Rudolph Jones.** Dr. Jones was selected to head the university after the retirement of Dr. Seabrook in 1956. He had been a public schoolteacher and principal, and later came to Fayetteville State in 1952 as a dean. Under his administration, the school charter was changed in 1959 to allow additional majors to be added, including a number of non-teaching degrees. The "Teachers" portion of the name was dropped, and additional buildings were added to accommodate the growing student population. Dr. Jones had two other buildings in the planning process at the time of his retirement in 1969. He was named president emeritus in 1976. He died in 1998.

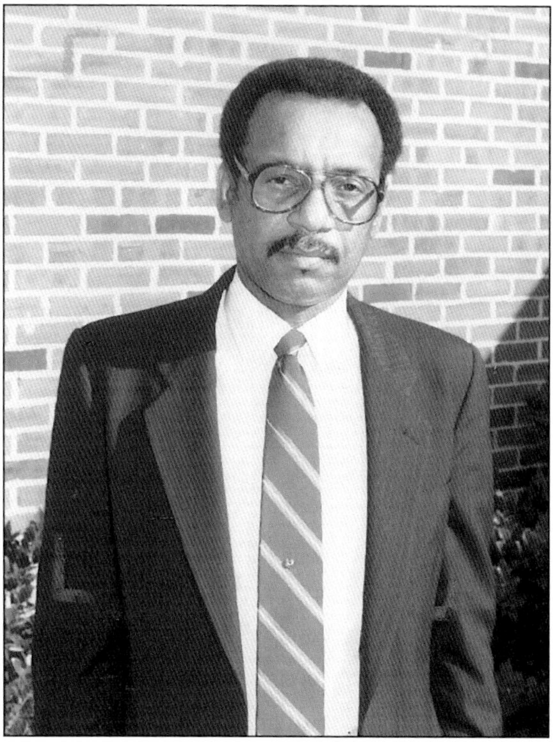

Dr. Charles Lyons. Dr. Lyons became president of Fayetteville State in 1969, upon the retirement of Dr. Jones. He had served at a number of other schools before arriving in Fayetteville. That same year, Fayetteville State was designated a regional university. In 1972, Lyons was named chancellor after the university became part of the UNC System. In athletics, the Broncos won their first Central Intercollegiate Athletic Association (CIAA) Tournament in 1973 and also established a championship golf program. Dr. Lyons became a major player in the CIAA, helping it to maintain its prominence after several schools left to form another conference. He resigned in 1987.

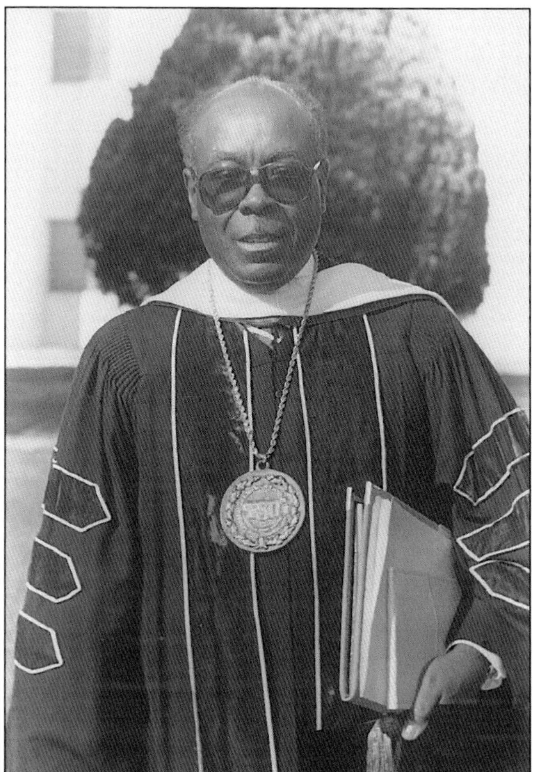

Dr. Lloyd V. Hackley. Dr. Hackley came to Fayetteville State after a stint at Arkansas–Pine Bluff. He took over shortly after the university was upgraded to a comprehensive university. A lot of money was poured into the campus to sustain its new status. The student body grew by more than 30 percent. For the first time, it passed the 3,000 and 4,000 marks. New masters and doctoral programs were added. During his tenure, Dr. Hackley took advantage of the new status to promote the university to other ethnic groups. This led to a major increase in the number of white students in the student body; this accounted for much of the increase in student population. Dr. Hackley resigned in 1995 to head the State Community College System.

DR. DONNA BENSON. Dr. Benson was named interim chancellor after the departure of Dr. Hackley. She was the first woman to head the university, even in an interim position. She brought a new atmosphere to the campus in the brief months that she was in charge. Her demeanor endeared her to the student body and allowed them great access to her. During the time when she was being considered for a permanent chancellorship, Dr. Benson was involved in an auto accident, in which she suffered severe injuries. Although she later fully recovered, she withdrew her name from consideration for the posts at Fayetteville State and Winston-Salem State. She is still likely to be the first black woman to be a permanent chancellor.

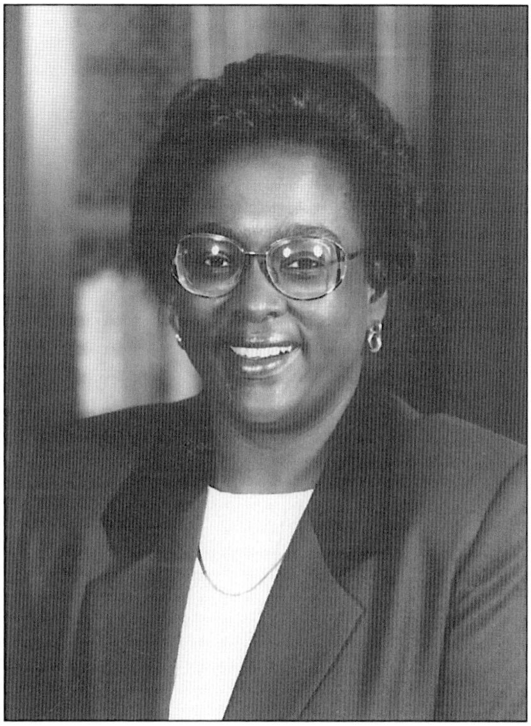

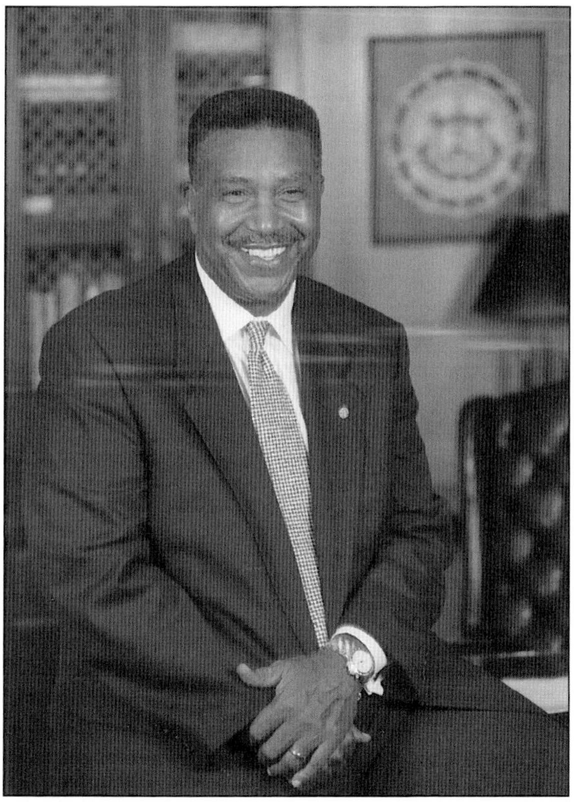

DR. WILLIS B. MCLEOD. Dr. McLeod graduated from Fayetteville State in 1964 and returned in 1995 as chancellor. As a student, he was a football player and student body president. He was one of the leaders of the civil rights marches. His career in education took him from the classroom to several superintendent positions. In 1987, he was a finalist in the search for the replacement for Dr. Lyons, and in 1995, he was chosen to become the leader of his alma mater. He is the first graduate of the university to head it in more than 100 years. Dr. McLeod brings a renewed spirit to the school. As a proud Bronco, he often leads the students in cheers at games. While this has yet to translate into wins, it is a refreshing sight. Under Dr. McLeod, Fayetteville State, in 1996, awarded its first doctoral degrees.

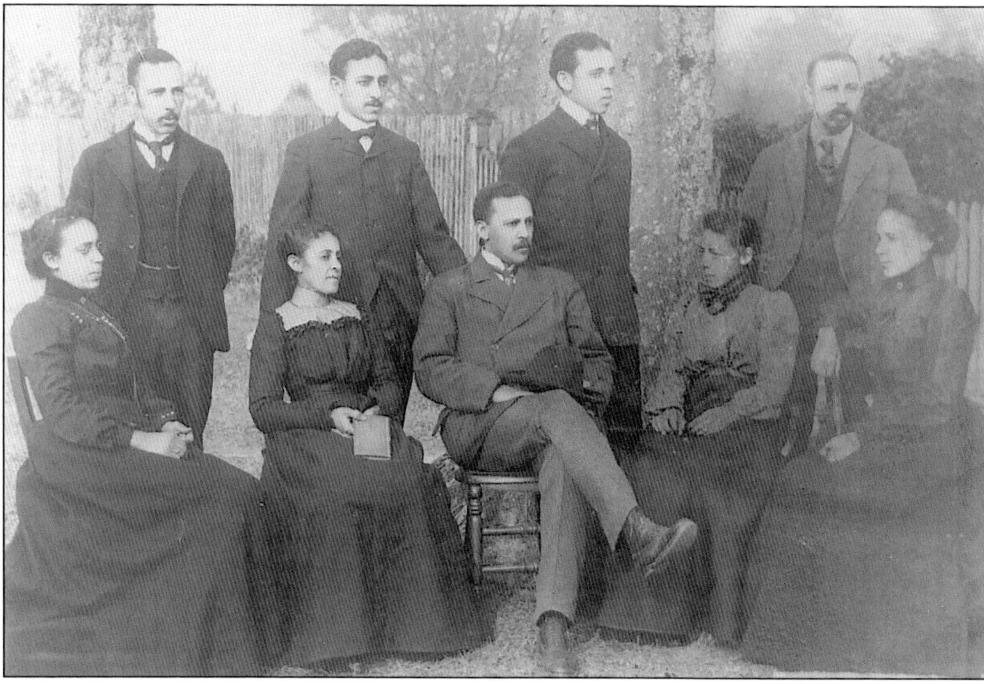

The Williston Family. The following six images are of prominent families that have four or more Fayetteville State University graduates.

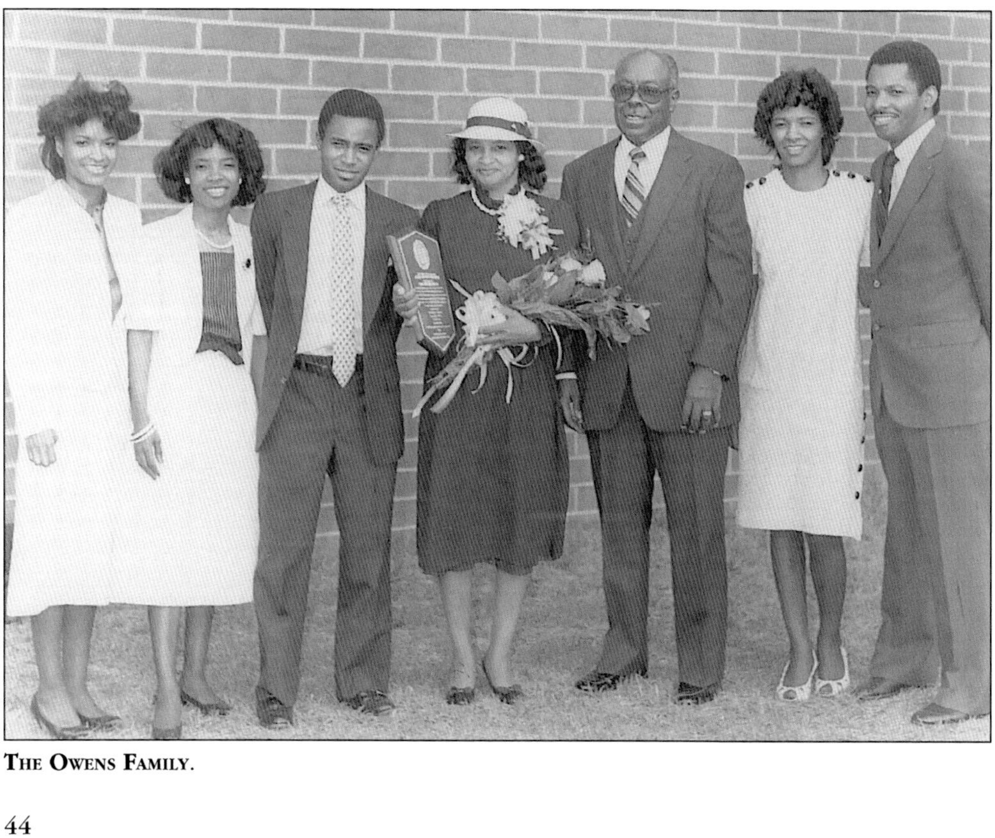

The Owens Family.

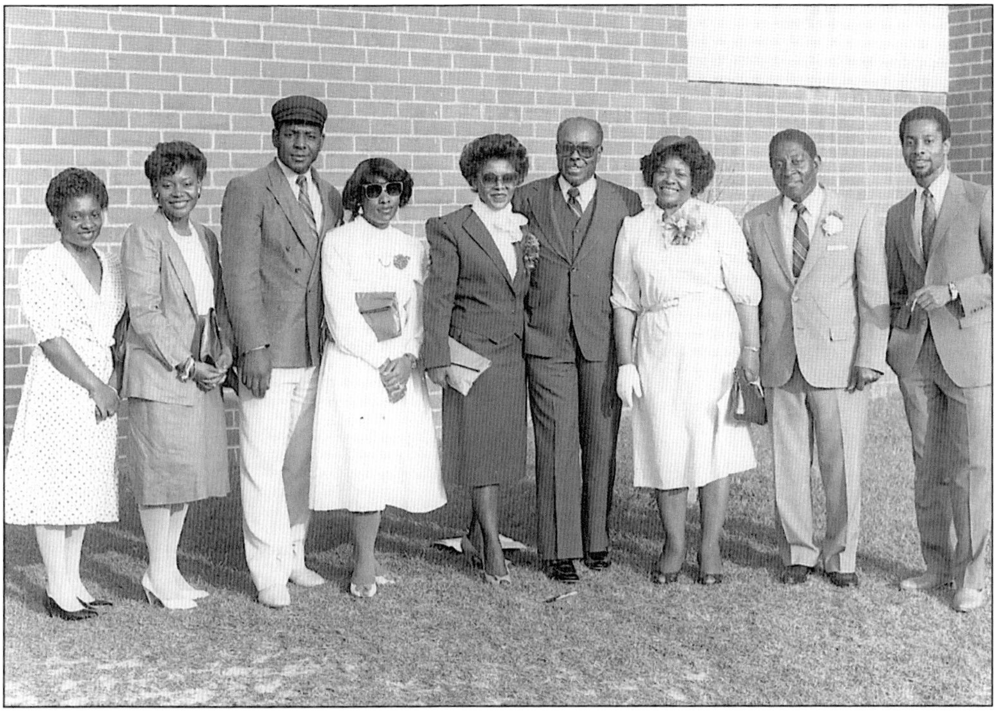

THE WRIGHT FAMILY.

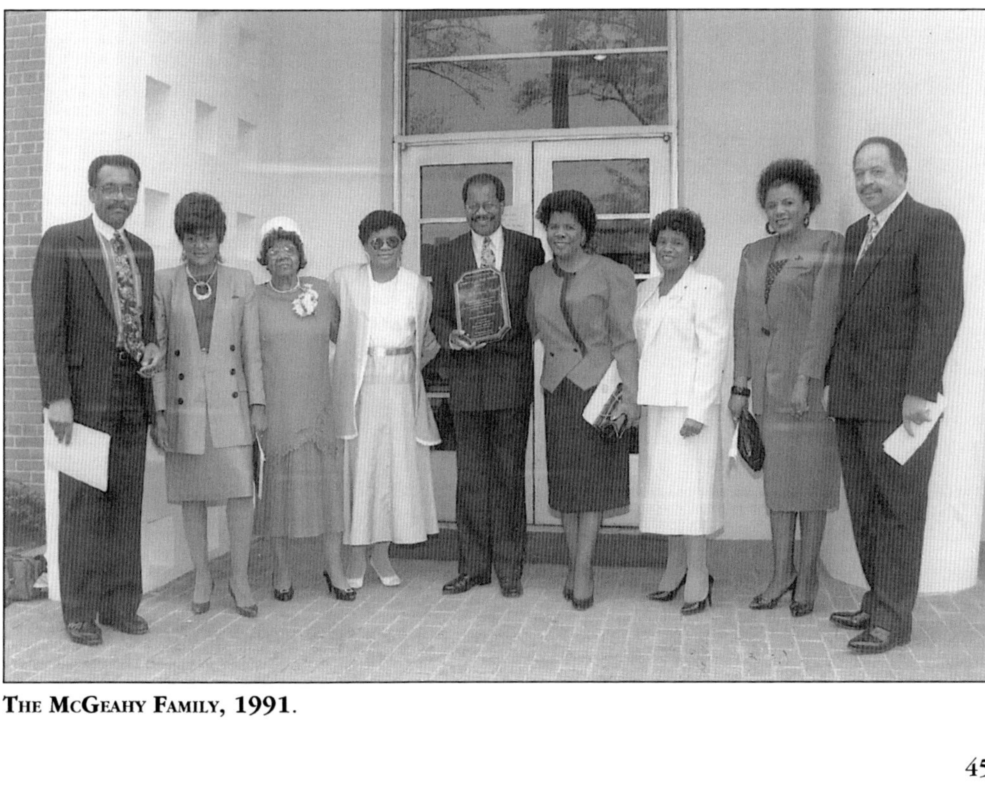

THE MCGEAHY FAMILY, 1991.

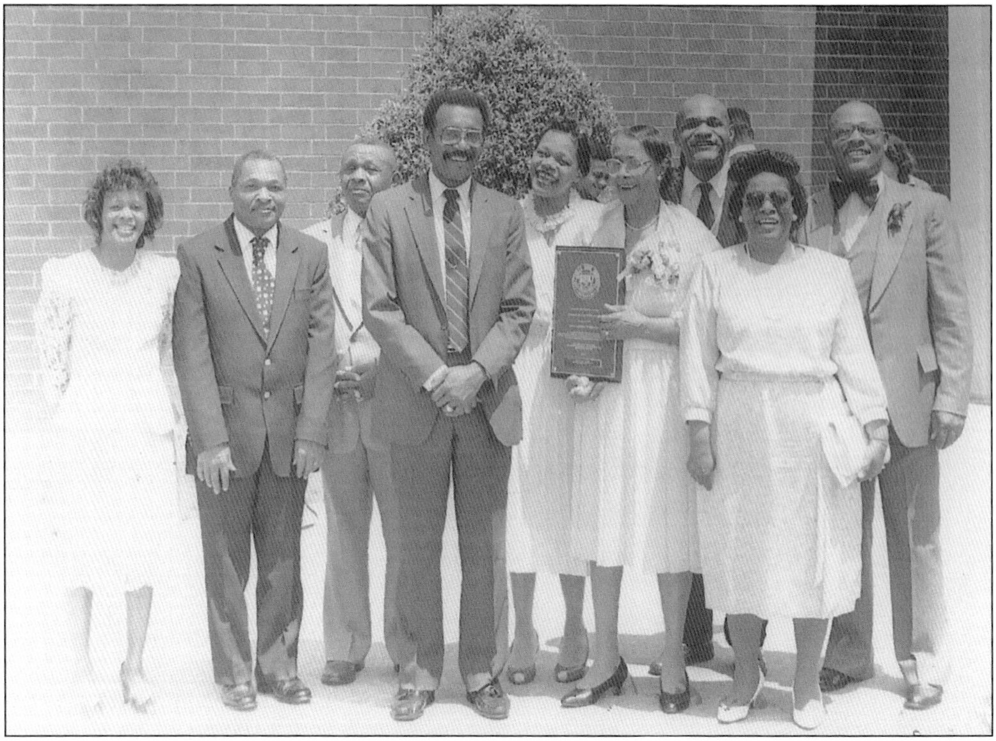

THE WILLIAMS FAMILY.

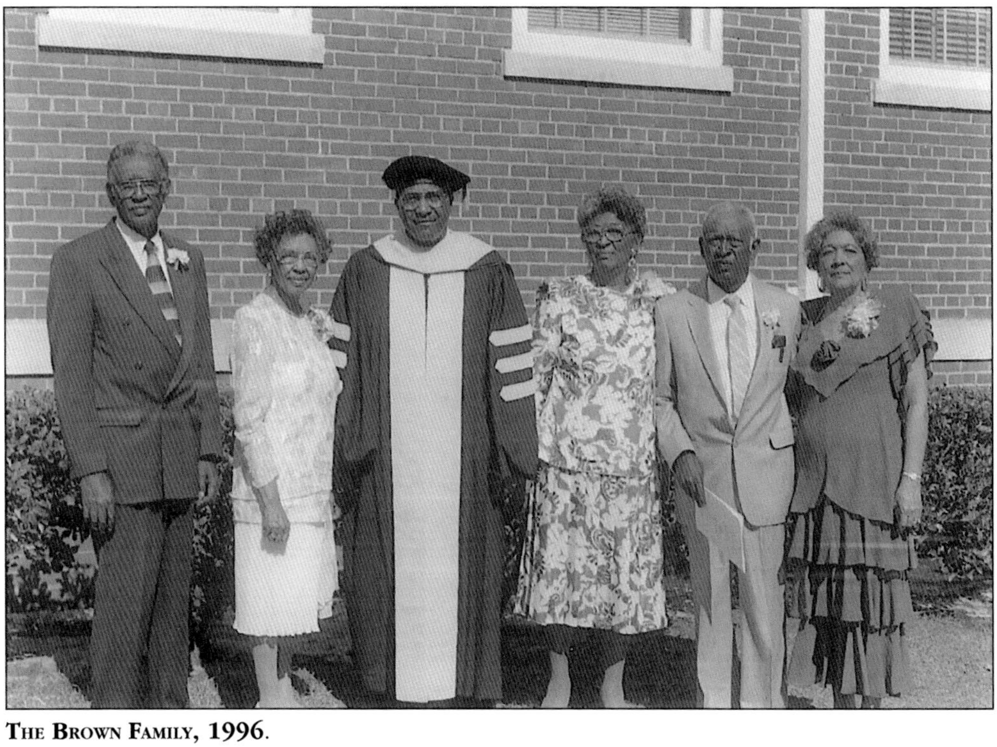

THE BROWN FAMILY, 1996.

Four

Defunct Schools

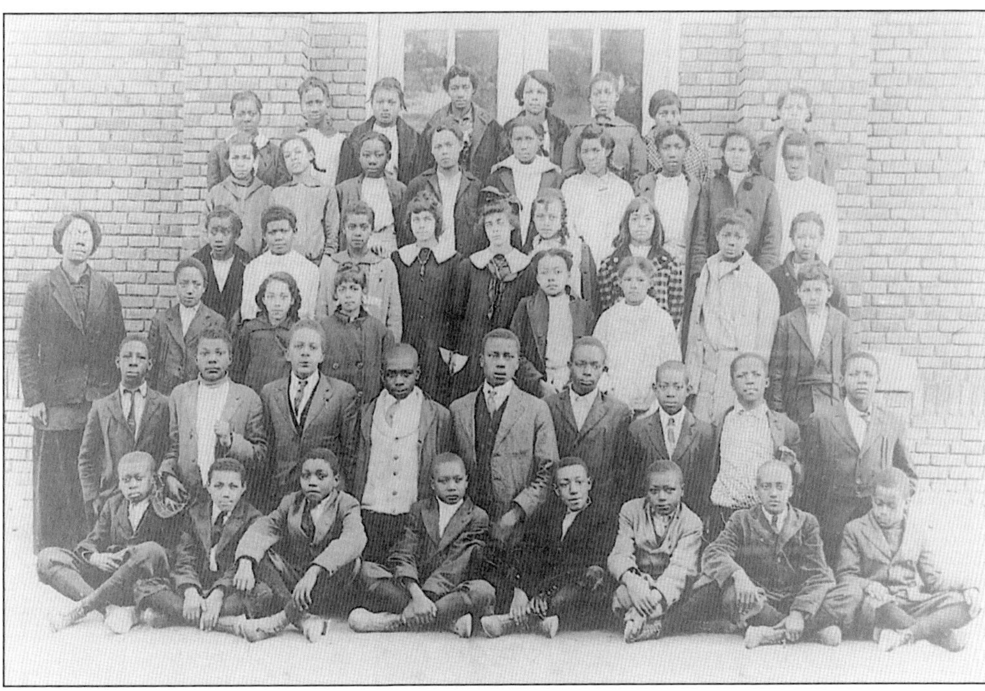

Orange Street School Students.

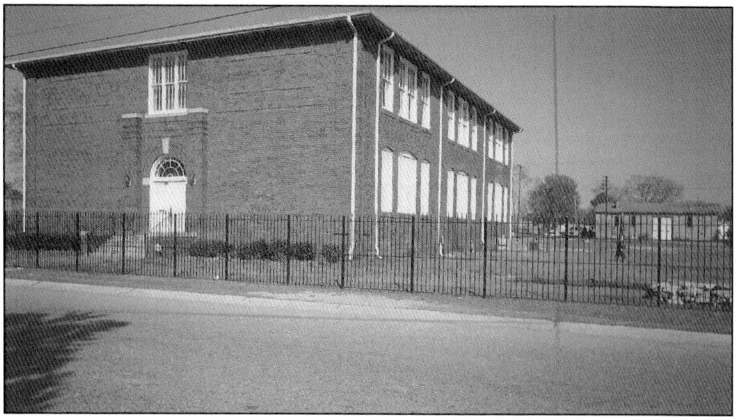

Orange Street School. Built in 1912 and closed in 1953, it was the first city school for blacks. The school also formerly housed E.E. Smith High School.

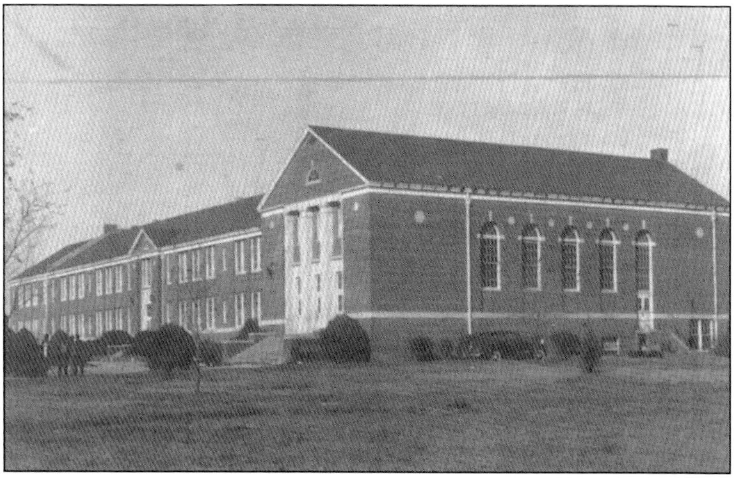

Newbold Laboratory School. This image shows Newbold's school and gymnasium. The school was built during the 1930s and closed during the 1960s.

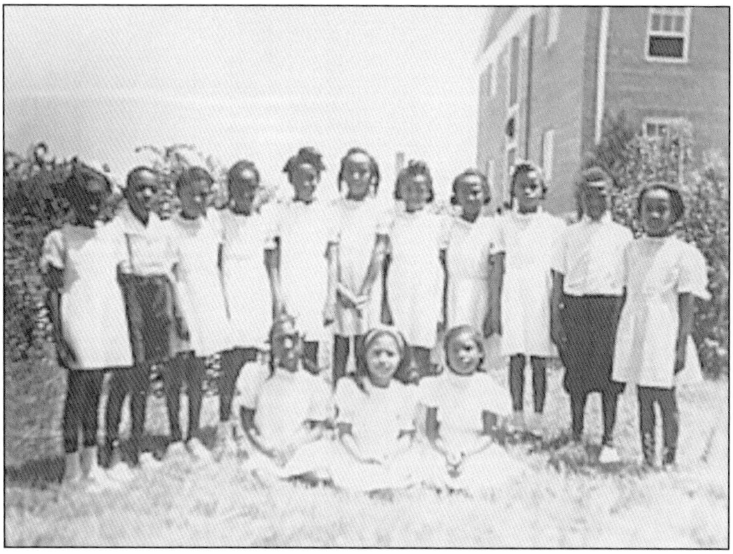

Newbold School Students.

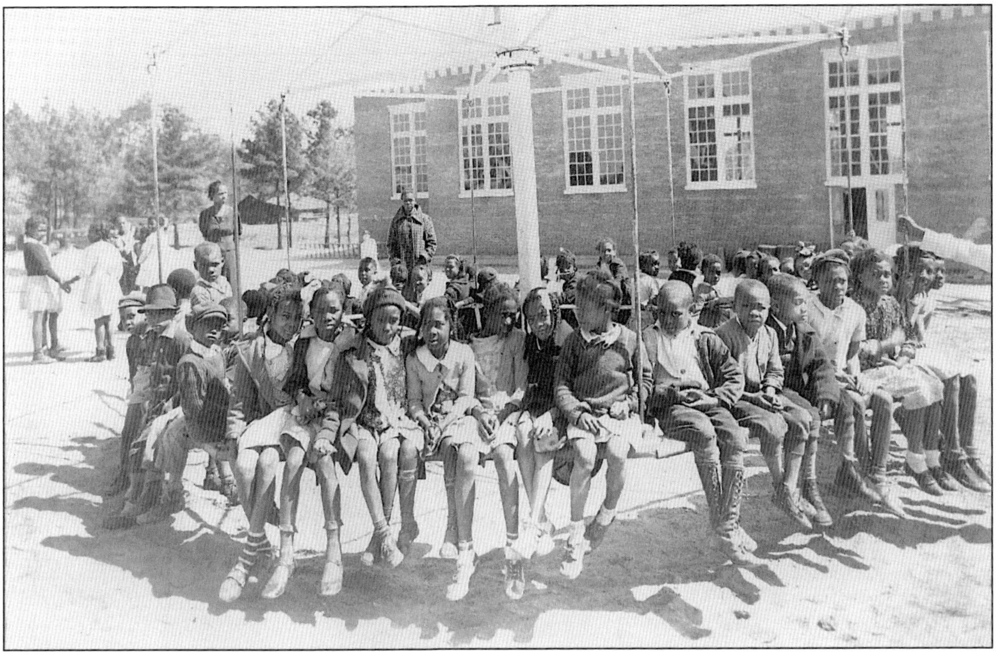

Newbold School Students, 1950. This view shows a group of students and student teachers enjoying the school's large recreational swing.

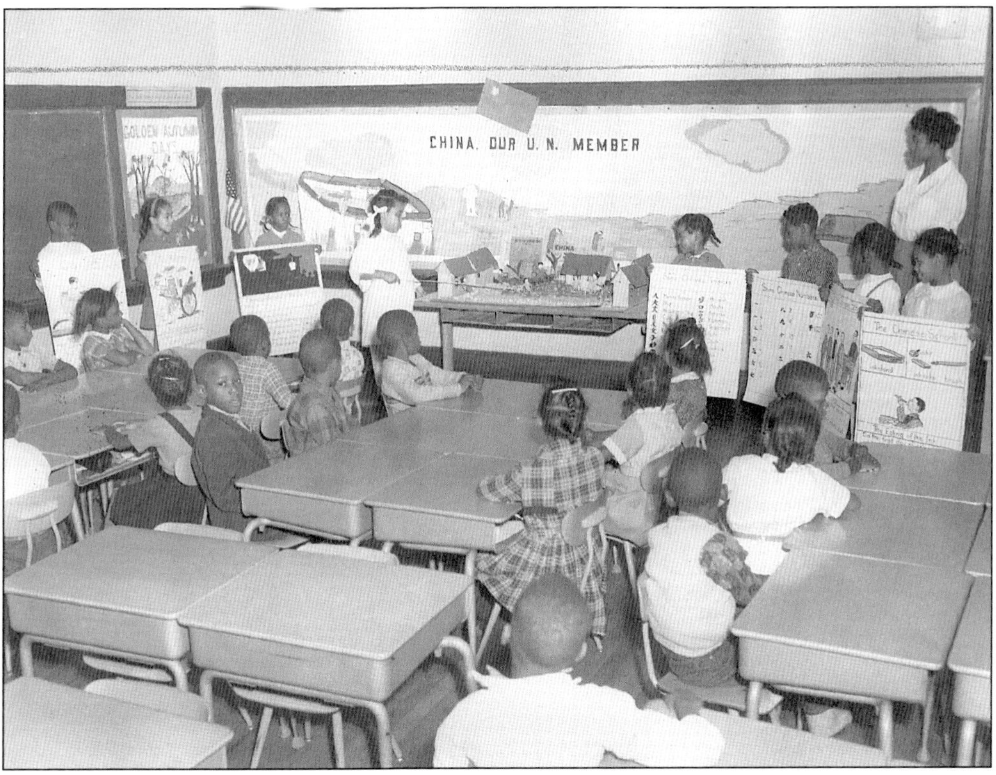

Newbold School Students Participating in United Nations Day, 1954.

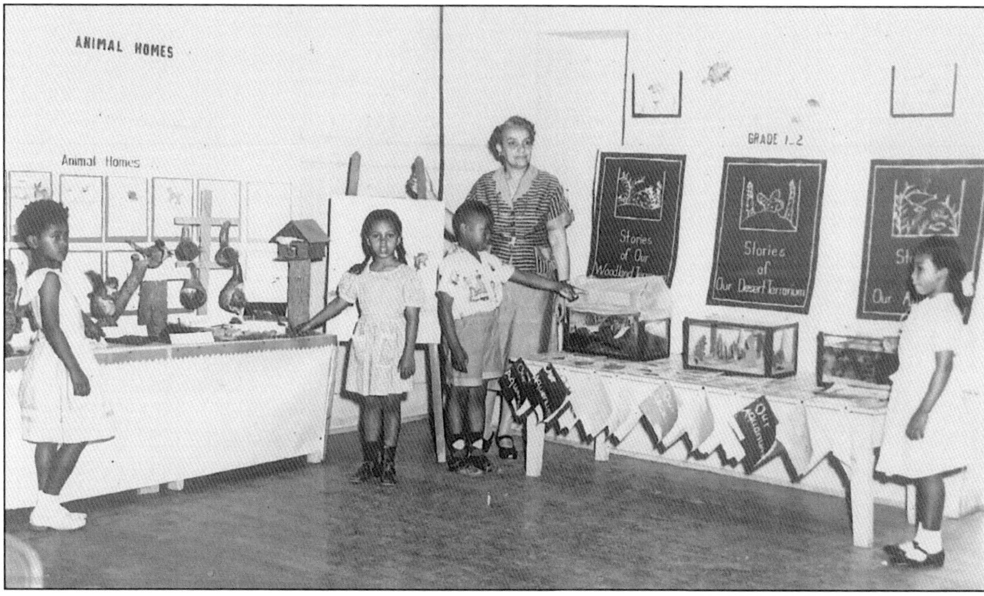

Newbold Students, 1955. These students are displaying their science exhibits for Miss Helen A. Hucles's class; those identified are Edwena Farmer, Roberta Gibson, William McKoy, and unidentified.

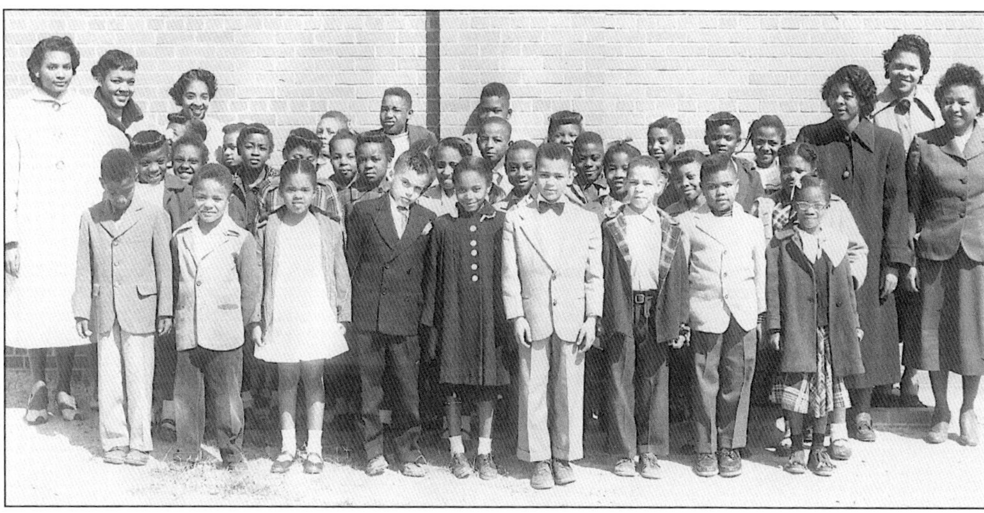

Newbold Students, 1953. Mrs. Eloise McNeill Haith is pictured here with her students and her student teachers.

Five

Fayetteville State University Athletics

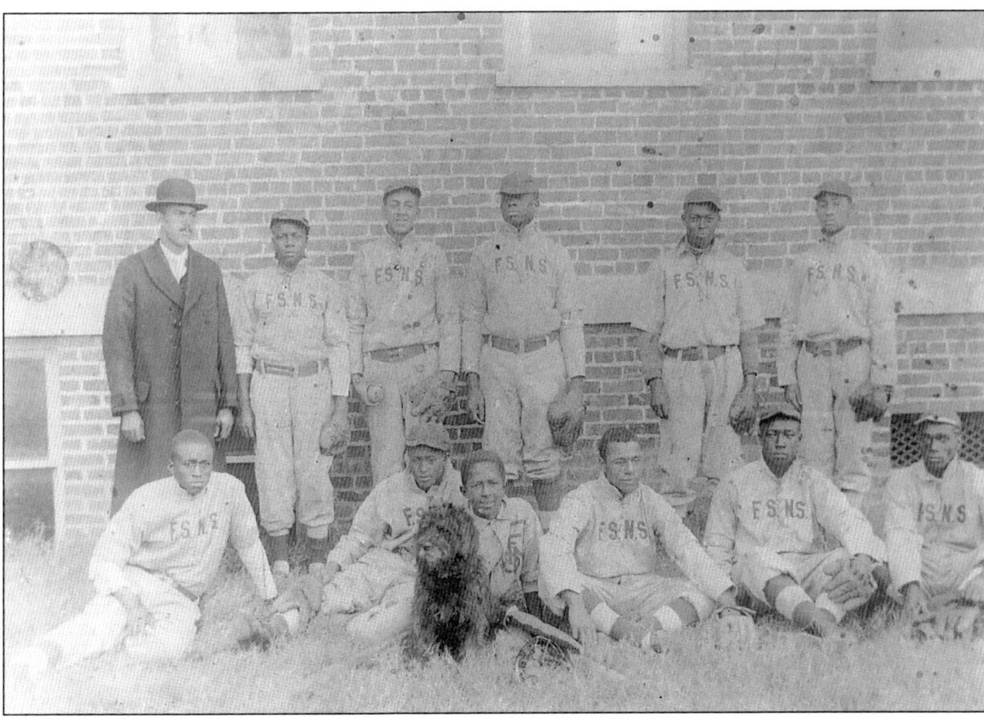

Baseball Team, 1910.

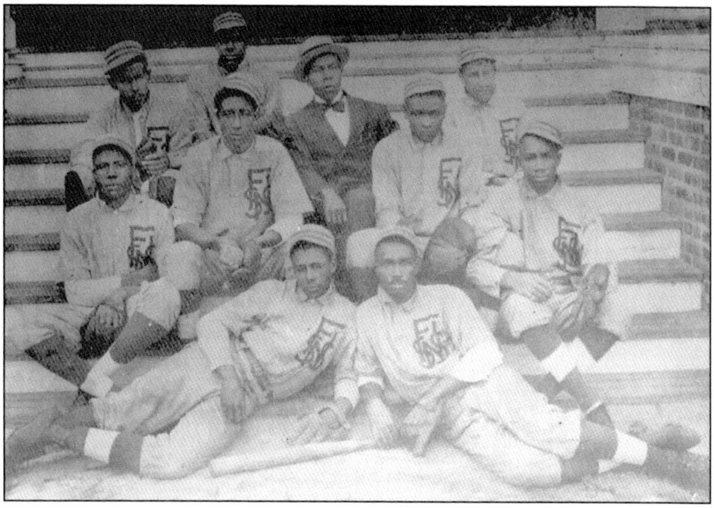

Baseball Team, 1916.

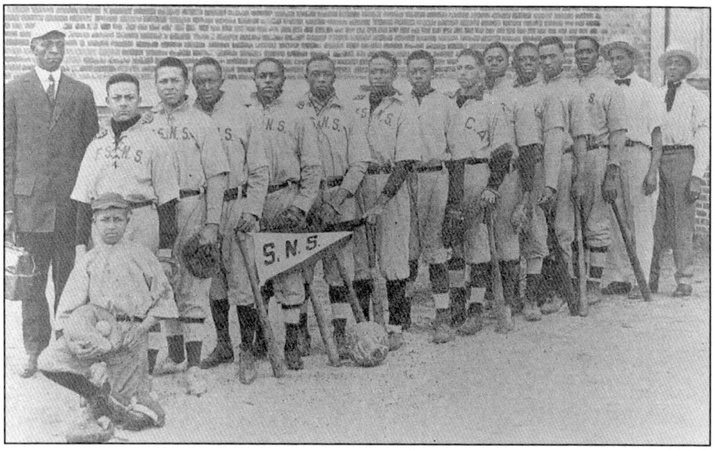

Baseball Team, 1918.

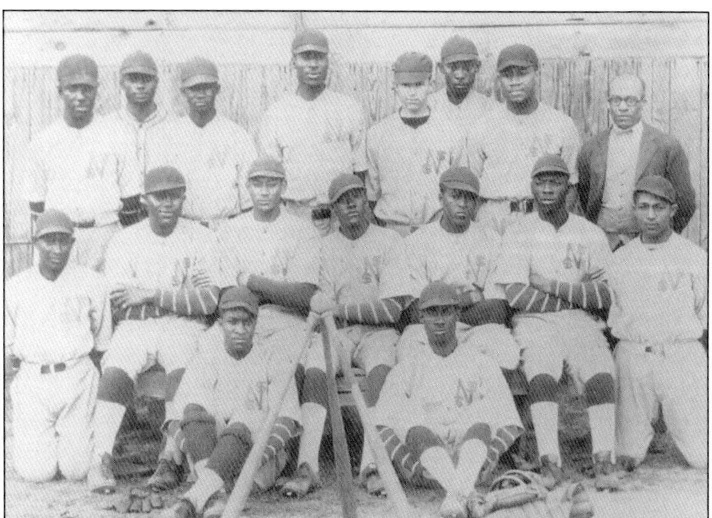

Baseball Team, 1927.

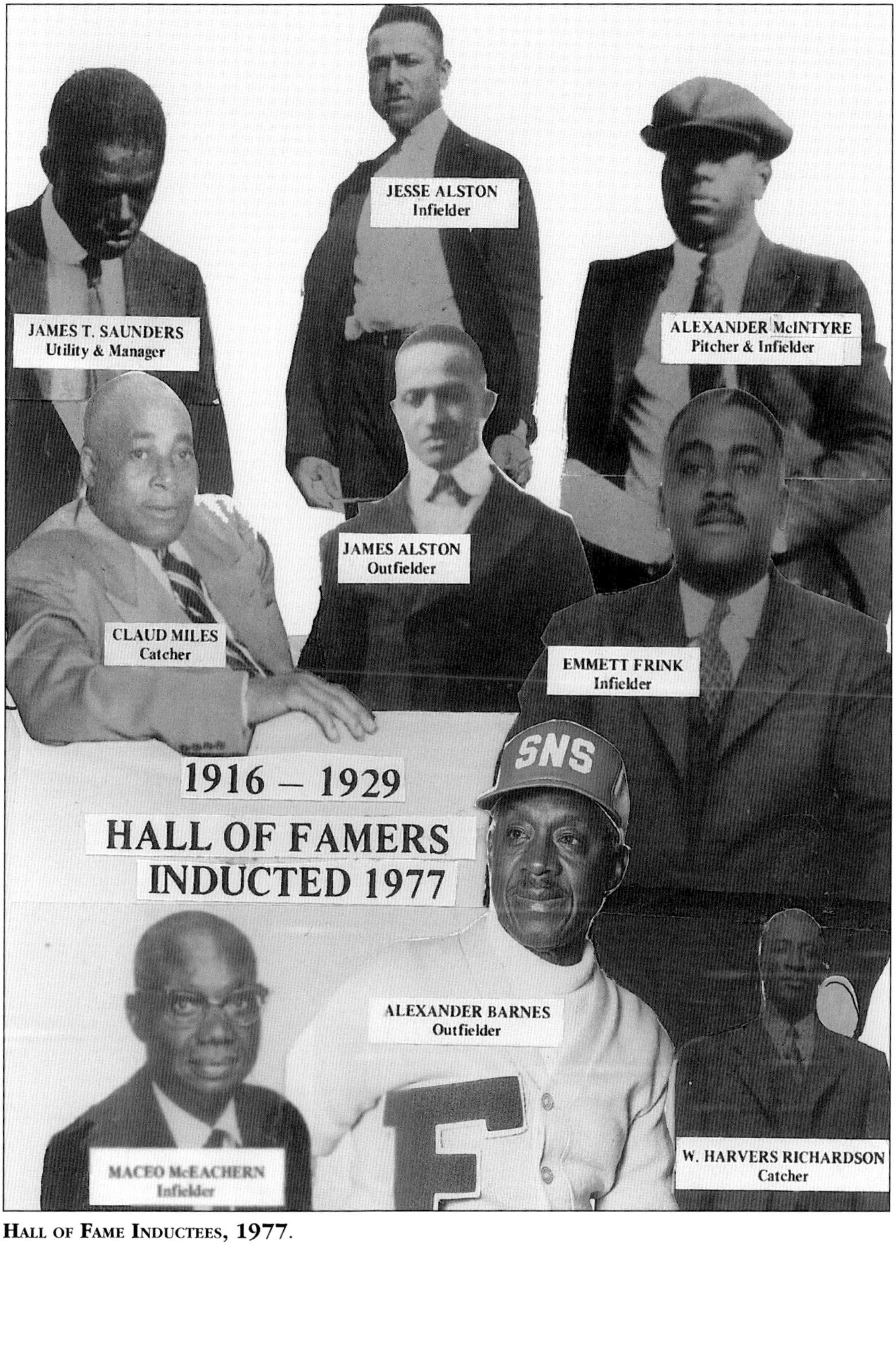

Hall of Fame Inductees, 1977.

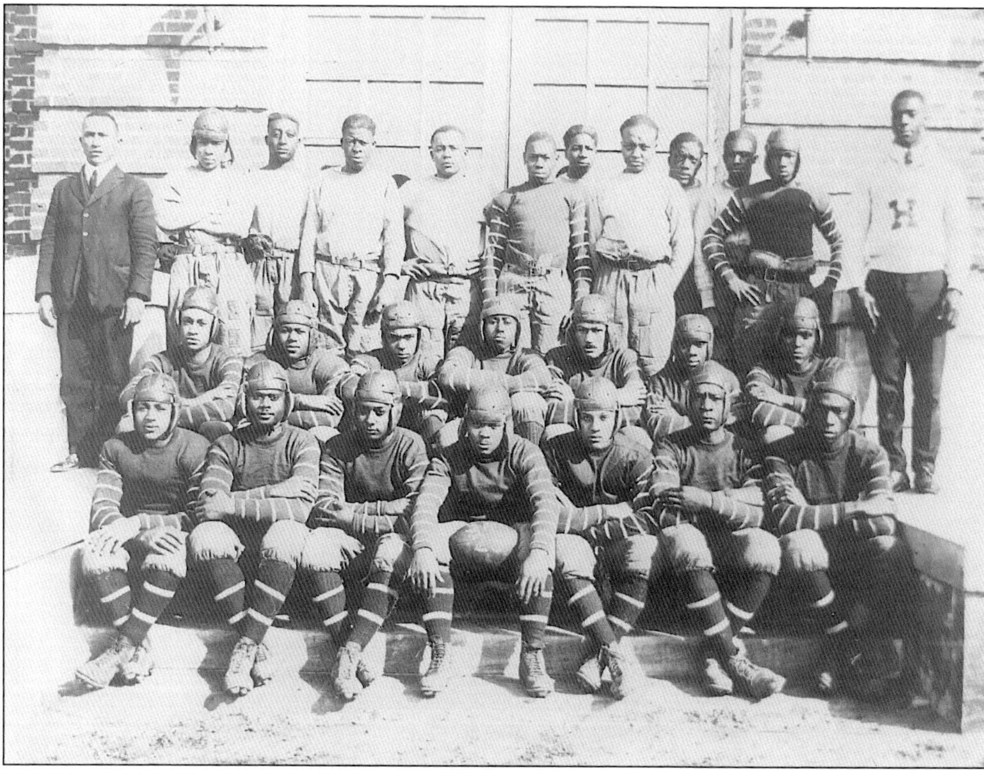

Football Team, 1925.

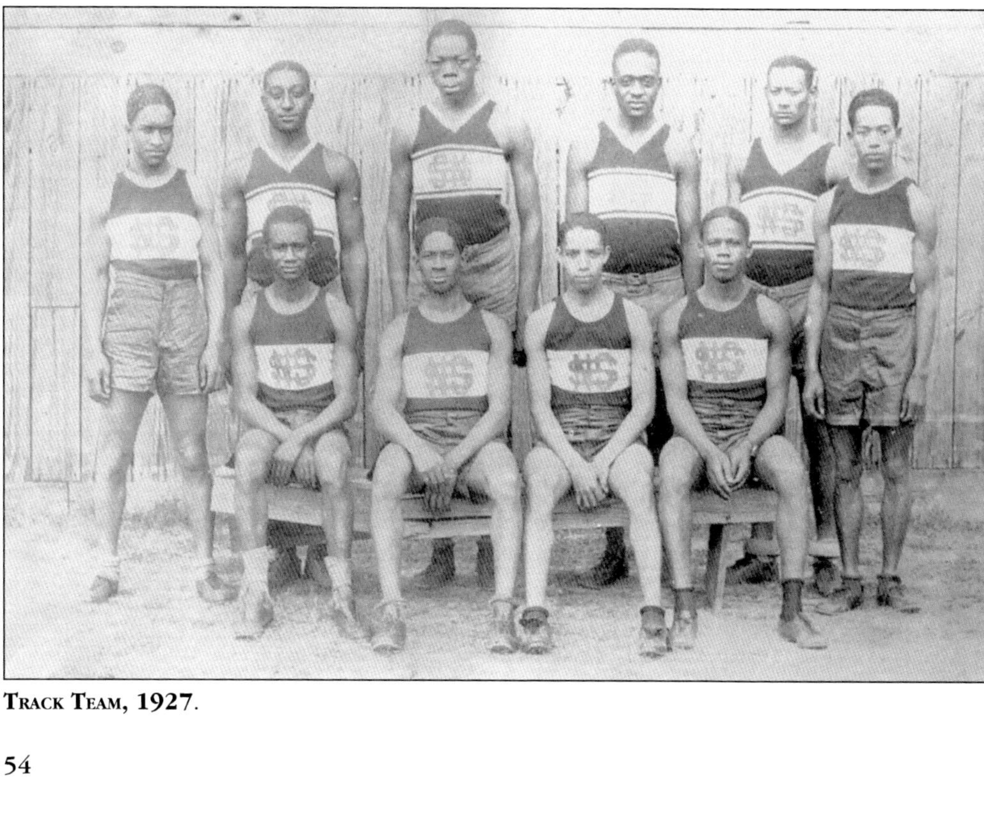

Track Team, 1927.

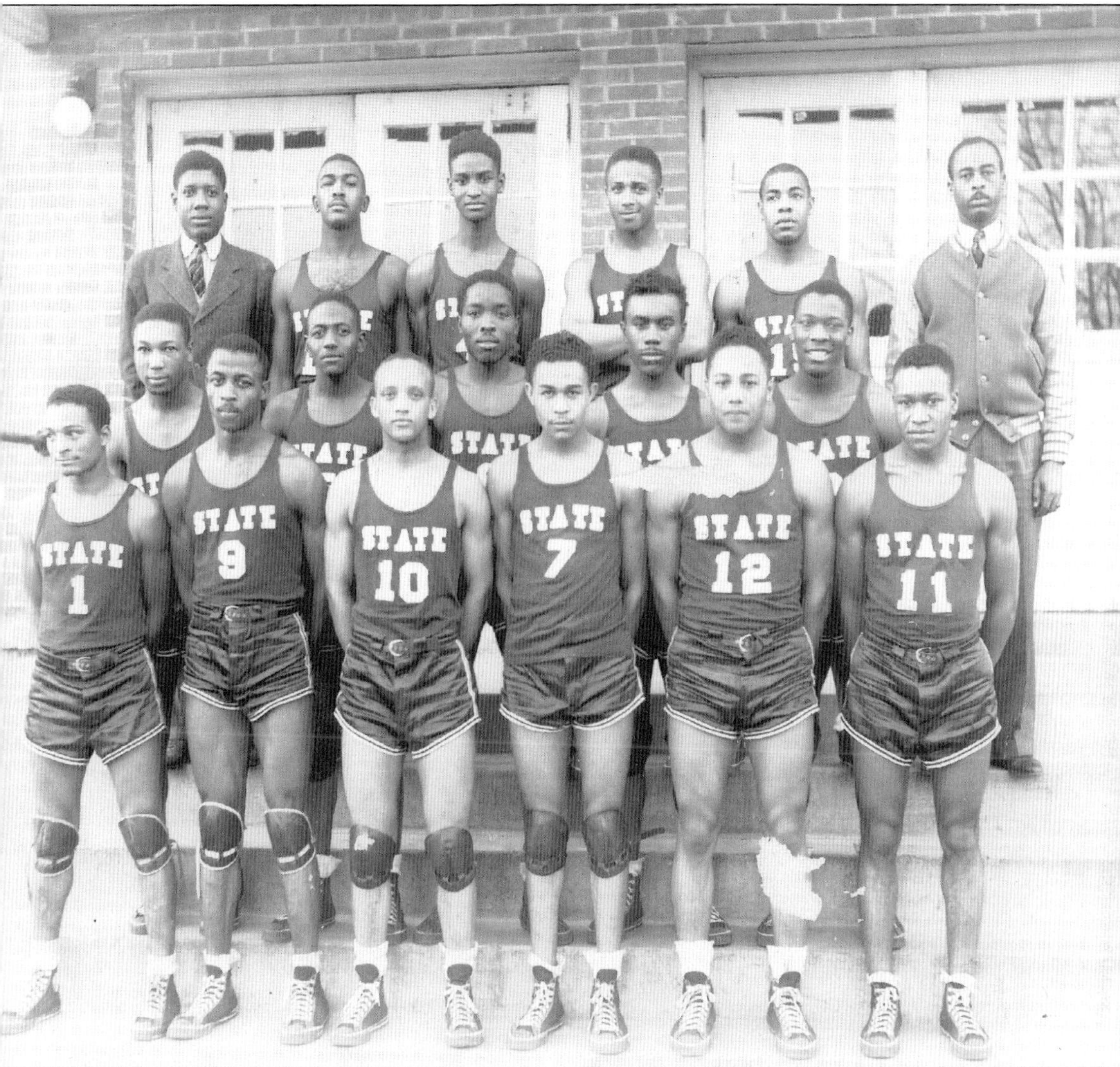

BASKETBALL TEAM, 1940. The 1940 Fayetteville State Broncos basketball team was not only successful, but it featured a number of future great professionals. Number 1 is Dennis T. Carter, who later became a great coach at E.E. Smith. Number 11 was a professor at Fayetteville State for over 35 years. Number 9 is Jerry Johnson, who is one of the leading basketball coaches in America; in 42 years at LeMoyne-Owens College, he has won 769 games. The second player from the left in the second row is Thelbert Torrey, who served on the city council for 12 years. The second player from the right is Roy McNeill Sr., whose two sons were stars at Fayetteville State; he attends nearly every game that Fayetteville State plays. The team was coached by Mr. Henry Black (third row, right), who brought most of the team with him after leading them to a high school national championship in 1939. Thelbert Torrey (second row, second from left) became a member of the Fayetteville City Council. Coach Black coached at Fayetteville State until they discontinued sports for the duration of World War II.

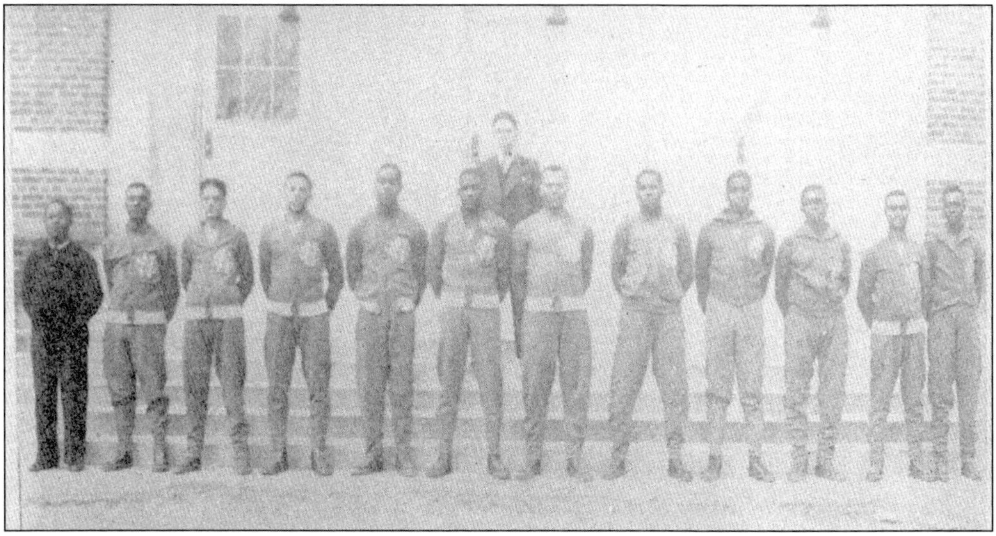

Basketball Team, 1935.

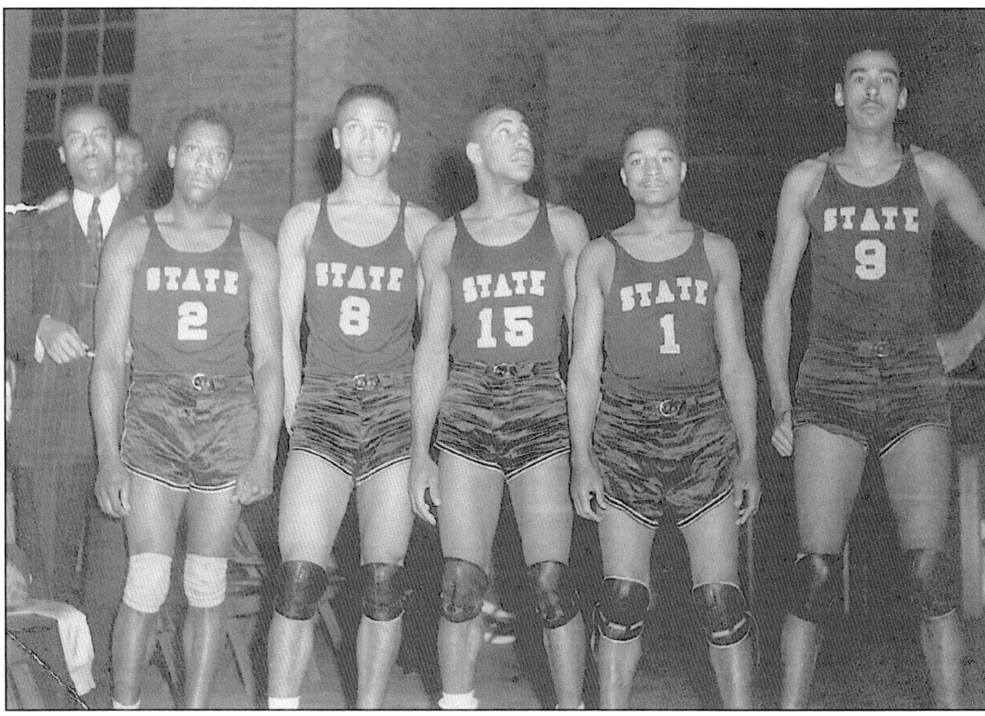

Basketball Team, 1941. This Fayetteville State team was the Eastern Collegiate Athletic Conference champions.

William Gaines. William A. "Gus" Gaines arrived in Fayetteville in 1945. He had been an All-CIAA and All-American football player at North Carolina College and was hired to serve as head coach of every program at Fayetteville State. Gaines set out to build a quality program for the Broncos. Because most men were still away at war, he began with the women. The women's basketball team was one of the most dominant in America. From there, he built a men's program in football and basketball. Gaines accumulated 300 victories faster than any coach in North Carolina history and holds the national record for most victories in a season with 44. He guided the Broncos to five Eastern Intercollegiate Athletic Conference (EIAC) Championships in basketball and two in football. Fayetteville State honored him in 1996; his portrait hangs over the basketball arena.

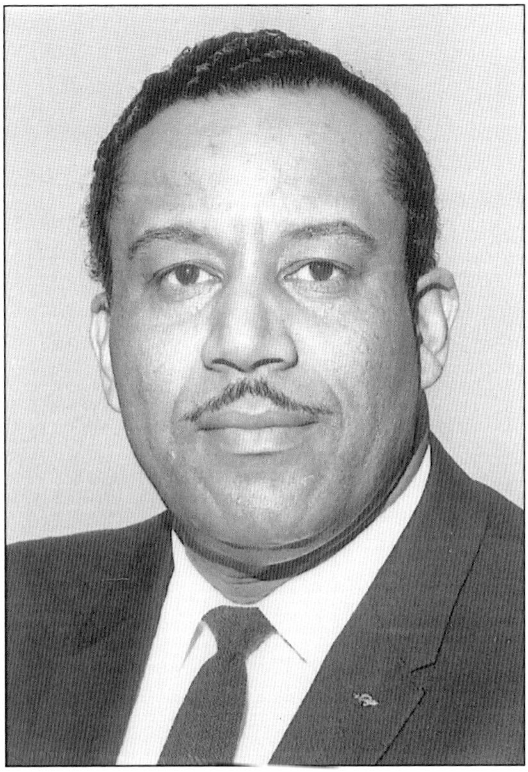

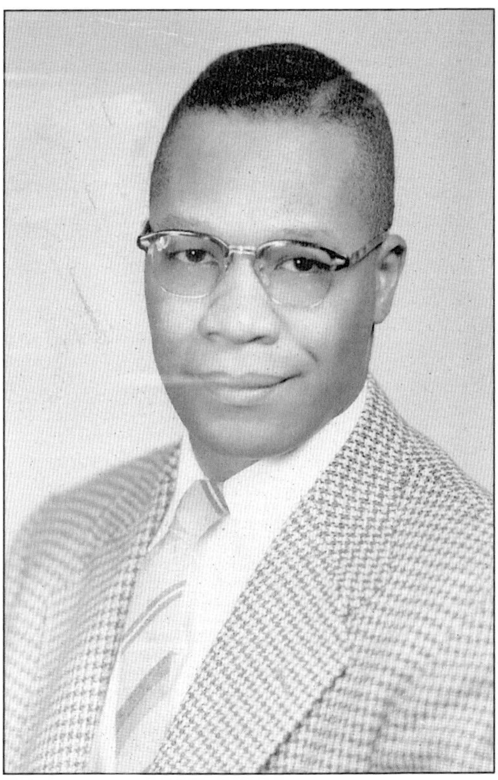

Coach Harold L. Scott. Coach Scott is a native of Pittsburgh, Pennsylvania, and a graduate of West Virginia State College. He earned a masters degree from Pittsburgh. Coach Scott came to Fayetteville State in 1947 as a physical education instructor and assistant coach to the football, basketball, and baseball teams. He established and coached the first modern-era track team at Fayetteville State in 1954. His team was the first Fayetteville State team to go to the CIAA, Penn Relays, and Madison Square Garden. He was promoted to athletic director in 1957 and served in that capacity for 12 years. He was the Fayetteville State liaison to the Red Cross and was responsible for the certification of physical education majors. He chaired the Physical Education Department from 1961 to 1970 and was the president of the CIAA for one year. In 1973, he was the first director of the National Youth Sports Program (NYSP). Coach Scott was later inducted into the FSU Hall of Fame.

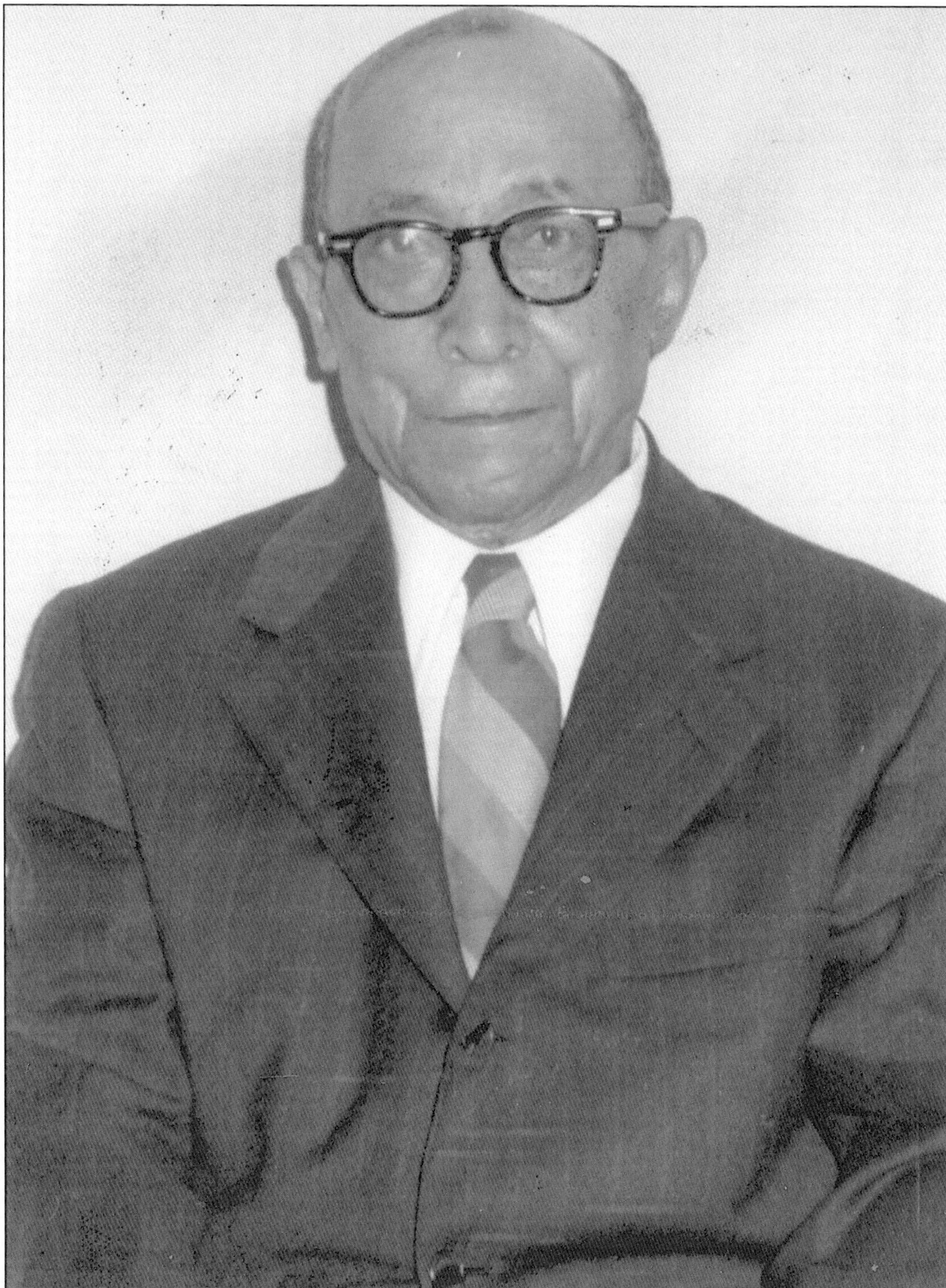

James Coppage. James Coppage is the first known coach at Fayetteville State. A graduate of Hampton Institute, he joined the staff in the 1920s as a vocation teacher. He used his athletic experience to assist the Broncos football, basketball, and baseball programs. Unfortunately, there are no complete records from his coaching career, but it is safe to say that he built a quality program for his day. Fayetteville State was a power in baseball in the 1920s and 1930s under his guidance.

Laurette Taylor. Miss Taylor joined the Fayetteville State staff in 1944 and has served as a dormitory director, physical education instructor, and women's basketball coach. She strived to build school spirit and comradery among faculty and students. All of her teams were academically and athletically sound. Most Broncos remember her as the women's basketball coach, and she built Fayetteville State into one of the CIAA's dominating programs. Her 1975 and 1976 teams were runners-up in the CIAA Tournament. In 1975 and 1976, she earned Coach of the Year honors, and she was inducted into the CIAA Hall of Fame in 1982. Miss Taylor was a member of Evans Metropolitan AME Zion Church and served as a member of the Fayetteville Recreation Board.

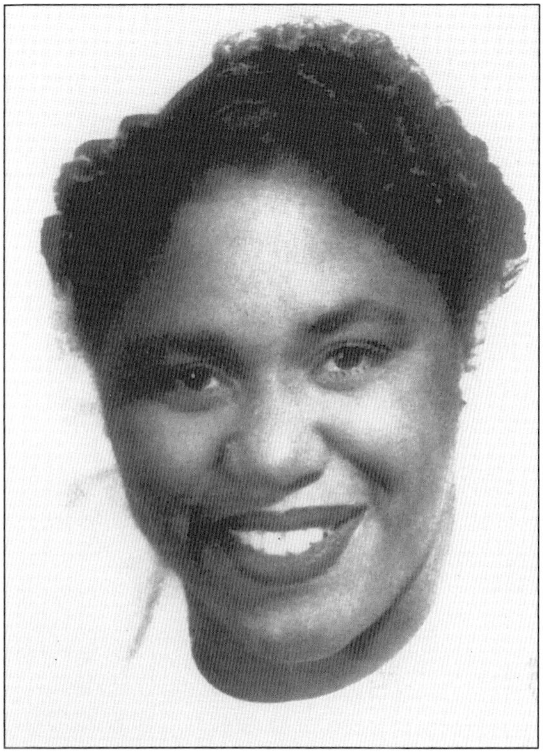

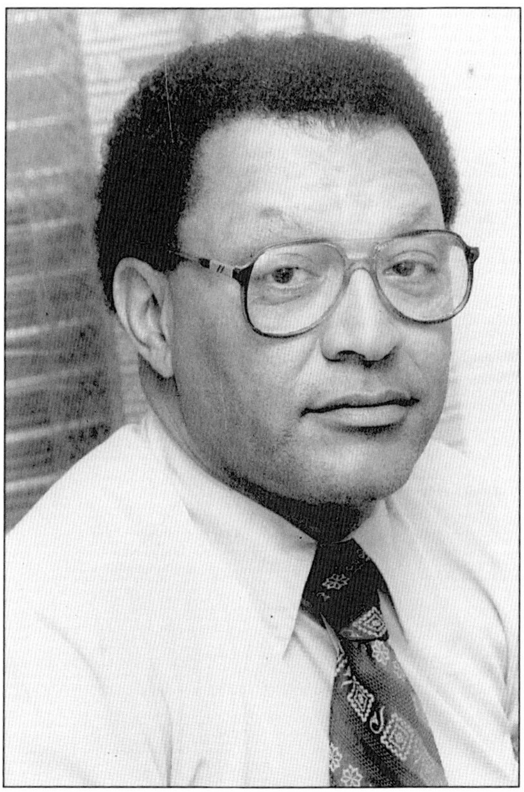

John Marshall. John "JD" Marshall joined the staff in 1980 as athletic director. He brought a wealth of knowledge to the program. A graduate of South Carolina State College, he served on numerous national committees. Under his administration, women's sports were given new focus. Softball was added in 1981, and the Lady Broncos captured the 1983 CIAA Championship. He introduced strong academic standards for student-athletes and paved the way for growth. Mr. Marshall made headway in taking the program to the community. He is the only representative of Fayetteville State to be a member of the Fayetteville Sports Club. He gained great contacts with the business community and opened doors that had never been attempted before. Serving admirably until 1989, Mr. Marshall was inducted into the National Collegiate Athletic Directors Association (NCADA) Hall of Fame in 1995.

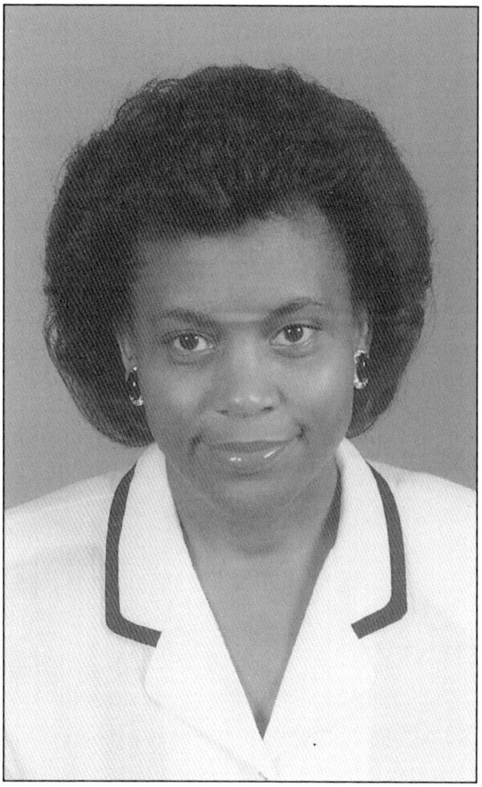

Peggy L. Green. Dr. Peggy L. Green came to Fayetteville State in 1985 as the women's basketball and volleyball coach. In addition to her coaching duties, she served on several NCAA committees. From 1989 to 1998, she served on the NCAA Division II Women Committee and chaired the committee from 1996 to 1998. She has been a member of the Management Council since 1995. Additionally, she is a member of the NCAA Minorities Opportunities and Interest Committee and chairs the Student-Athlete Involvement Project Team. Dr. Green is the first woman from FSU to hold a national athletic office, serving with great distinction. She has worked diligently on behalf of FSU student-athletes as the women's coordinator.

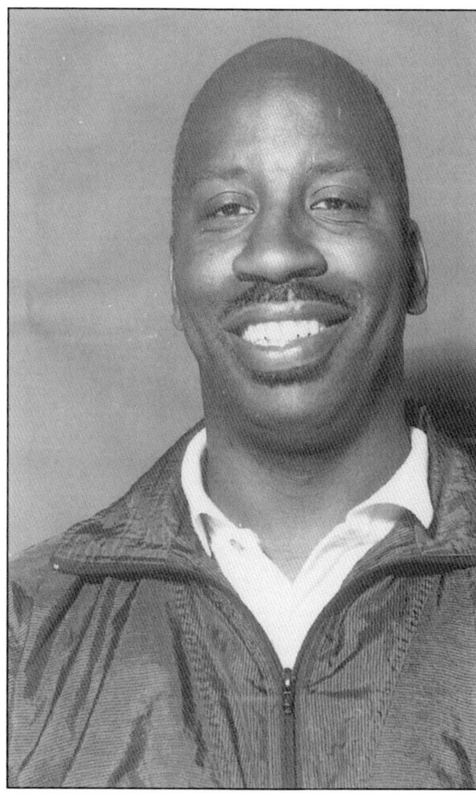

Eric Tucker. Eric Tucker made history in 1992, when he was named the head women's basketball coach at FSU. He is the first coach of a major sport from the local area in half a century. Tucker came from the junior high ranks, amid great criticism. He has proven his detractors wrong, guiding the Lady Broncos to the CIAA finals twice, and he has been named Coach of the Year twice. Tucker took the Lady Broncos to the NCAA Southeast Regionals in 1998, making it to the semi-finals. They posted their first undefeated record in the Southern Division of the CIAA. He has built a solid program that is ranked near the top of the CIAA each year. In eight years, Tucker has posted a 139-79 record, giving him the most victories by a Broncos women's coach.

Six

Fayetteville State University Athletes

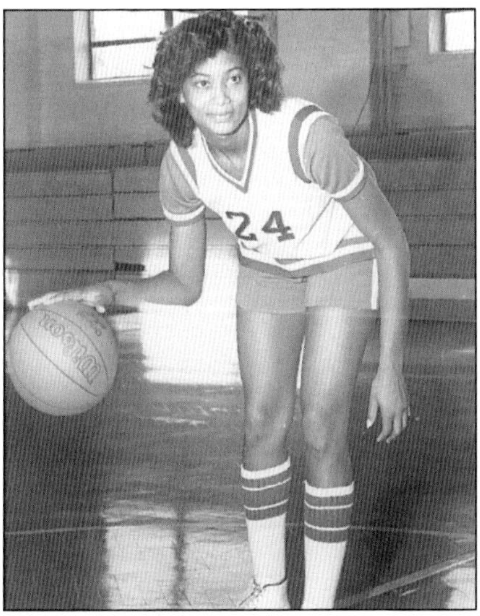

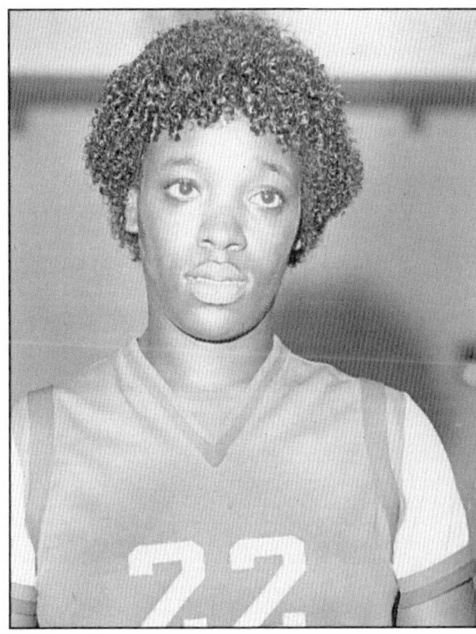

Left: Dianthia Morris. Dianthia "Dee" (Ford) Morris was an All-CIAA athlete in softball and basketball. She was blessed with exceptional skills, but her strongest asset was her leadership abilities. Where she led, the team followed; when she led, the team won. She applied the same principles to her studies and maintained a place on the Dean's List. As a senior in 1982, she hit 8-11 for the three-game championship against a favored Norfolk State and was named All-CIAA and to the All-Tournament Team. She was named All-CIAA in basketball three times. Dee is presently coaching volleyball and softball at Shaw University. Her volleyball team won the CIAA championship in the fall of 1995, and her softball team won the CIAA in the spring of 1996.

Right: Concethia Smith. Concethia "CC" Smith is one of the best players ever to play for FSU, in any sport. A deadly shooter from any point on the court, she was feared by many male players because she was never afraid to mix it up with them, and win. Her efforts made her the third-ranked career scorer, with 1,474 points. Her career average of 19.7 per game is the highest for a four-year player. She was named All-CIAA in 1981, 1982, and 1983 and was an Association of Intercollegiate Athletics for Women (AIAW) All-American. CC's skills were not restricted to basketball, for she was also a member of the Broncos softball team. Her natural position was the outfield, but she could play most positions. She was also a strong threat at the plate and an aggressive runner on the base paths.

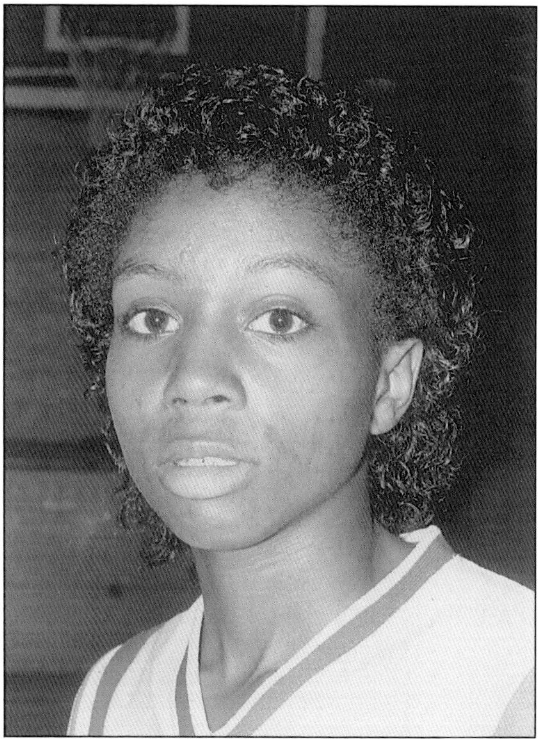

Joyce Vaughn Battle. Most people will remember Joyce Vaughn Battle as the left-handed point guard that starred at E.E. Smith and Fayetteville State. Not flashy, Joyce could get the most out of those around her. She earned All-CIAA honors and was named to the All-CIAA Tournament team as a junior. She was a member of two CIAA Southern Division championship teams. Battle was a member of the Black Conference of Sports Information Directors (BCOSIDA) College Division All-American Team. She also played tennis for the Broncos. Following graduation, Battle was a part of history. She was a professional basketball player in the failed National Women's Basketball Association, playing for the Virginia Express. The league folded after only five games. In 1988, she joined her former coach at Delaware State College, where she worked as an assistant.

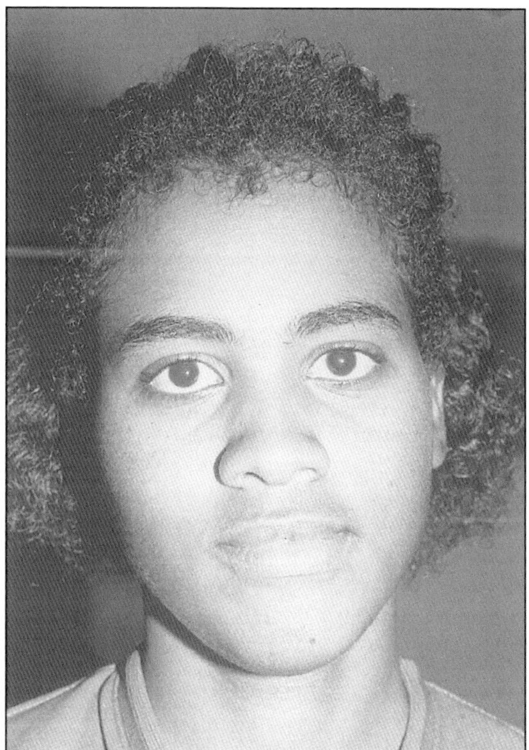

Dimple White. Seldom has such a talent chosen to attend a small college, but Dimple White decided to stay at home and become a Bronco. A graduate of Pine Forest High School, Dimple was highly touted. She earned All-State honors and played in the East-West All Star Game. She became an impact player as a freshman and continued to glow throughout her career. During the 1986 and 1987 seasons, she led the Broncos in rebounds and blocked shots. She finished her career with 1,171 points and had a career average of 13.1 points per game. White earned All-CIAA in 1986 and 1987 and earned BCOSIDA All-America honors as a senior.

ANNETTA FAULCON. Annetta Faulcon played for the Broncos from 1983 to 1986 and was a major force behind their success. The 5-feet, 11-inch lefthander was a deadly shot from the floor and a great rebounder. She played unselfishly, leading the team in assists during her sophomore year. As a junior and senior, she took on more of the scoring load. Her career 1,409 points places her in fourth place on the Broncos' scoring chart. She averaged 13.7 point per game over four years. Faulcon had a well-rounded game and was a strong player at both ends of the court. She led the team in rebounds as a sophomore and steals as a senior. Faulcon is well remembered for her winning smile and her leadership on and off the court.

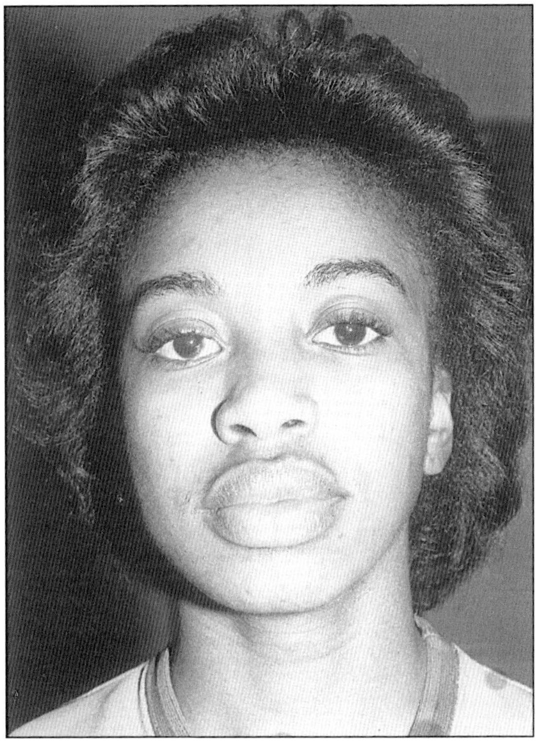

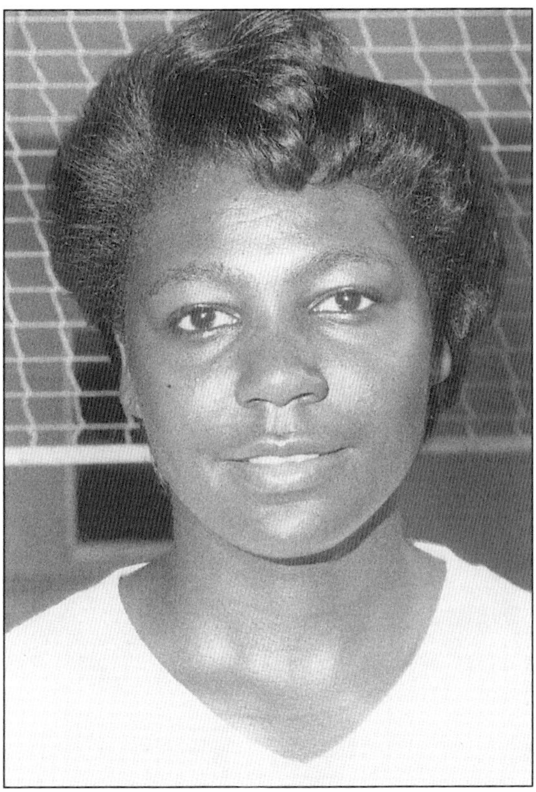

SHEILA SEWARD. A native of Henderson, North Carolina, Sheila is one of the best athletes in Fayetteville State history. She starred in volleyball, basketball, and softball. Her best sport was basketball. As a senior, she ranked seventh in the nation in scoring and rebounding. She was named All-CIAA as a junior and senior and was ranked first in the CIAA in rebounding as a senior and second in scoring. For her career, Sheila is ranked fourth in scoring with 1,643 points, and second with a scoring average of 16.3 points per game. She is the Broncos career-leading rebounder with 1,211 rebounds. She is also ranked fifth in career steals and second in career blocked shots. Sheila majored in intermediate education and is presently teaching and coaching in her hometown.

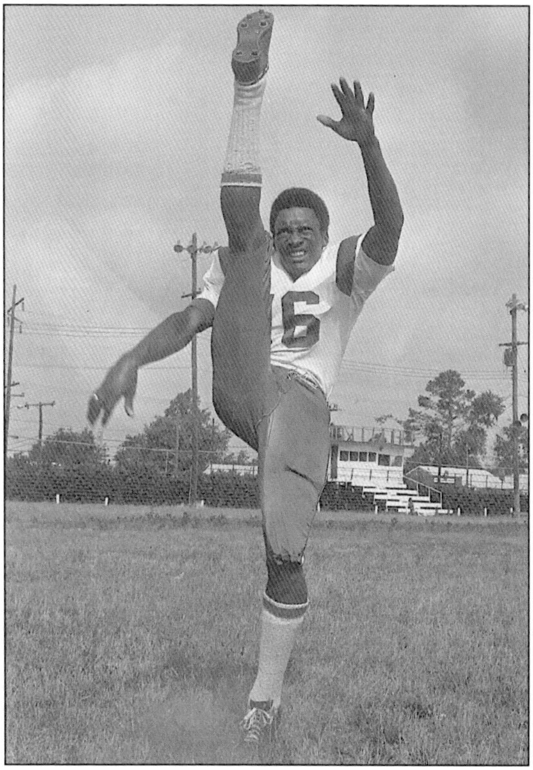

Kenny Gamble. Kenny Gamble is the all-time leading punter in Broncos history. As a senior, he led the nation in yards per kick. Blessed with a strong, flexible leg, Gamble kept Broncos opponents at bay. He could place the ball in the corner, burying them inside their 20-yard line. Even if the kicks were in the middle of the field, he had tremendous hang time, allowing his teammates to cover. Gamble played from 1969 to 1971. He averaged 44.5 yards per kick in 1971 and had a career average of 41.1 yards per kick. He earned All-CIAA and All-American honors. After graduating in 1972, he tried out with the Dallas Cowboys. During the training camp, an eye problem was discovered and he was cut. He has since pursued a career in education.

Blenda Gay. Blenda Gay was an all-time great in Broncos history. He was a defensive tackle who was nearly impossible to block. He was a common sight in opposing back fields. At 6 feet, 5 inches, and weighing 255 pounds, he was an intimidating physical specimen and was named All-CIAA and All-American. After graduating, Gay was signed by the Oakland Raiders, and he made it to the final cut in training camp. He made such an impression that he was picked up by the Philadelphia Eagles, where he made the team. He had an immediate impact with the new team and became a starter in his second year. Gay was an All-Pro performer until his untimely death in 1979.

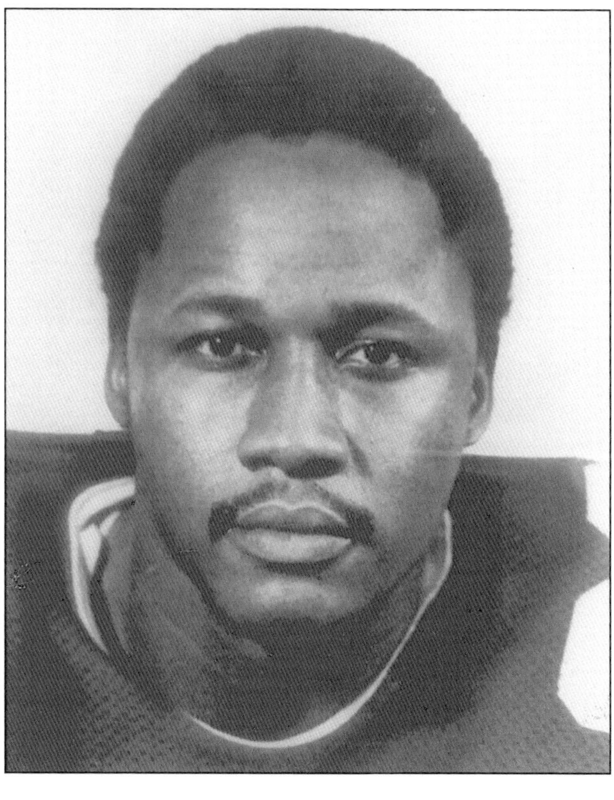

Sylvester Writter. Most people know him for another sport, but from 1971 to 1974, Sylvester Writter was a member of the FSU Broncos football team. He played offensive guard and tackle for four years and was a starter for the last three. He was a dominating blocker for the run and pass plays. For a man his size, he was surprisingly quick and often led on wide-running plays. Writter was named All-CIAA, All-National Association of Intercollegiate Athletics (NAIA) District 29, and NAIA All-American. He had tryouts with several professional teams. After giving up on football, he tried his hand at another sport—wrestling. He made a big splash in this venue, rising to the top of the game. Most people recognize him as the "Junkyard Dog" of the World Wrestling Federation, in which he had a very successful career, retiring in 1997. He then entered the business world, but was killed in an accident.

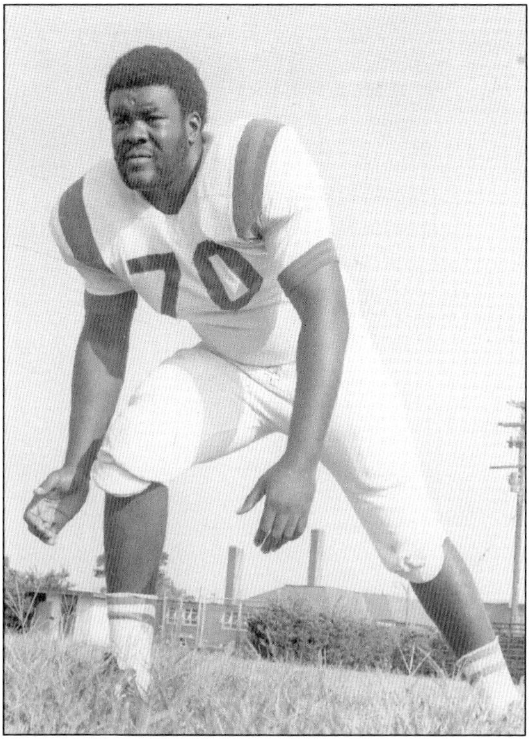

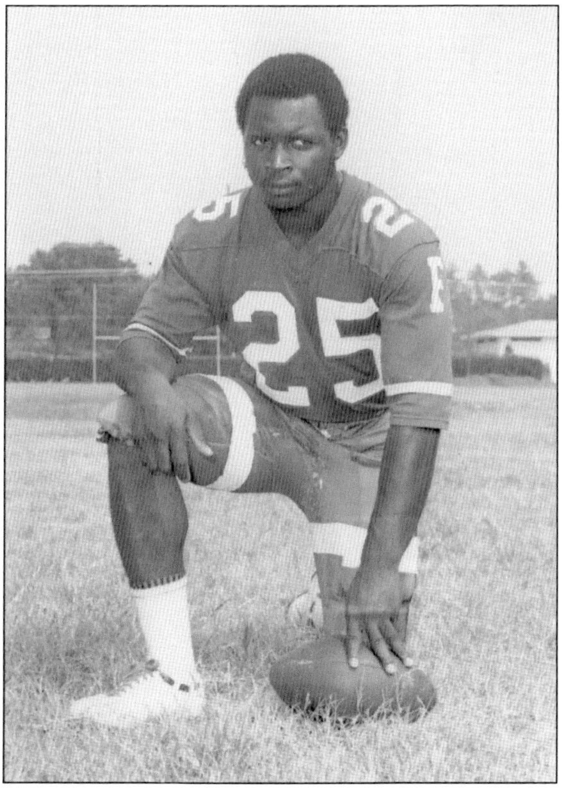

James Godwin. James Godwin established himself as a star in football and track at the high school level. He was all-conference in football and all-state in track. After graduating from Cape Fear High School, he enrolled at FSU. He had a great freshman year in both sports but was forced to sit out his sophomore year due to injuries suffered in an accident. When he returned, he again dominated both sports. In 1974, he became the Broncos' first 1,000-yard rusher. He still holds the record for touchdowns in a single game with four. Godwin's track career was even better than football. He was named All-CIAA three times as a long jumper, an event for which he still holds the FSU record. Godwin was inducted into the FSU Hall of Fame in 1997.

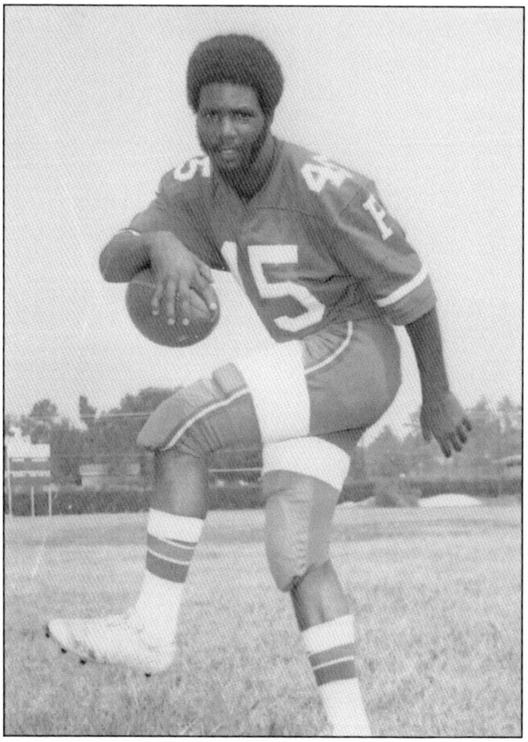

TIM HEATH. Tim Heath starred on a talent-laden football team at Seventy-First High School before he entered FSU. He had been a member of the Eastern 3-A champions as a junior and senior, and he came to the Broncos as a speedy runner and solid blocker. As a Bronco, he played a valuable role in the team's success under Coach Ray McDougal, serving as a back-up to both James Godwin and Glenn McKoy. Following graduation, Heath entered the field of education and coaching. After several years as an assistant, he was named head coach at Lumberton High School. He built a winning program there before moving into administration. He is now a principal.

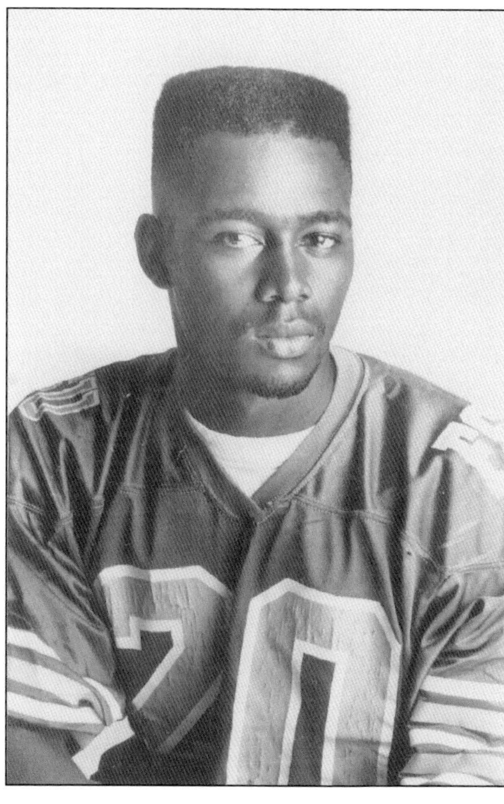

CLIFTON DAVIS. Clifton Davis holds nearly every rushing record that is kept for the Broncos. At only 5 feet, 9 inches and 180 pounds, he hardly fits the profile of one of the most dominating runners at any school. He played for the Broncos from 1991 to 1994. In 1992, he rushed for 265 yards in one game, which was part of his career best—1,591 yards for the year. He scored 17 touchdowns on the ground that year. Over his career, Davis rushed for 3,709 yards, which places him 14th among black college rushers. He scored 29 rushing touchdowns and averaged 106 yards per game and 5.1 yards per carry. He recorded 13 games of more than 100 yards and 5 games of more than 200 yards.

Alton Cogdell. Alton Cogdell, left, was the driving force behind the Broncos drive to the CIAA championship in 1973. A St. Paul's native, Cogdell played both small forward and shooting guard at 6 feet, 5 inches. He was a deadly shooter with great range and had the ability to take the ball inside. Although many of his records were lost, it is known that he led the team in scoring in 1974 with 530 points and 21.1 points per game. Cogdell was named to the All-CIAA team in 1973 and 1974. He was named All-NAIA in 1974. After his playing days at FSU, he had a tryout with the Baltimore Bullets. Coach Otis Hawkins is pictured on the right.

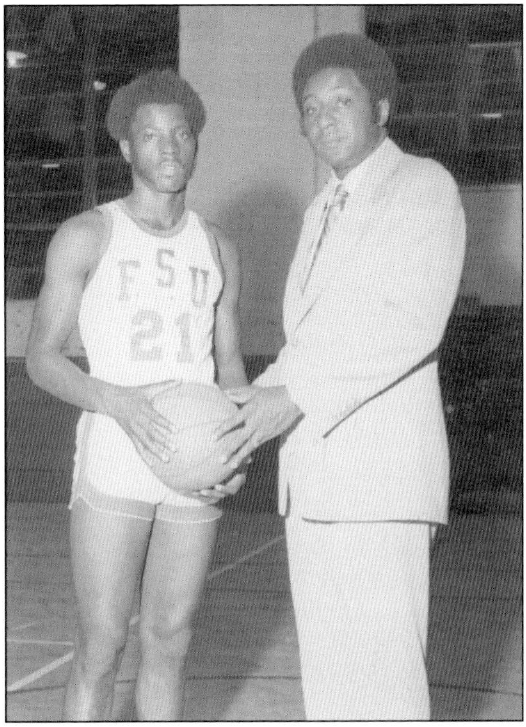

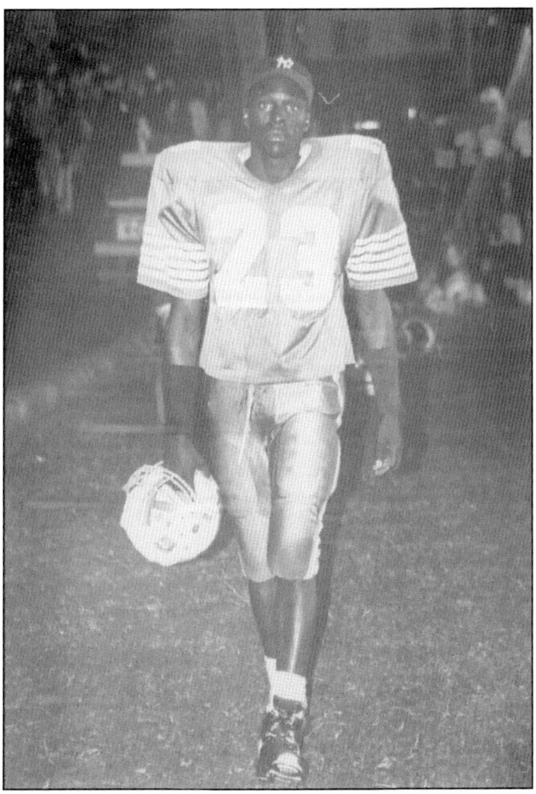

Darrell Armstrong. Darrell Armstrong came to FSU as a kicker on the football team. He had a successful career and set the school record for longest field goal, 47 yards—he would later tie that record. One rarely suspects an intramural program to be a hotbed of talent for basketball but that was where Armstrong was displaying his other talents. He was discovered by the intramural director, who was appointed interim basketball coach after the head coach left and took most of the team with him. Armstrong joined the FSU team and proceeded to lead them in scoring for three years. He was named All-CIAA in 1991. After his playing days were over at FSU, he still dreamed of playing in the NBA. His prayers were answered in 1995, when he joined the Orlando Magic. Darrell is one of the most respected players in the NBA.

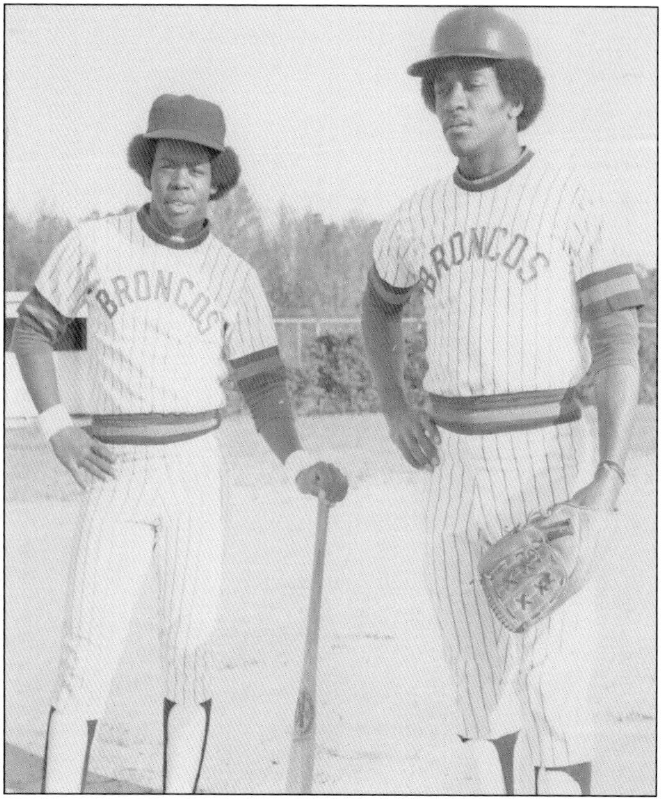

George Ellis. George Ellis, left, came to FSU as a baseball player during a time when the Broncos were a power in the CIAA. Ellis helped to lead the Broncos to their only CIAA championship in 1977. Unfortunately, the decision was made to eliminate the baseball team later that same year. Ellis transferred to Methodist College to complete his career. After graduating, Ellis pursued a career in education. He worked as a classroom teacher, assistant principal, and principal. He now works in the administration office of the Cumberland County School System.

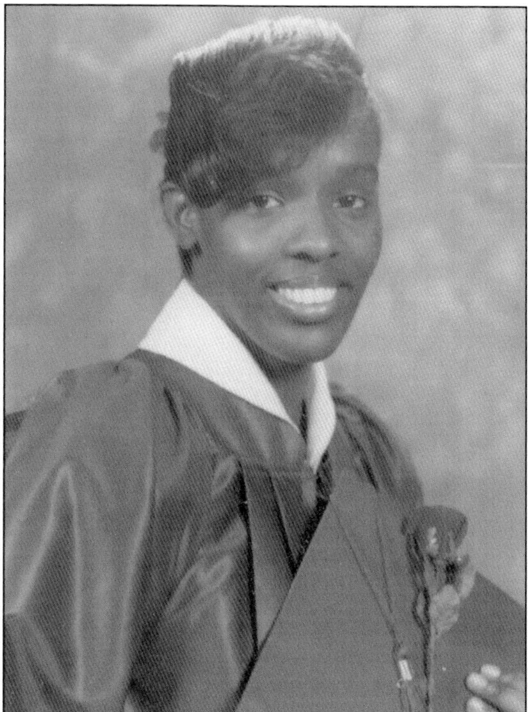

Beverly Hick. Beverly Hick epitomized what being a student athlete was all about. She starred on both the volleyball and softball teams, starting on the teams her freshman year. She made All-CIAA in both sports and was also a honor student. In her spare time, she served as statistician for the women's basketball team. What really set Beverly apart was her natural ability to lead. She was named captain of the softball team as a sophomore and held the position for two years. As a senior, she was elected student body president. Due to her added responsibility, she refused to serve as captain. Her teammates voted her honorary captain out of respect. Her team name was changed to "Madame President" in honor of her leadership on the team and over the student body.

Vincent Reid. Vincent Reid was the first real star in golf for Fayetteville State. He came to college with strong skills and played a dominating game. He won medalist honors in 1974 and 1975 en route to helping the Broncos to their first two CIAA championships. He served as team captain for three years and provided strong leadership. After graduating, he played on the mini-tour for several years, but never earned his PGA card.

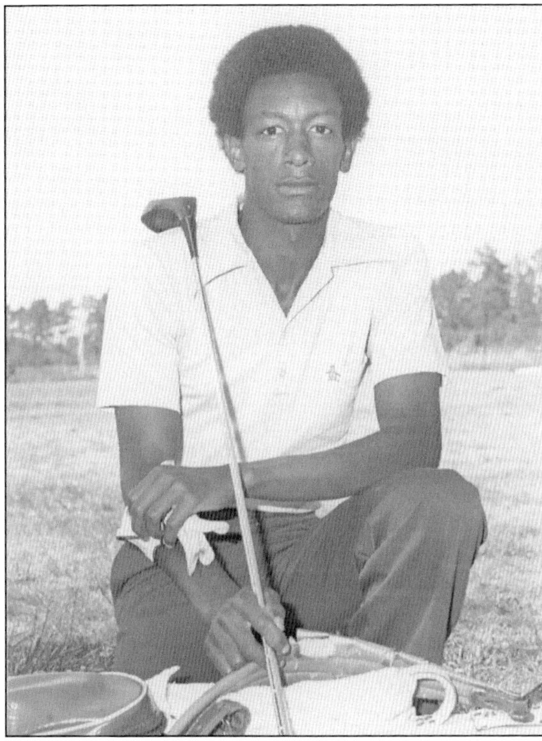

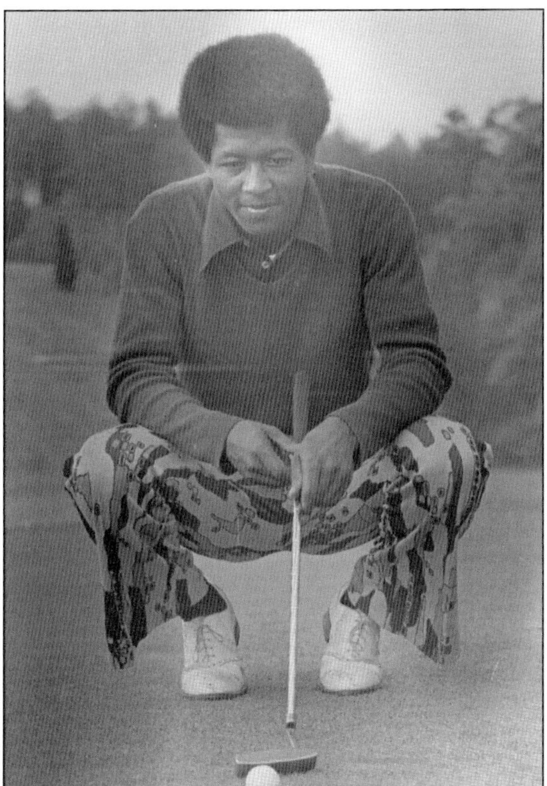

Andre Springs. After the departure of Vincent Reid, Fayetteville State's golf fortunes fell to Andre Springs, who arrived during Reid's senior year. He played in the shadow of Reid for one year, then burst into his own. Springs held the limelight for three years, winning CIAA Medalist honors three consecutive years. He was named to the All-CIAA Tournament Team in 1979, the first year it was selected. In 1976, he was named Most Valuable Golfer, and in 1978, he was named NAIA All-American. Following graduation, Springs played on the mini-tour for a while before going into coaching. While at Livingstone, his team broke the Broncos string of consecutive championship seasons.

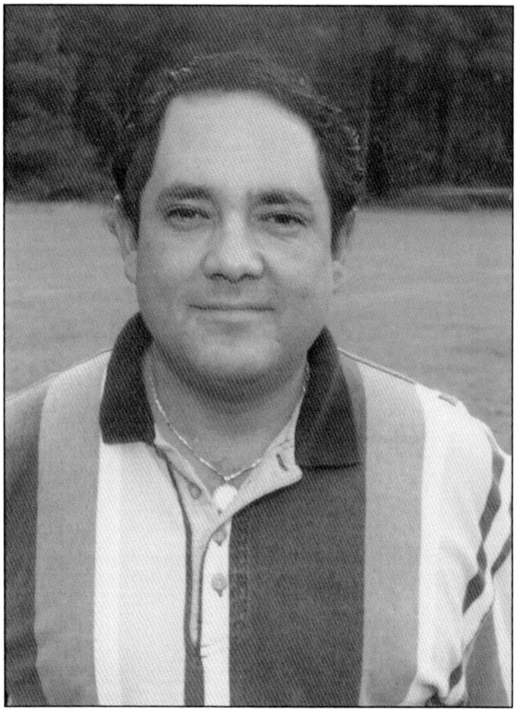

Lorenzo Juarez. Lorenzo Juarez arrived on Fayetteville State's campus after a military career. While in the military, he had developed a strong golf game and was All-Army. He brought that game to FSU and proceeded to dominate the CIAA for four years. He won medalist honors four consecutive years, including spring and fall championships in 1992–93. He helped the Broncos to four CIAA titles and two National Minority Intercollegiate Golf Championships. Juarez was Most Valuable Golfer in 1993 and 1994. He was named to the Golf All-American team in 1994.

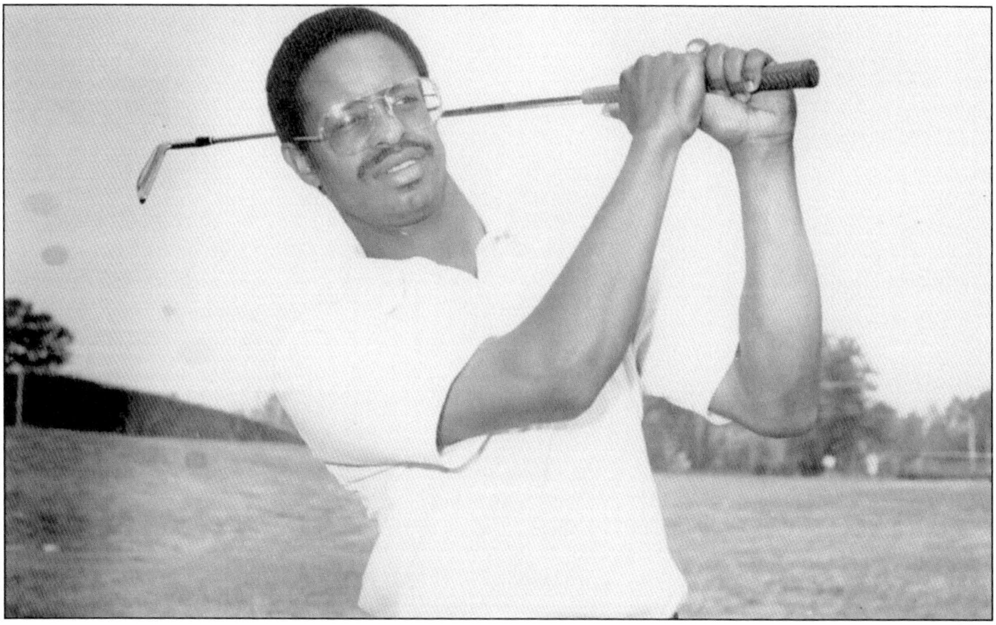

Tony Terry. Tony Terry followed Reid and Springs as the top Bronco golfer. As a Bronco, he often placed second to Springs, and even beat him on occasion—that meant he was finishing at or near the top in competition. In 1980, he won the CIAA championship and then finished second to Richardo Stevens, another Bronco, as a senior. He was named to the CIAA All-Tournament Team in 1980. Terry was a student of the game and had a coach's approach to golf. He was a team leader and also a good student.

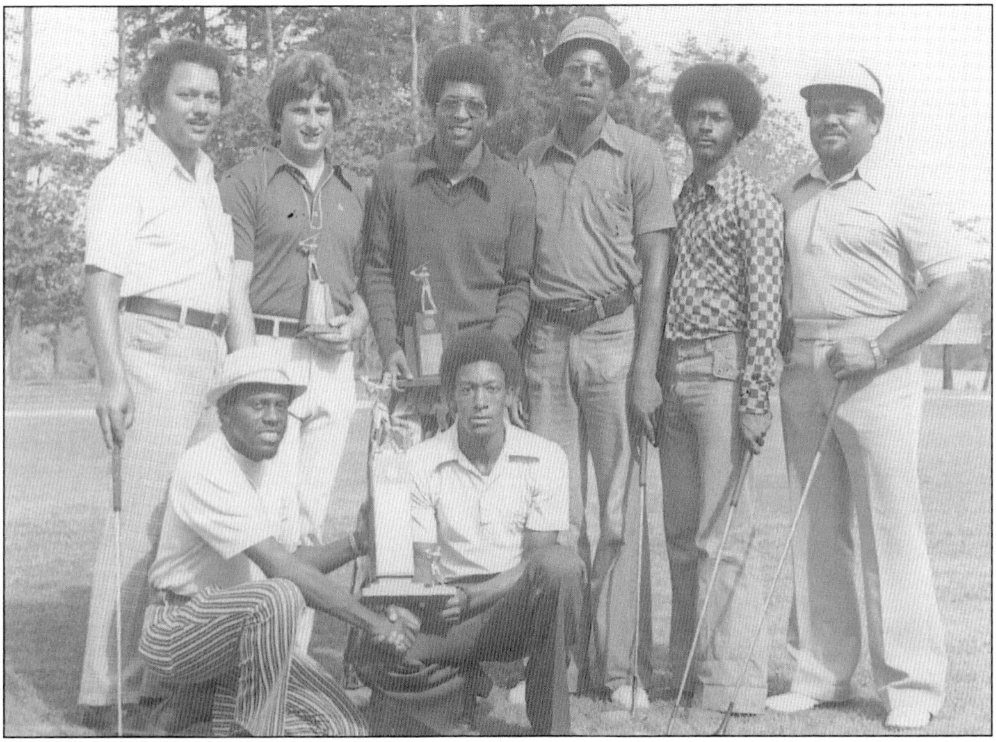

Dr. Moses Walker and the 1975 CIAA Champions.

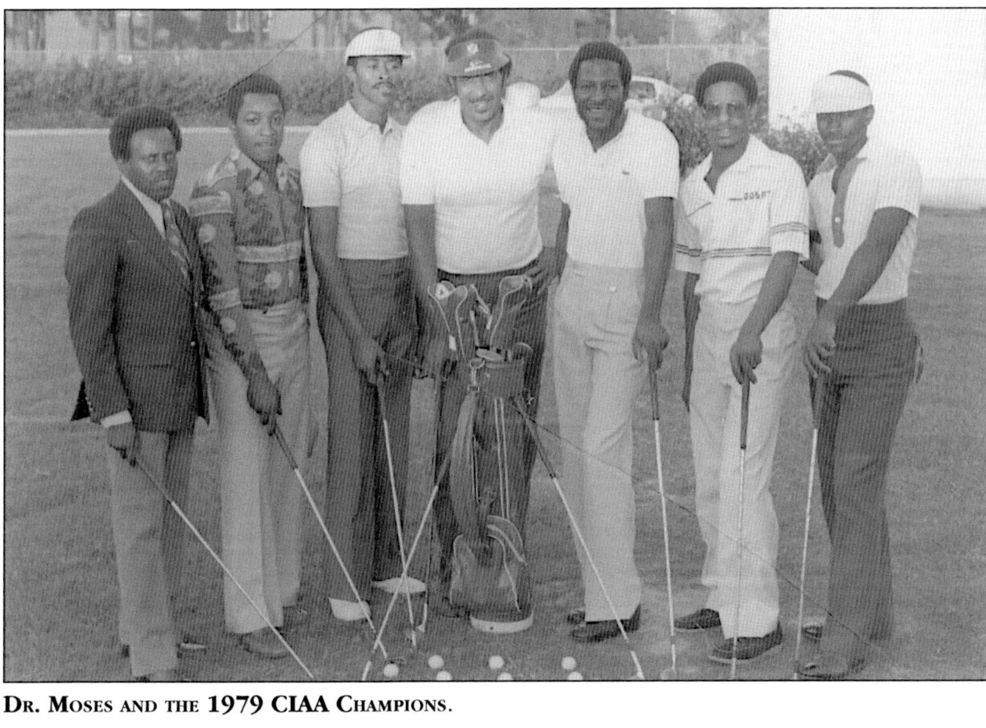

Dr. Moses and the 1979 CIAA Champions.

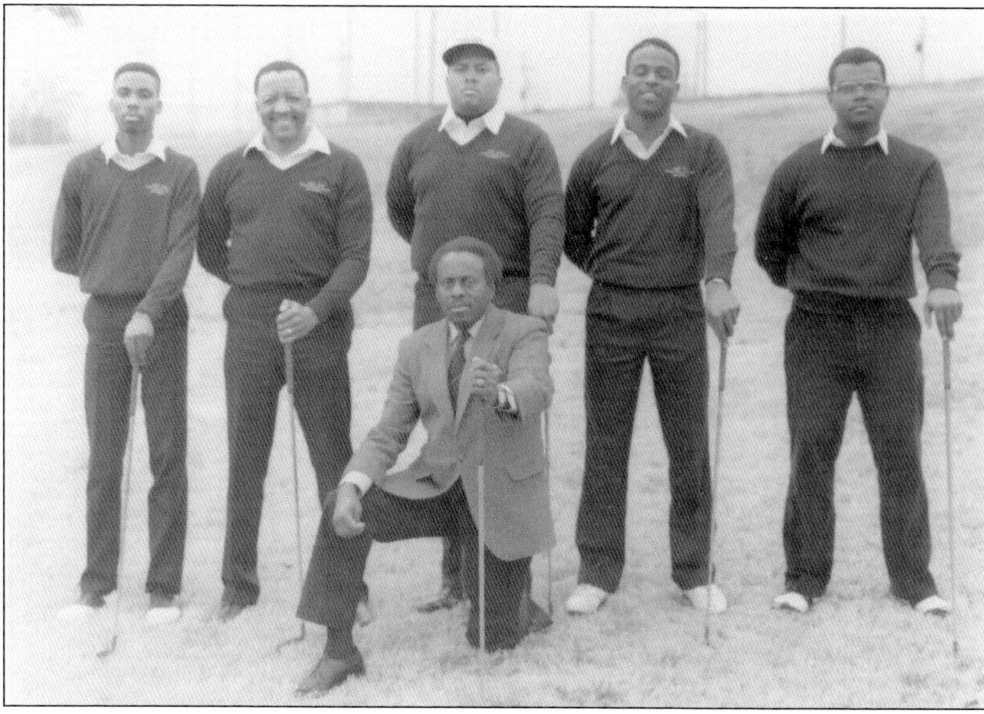

Dr. Walker and the 1987 CIAA Champions.

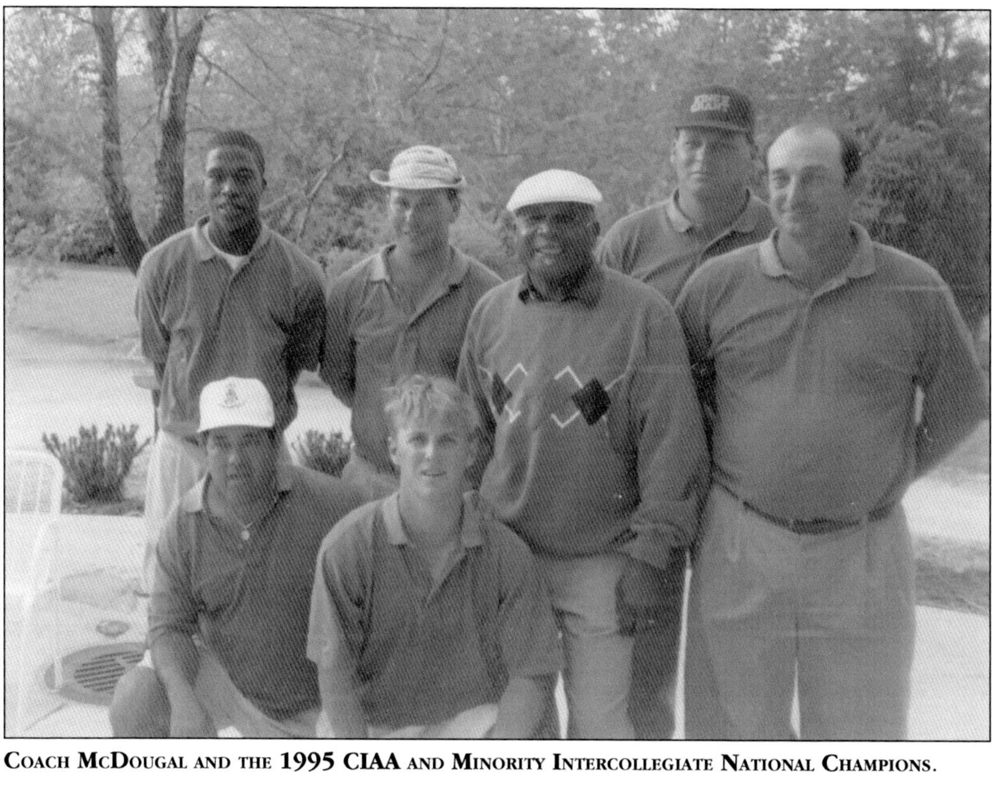

Coach McDougal and the 1995 CIAA and Minority Intercollegiate National Champions.

Dr. Walker. Dr. Walker is possibly one of the best self-taught golfers in the world. With a lot of hard work, he became a scratch handicap, without ever taking a professional lesson. He was selected to coach golf at Fayetteville State in 1973. Two years later, he had the CIAA medalist champion, and after three years he won the first of his 13 CIAA Golf championships. He coached the Broncos to 12 consecutive conference championships and won CIAA Coach of the Year in eight consecutive years—and a total of nine times. He has produced five conference champions, four teaching pros, and eight mini-tour pros. His playing, coaching, and other contributions to golf have earned him a place in the National Black Golf Hall of Fame.

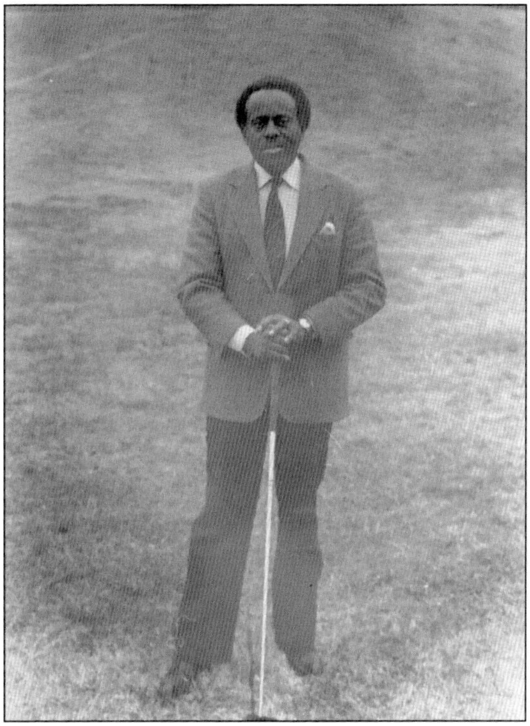

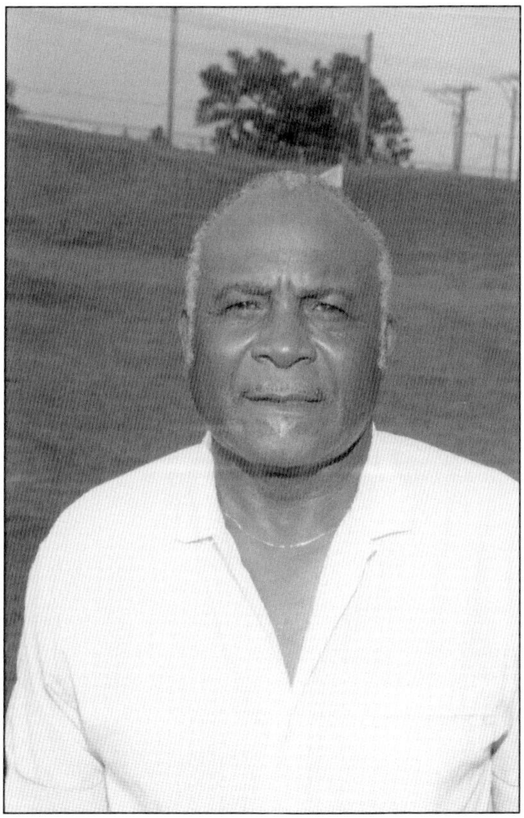

Raymond McDougal. Raymond McDougal joined the FSU staff in 1970 as a football coach. He has won more football games than any other coach in Bronco history. Upon assuming the Bronco helm, McDougal began to produce immediately, posting his first winning record in 1971 and earning NAIA Coach of the Year for his efforts. He also posted winning seasons in 1972, 1975, and 1976, with back to back 7-3 seasons. He was voted NAIA Coach of the Year in 1971, 1973, and 1975, and CIAA Coach of the Year in 1975. In 1993, he was named head coach of the Bronco golf team. He produced four consecutive CIAA championships and two national championships. He has been named CIAA Coach of the Year three times.

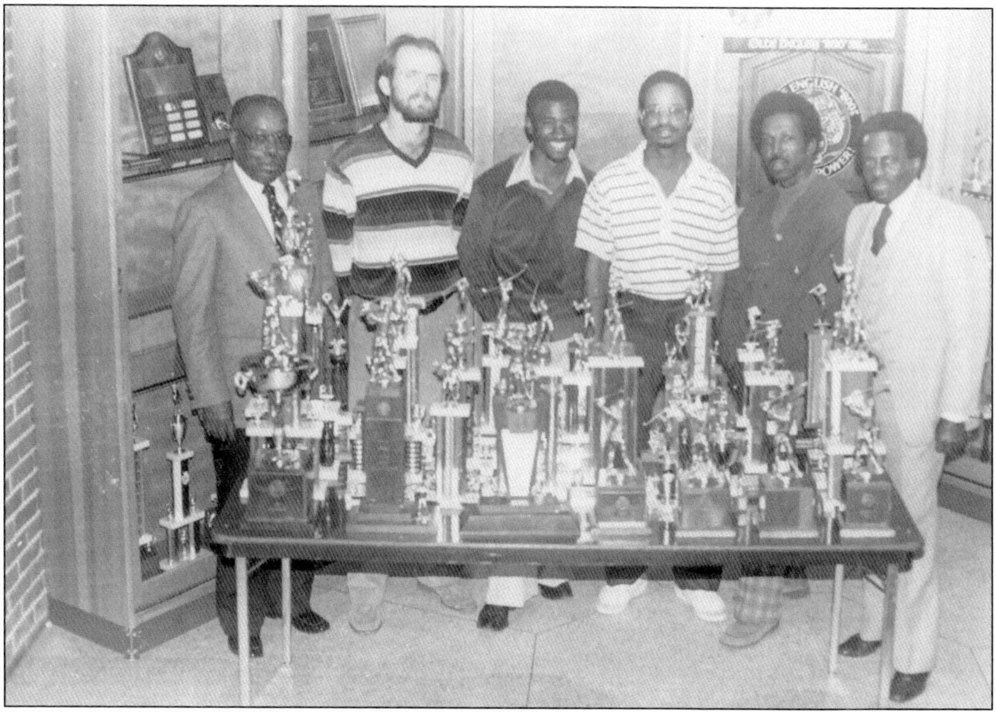

Coach Walker and the Golf Team. In this photograph, Coach Walker and his victorious team present trophies to Dr. Lyons.

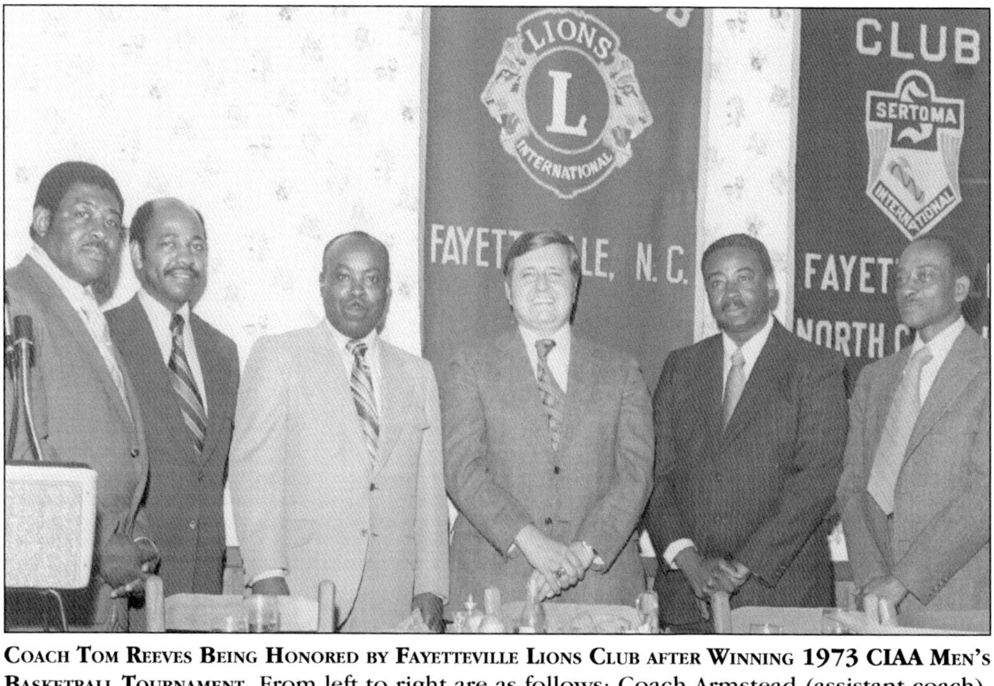

Coach Tom Reeves Being Honored by Fayetteville Lions Club after Winning 1973 CIAA Men's Basketball Tournament. From left to right are as follows: Coach Armstead (assistant coach), two unidentified men, Tom Council, Dr. Charles Lyons, and Coach Tom Reeves. Coach Reeves died just week later.

Seven

555th Airborne and 2nd Rangers

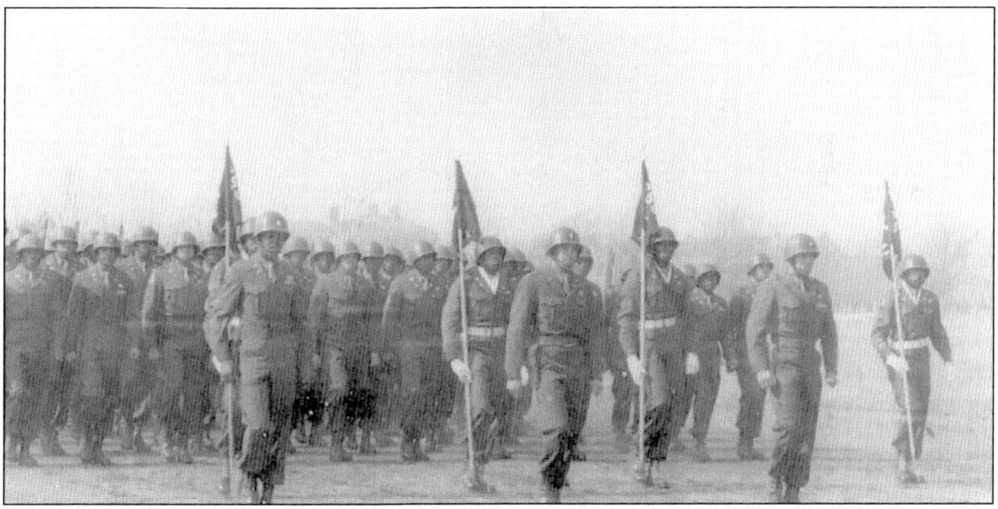

555th Airborne Division. During World War II, the United States Army was segregated. Most of America is familiar with the Tuskegee Airmen, the courageous and highly skilled fighter pilots of the era, but far less is known about the 555th, because it was not allowed into combat. These men were used in a "special mission" as smoke jumpers to defend against Japanese balloon bombs. Still, this proud group of warriors distinguished themselves in the ranks and later during the Korean War as members of the Rangers.

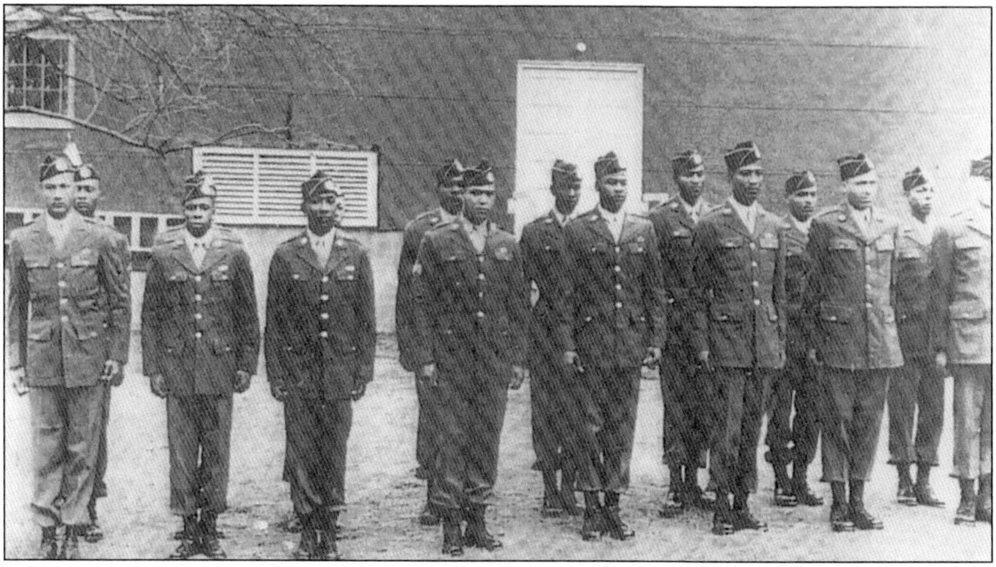

Graduation Day for the "Sweet Sixteen," February 18, 1944. The first African-American paratroopers in the history of the U.S. Armed Forces, these proud pioneers are, from left to right, as follows: (front row) First Sergeant Walter Morris, Sergeant Jack. D. Tillis, Sergeant Leo D. Reed, Sergeant Daniel C. Weil, Staff Sergeant Hubert Bridges, Technical Grade IV Alvin L. Moon, Sergeant Ned D. Bess, and Sergeant Roger S. Walden; (back row) Corporal McKinley Godfrey Jr., Sergeant Elijah Wesby, Sergeant Samuel W. Robinson, Staff Sergeant Calvin K. Beal, Staff Sergeant Robert F. Greene, Staff Sergeant Lonnie M. Duke, Sergeant Clarence H. Beavers, and Sergeant James E. Kornegay.

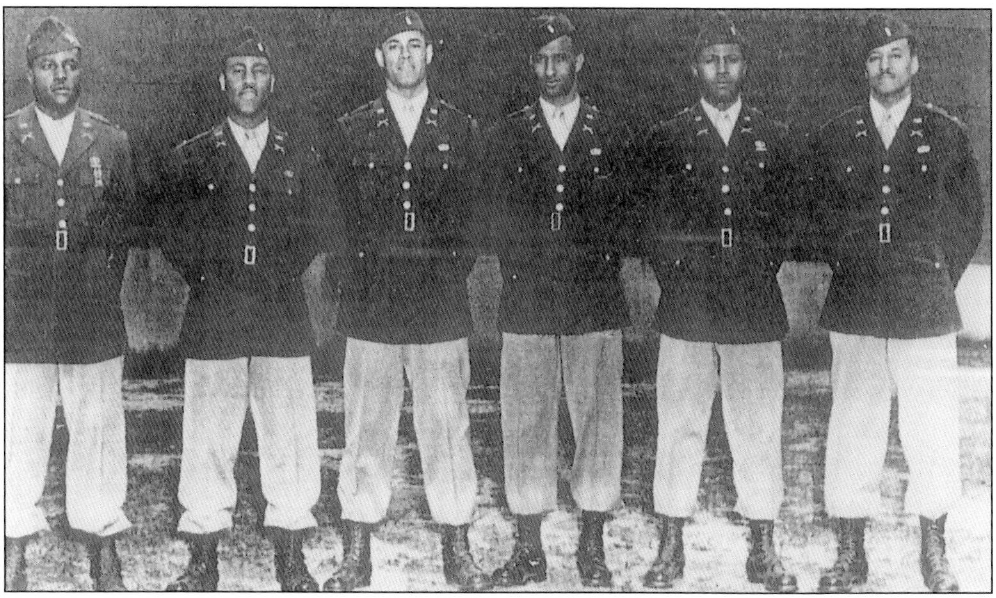

First Officers of the 555th. These officers are, from left to right, as follows: Lieutenant Jasper E. Ross, Second Lieutenant Clifford Allen, Second Lieutenant Bradley Biggs, Second Lieutenant Edwin H. Wills, Second Lieutenant Warren C. Cornelius, and Second Lieutenant Edwin Baker.

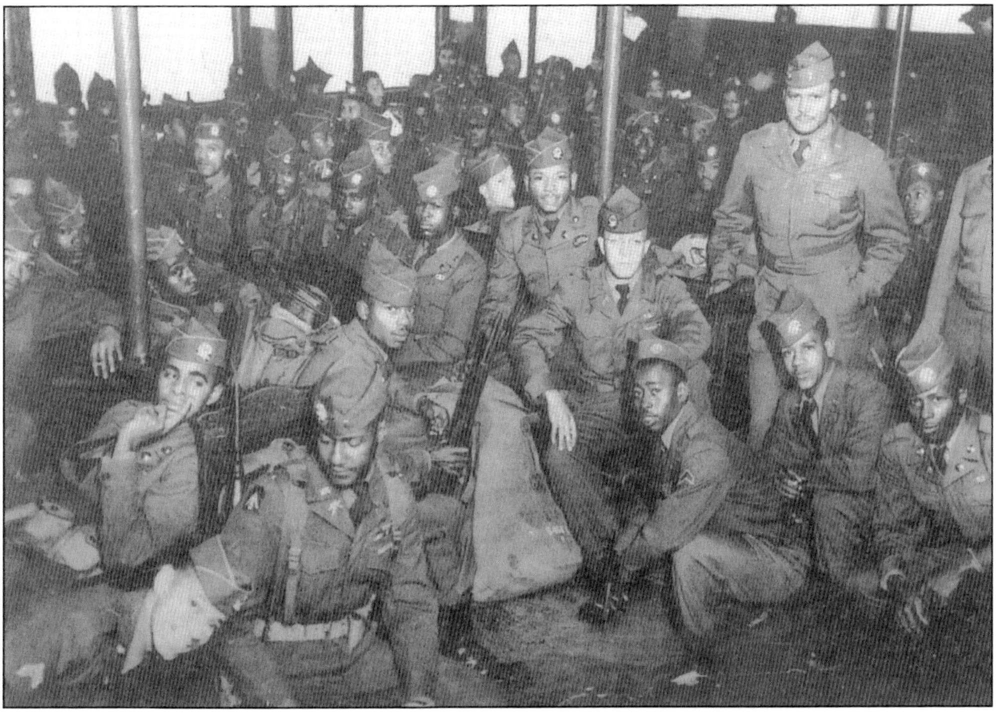

THE SECOND RANGERS EN ROUTE TO KOREA IN 1950.

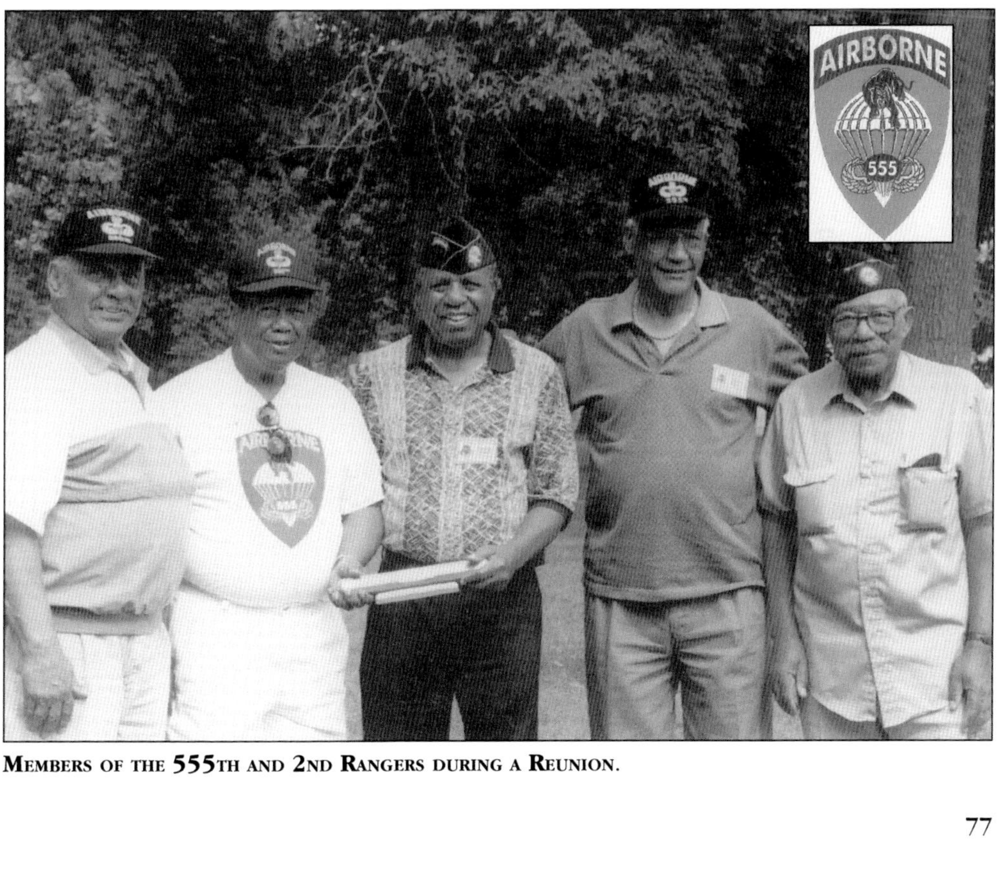

MEMBERS OF THE 555TH AND 2ND RANGERS DURING A REUNION.

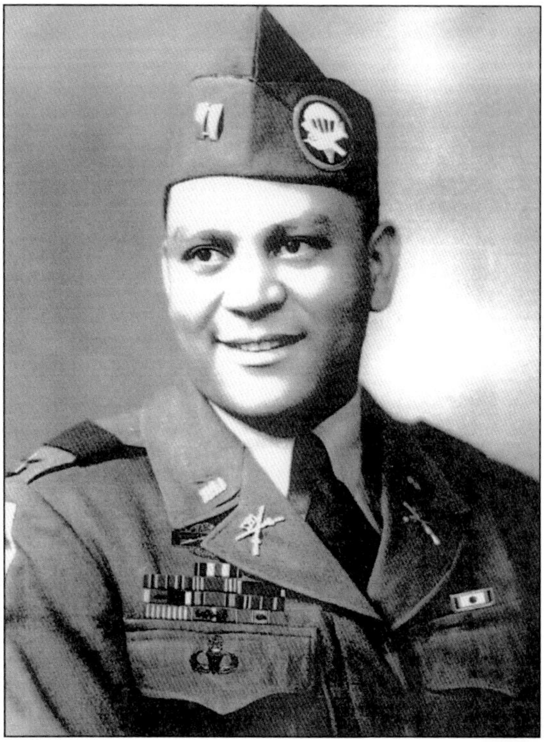

Major Warren Allen. Major Warren Allen came to Fayetteville with the military in the late 1940s. In 1944, Allen went to officer candidate's school and parachute school. He was assigned to the 555th Airborne at Fort Bragg. After Ranger School, Allen was named company commander. In December 1950, the unit was shipped to Korea and was involved in a major fire-fight five weeks later. Lieutenant Allen and the all-black 2nd Rangers engaged a unit of North Koreans, driving them from their position. The Koreans counterattacked, and as Allen rallied his troops, he was hit by shrapnel. The shrapnel was deflected by a map and a Bible prayer book that he carried in his pocket. Allen was honored with a Silver Star. Allen retired in 1962 with the rank of major. He started an electronics business in Washington, D.C., which he operated until his death in 1973.

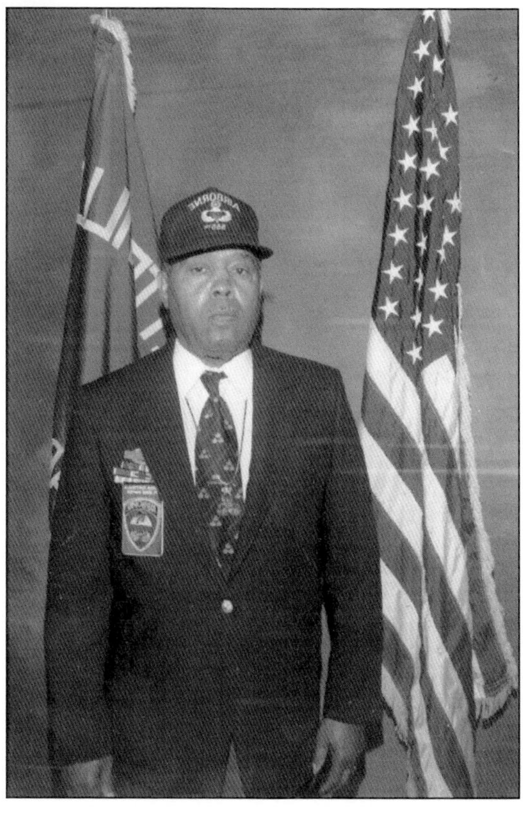

James L. Lawrence. First Sergeant James Lawrence is a former member of the 555th and the 2nd Rangers. During the Vietnam War, he served as a platoon sergeant in the 173rd Airborne Brigade. While on a mission in 1966, his platoon came under heavy enemy fire. Sergeant Lawrence took command of the lead element and pursued the retreating force. When the enemy counterattacked, he flanked the enemy, without regard for his own safety, and was wounded, but refused assistance until the battle was won. For his valor, Sergeant Lawrence was awarded the Silver Star.

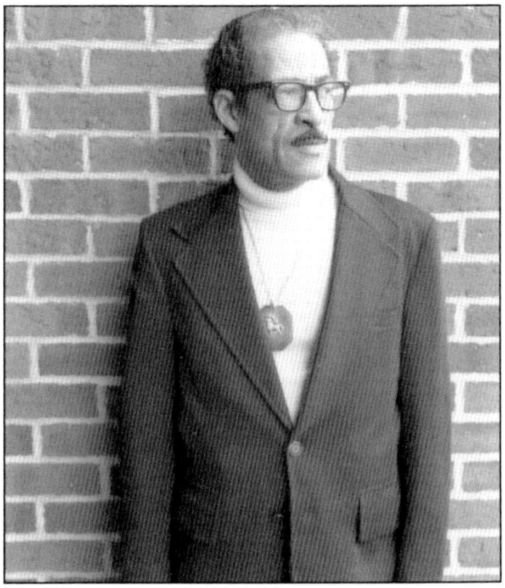

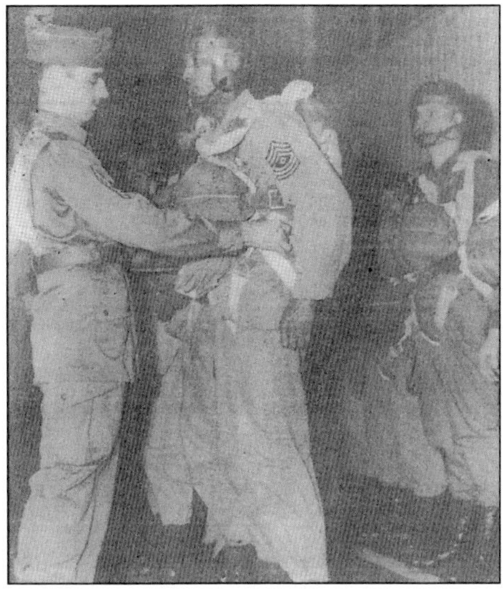

Left: **George Barnes**. George Barnes was a 30-year veteran of the army and a member of the all-black 555th Airborne Infantry (Triple Nickel) and the 82nd Airborne Division. He set a record as an air-delivery officer with 94 drops without a malfunction. He maintained close ties to the military and participated in local veterans groups. Barnes has been a part of public radio in Fayetteville almost since WFSS signed on the air. As one of the great jazz minds in the city, he has a personal collection that is unmatched. As a volunteer, he served as a librarian for the station for many years, maintaining its collection of more than 4,000 records. At age 77, Barnes was one of the oldest and most tenured volunteers at WFSS, with nearly 20 years of service. He was also active at St. Ann's Catholic Church.
Right: **Walter Morris**. Walter Morris was a member of the 555th Airborne Infantry and was selected as the first enlisted member of the 555th, and thus officially the first black paratrooper when the unit was activated at Fort Benning, Georgia. He moved to Fort Bragg along with the unit and later reached the rank of master sergeant.

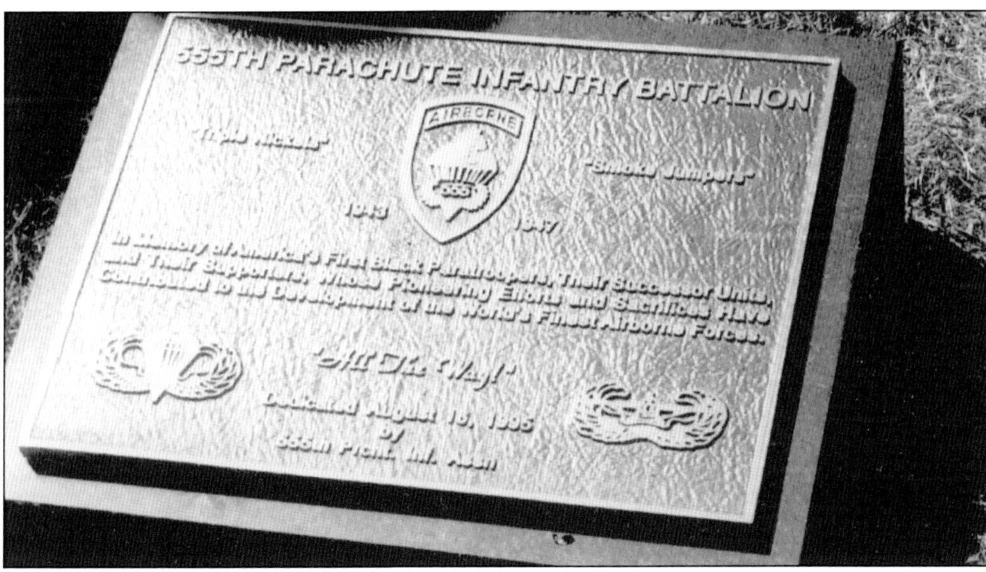

The Official 555th Grave Marker.

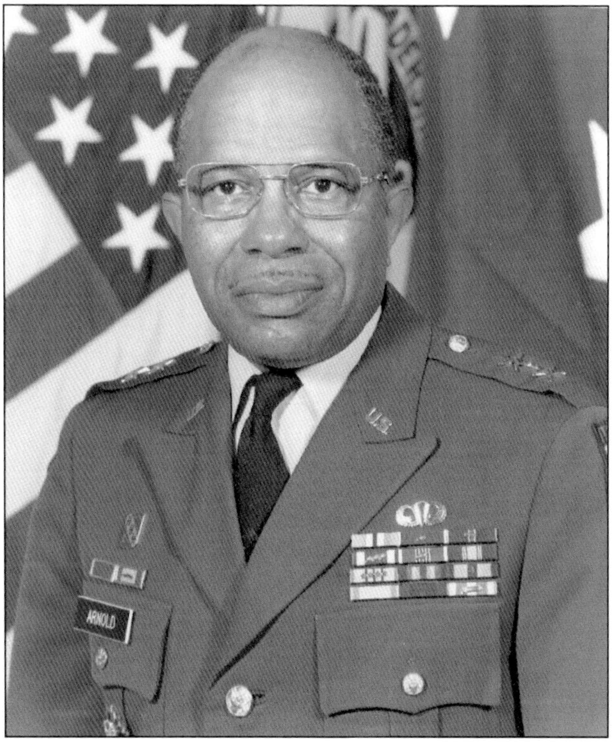

General Wallace C. Arnold. General Wallace is a native of Washington, D.C., and earned his degree from Hampton University. He served in a number of command positions during his career and was awarded the Legion of Merit with an Oak Leaf Cluster, the Meritorious Service Medal with four Oak Leaf Clusters, the Bronze Star, the Parachutist Badge, and the Army Commendation Medal with an Oak Leaf Cluster. General Arnold, who has served as the commanding general, First Reserve Office Training Corps Region at Fort Bragg, has been appointed commander of cadets. He assumed that post in April 1990, and in 1993, he was named commander of cadet training, covering all areas of ROTC and academies.

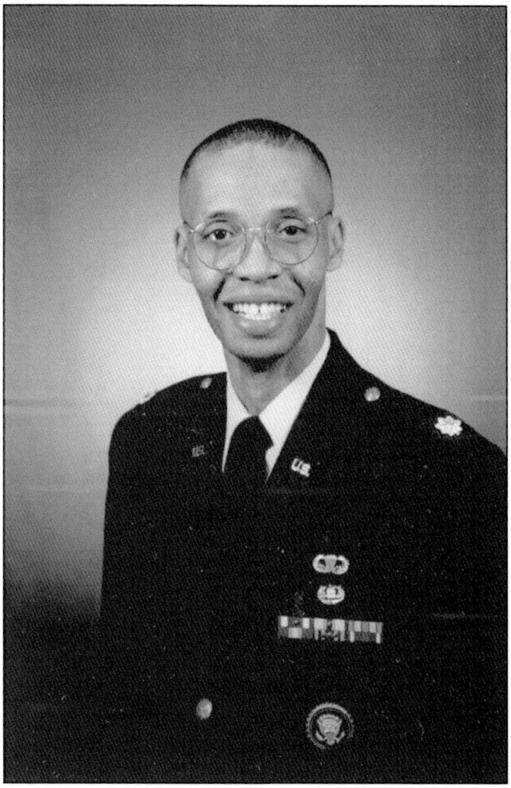

Lieutenant Colonel Will A. Gunn. Lieutenant Colonel Gunn served as the staff judge advocate of the 23rd Wing, Pope Air Force Base, North Carolina. Following graduation (with military honors) from the Air Force Academy in 1980, Lieutenant Colonel Gunn began his military career in the Academy's Minority Affairs Office, advising candidates on admission to the academy. In 1983, he entered Harvard Law School and was elected president of the Harvard Legal Aid Bureau. He graduated cum laude from Harvard in 1986. In 1990, Lieutenant Colonel Gunn was selected as a White House Fellow, serving on the White House staff as an associate director of Cabinet Affairs. He assumed his present duties at Pope Air Force Base in July 1996, where he is the judge advocate general (the first black to serve in that capacity at Pope Air Force Base).

Eight

Churches

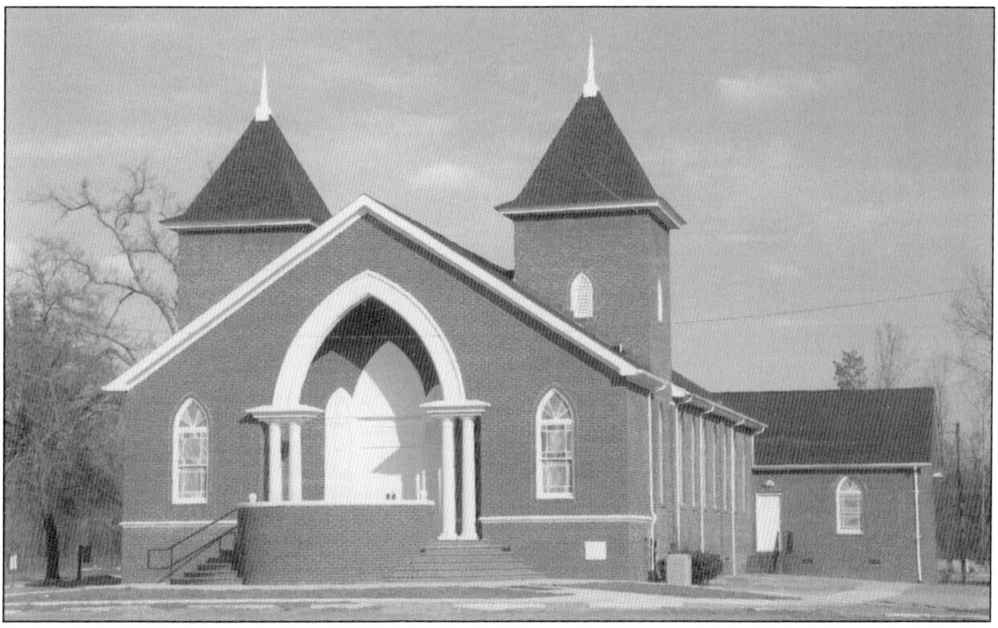

Savannah Baptist Church.

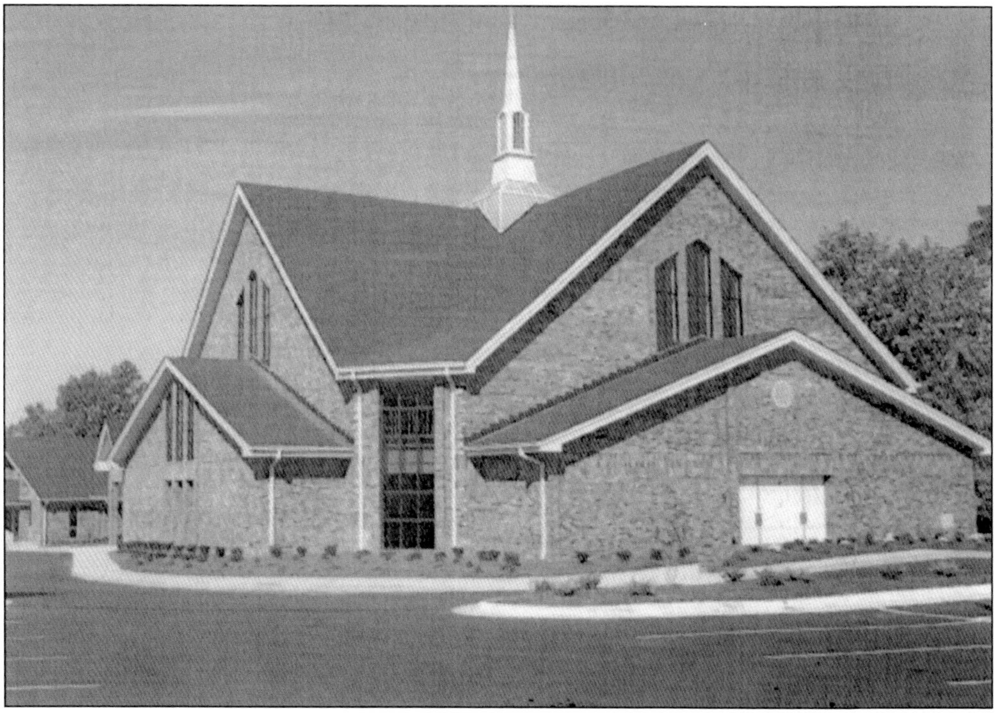

Lewis Chapel Baptist Church.

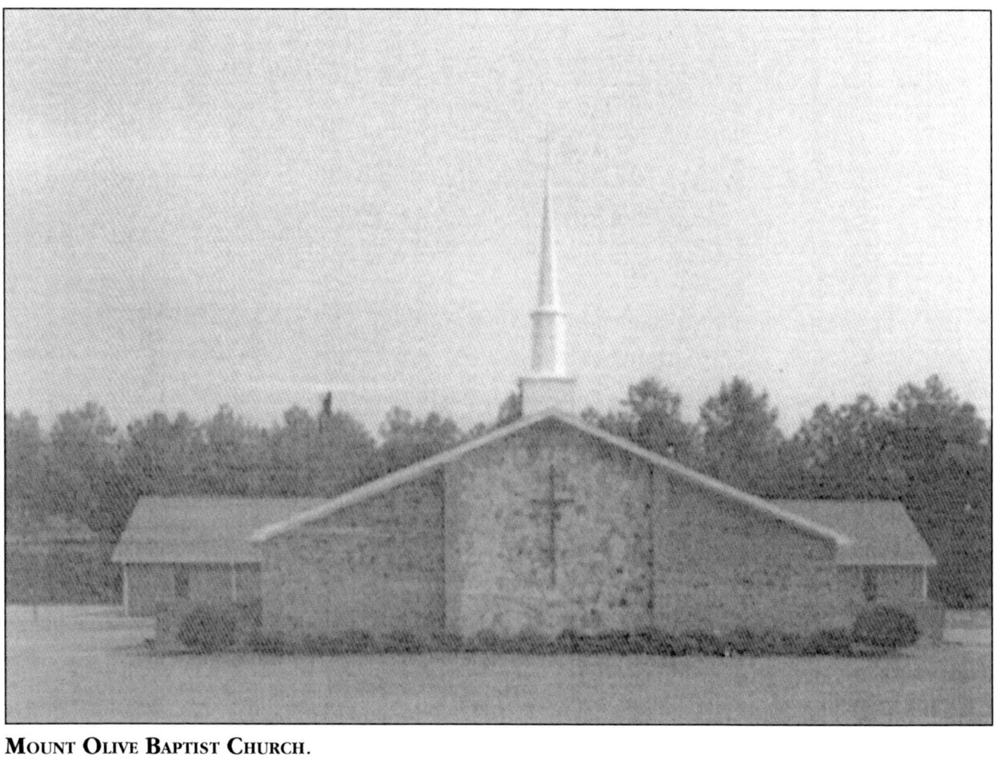

Mount Olive Baptist Church.

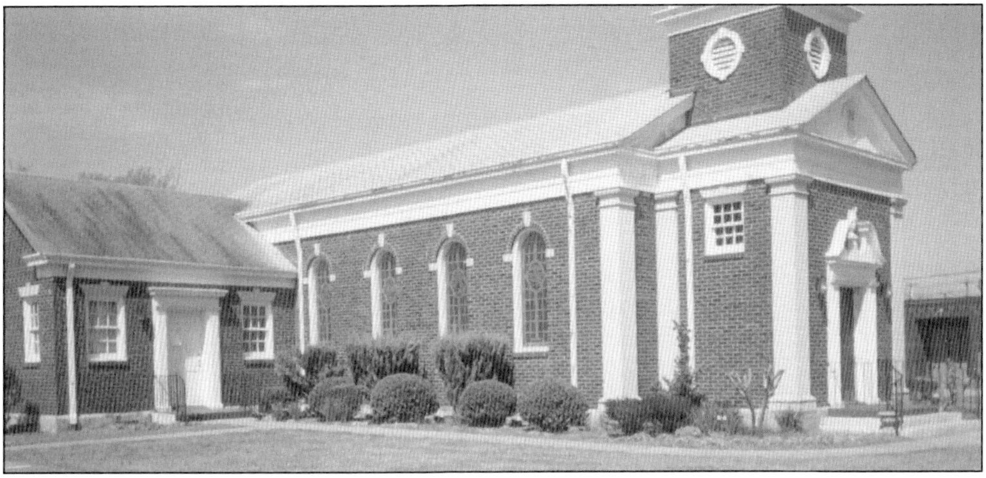

St. Ann's Catholic Church.

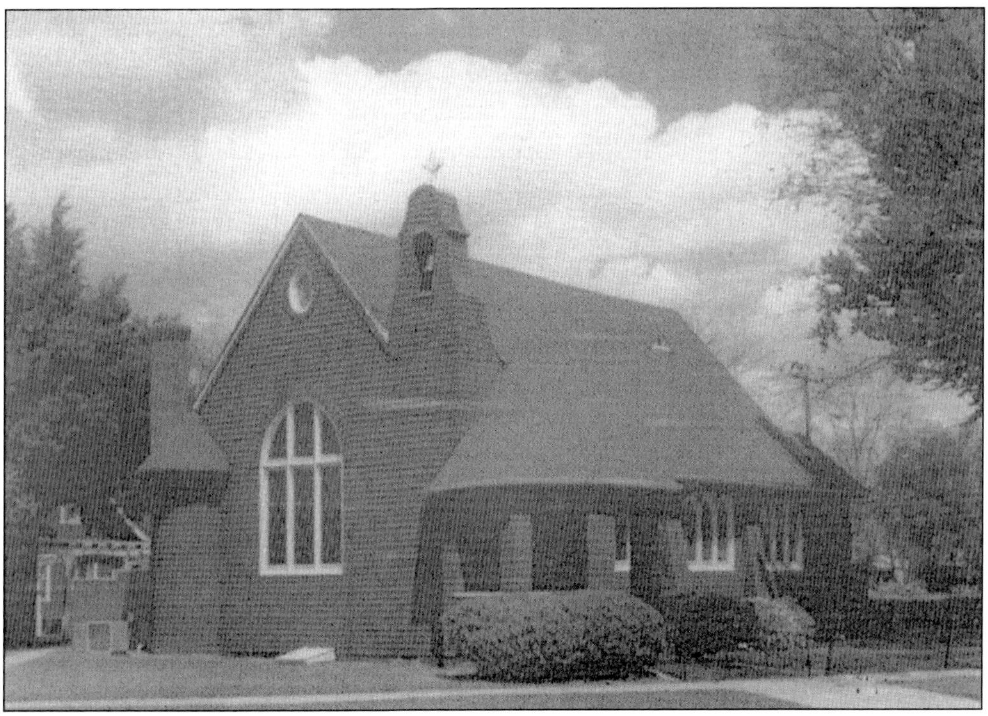

St. Joseph's Episcopal Church.

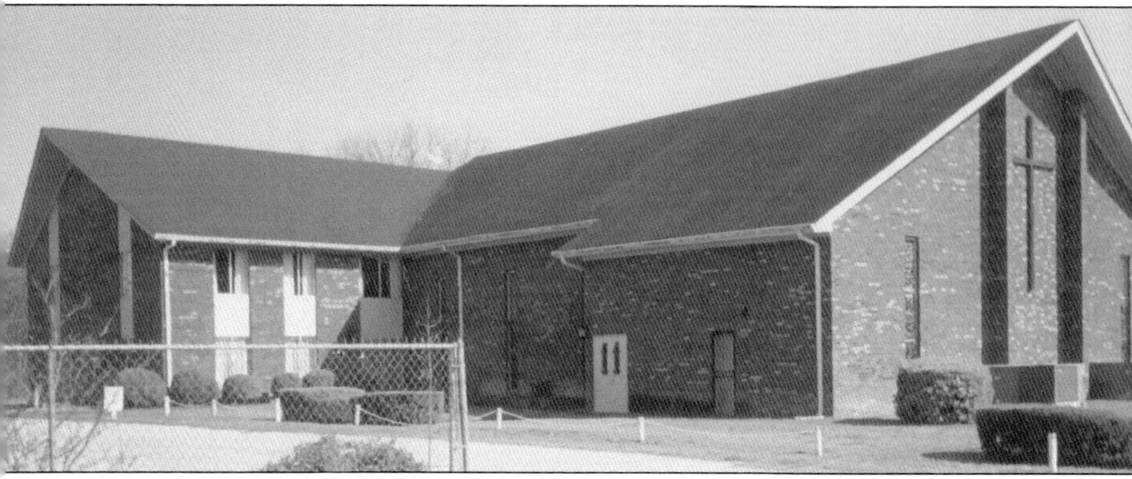

St. Luke AME Church.

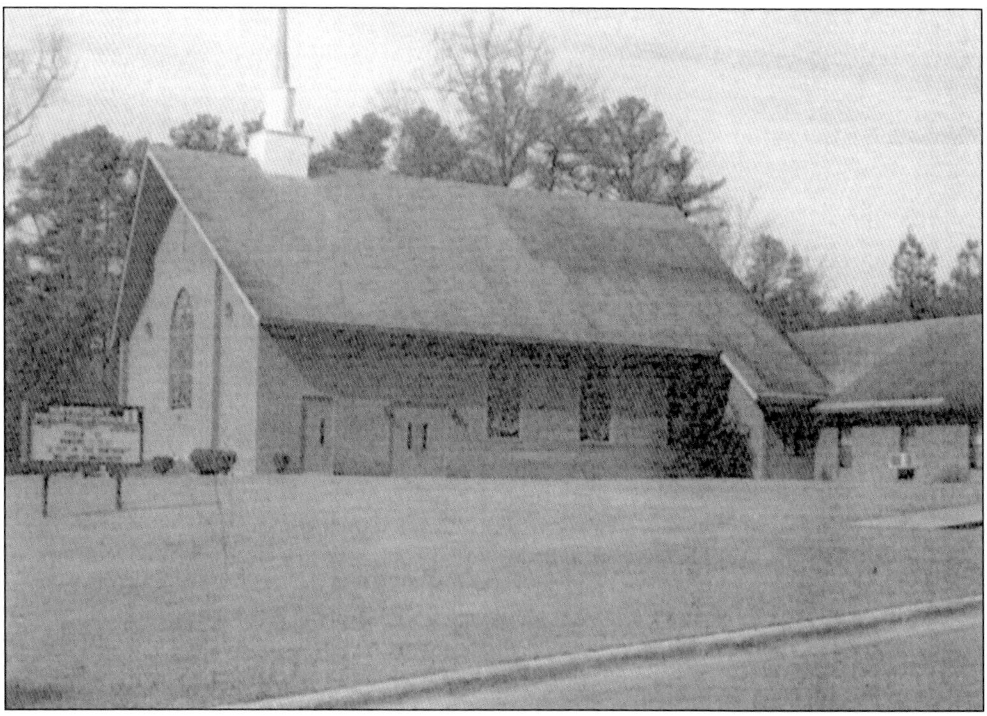

Haymount Presbyterian Church.

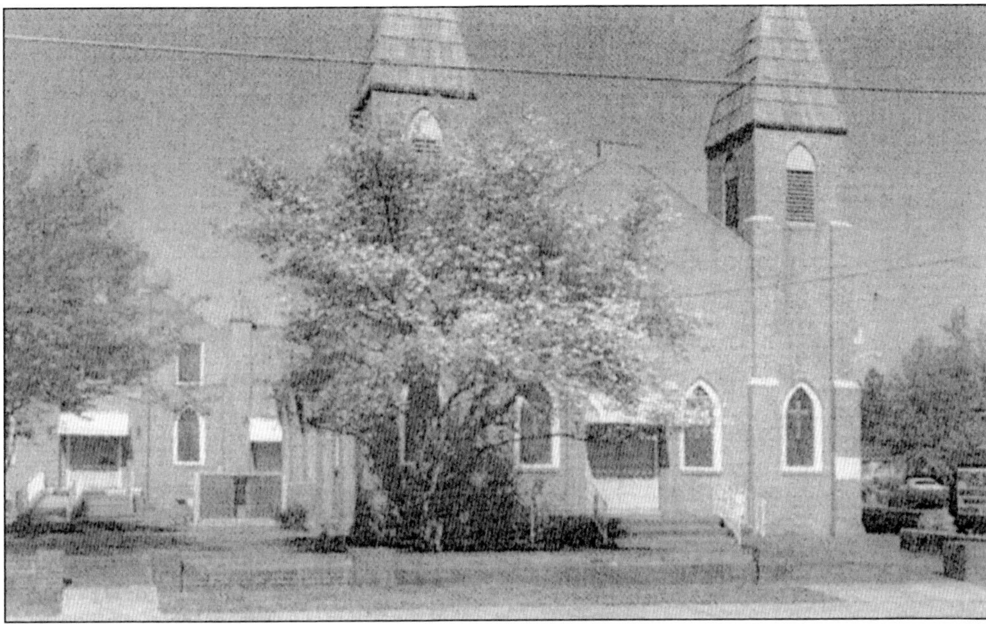

SECOND BAPTIST CHURCH.

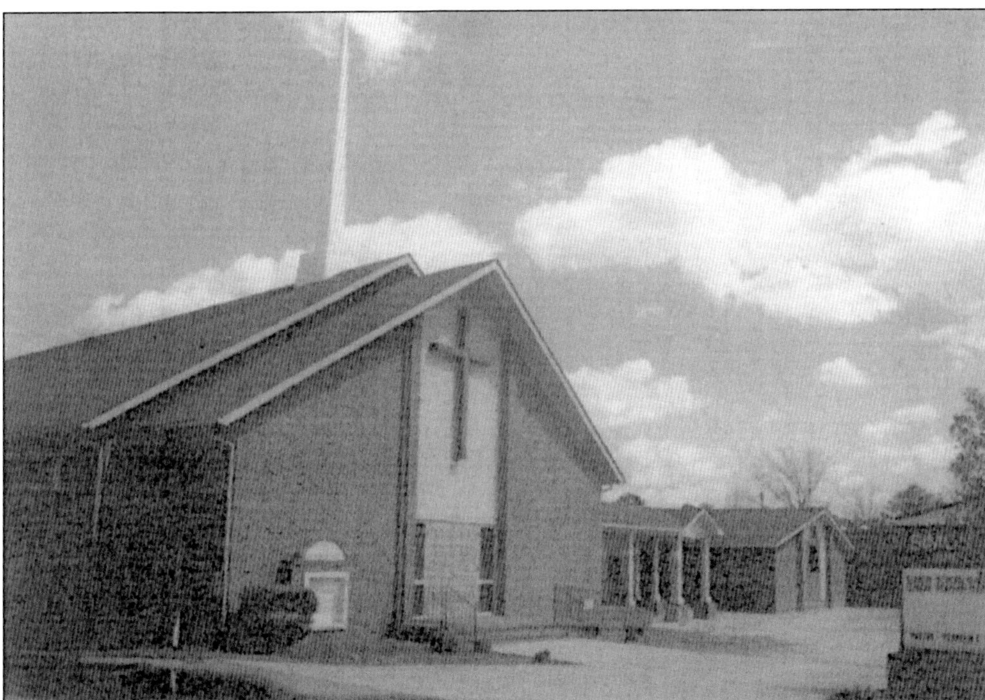

SIMON TEMPLE AME ZION CHURCH.

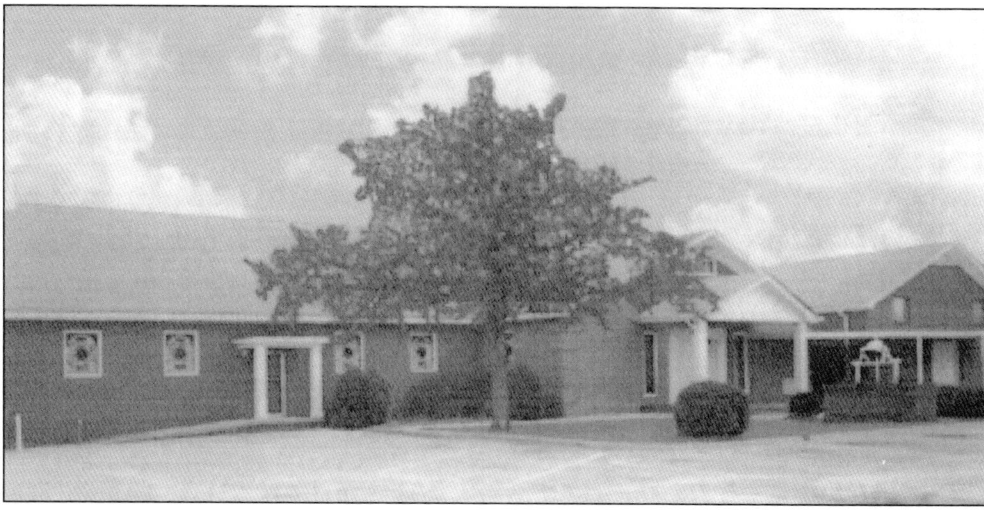

Williams Chapel Baptist Church.

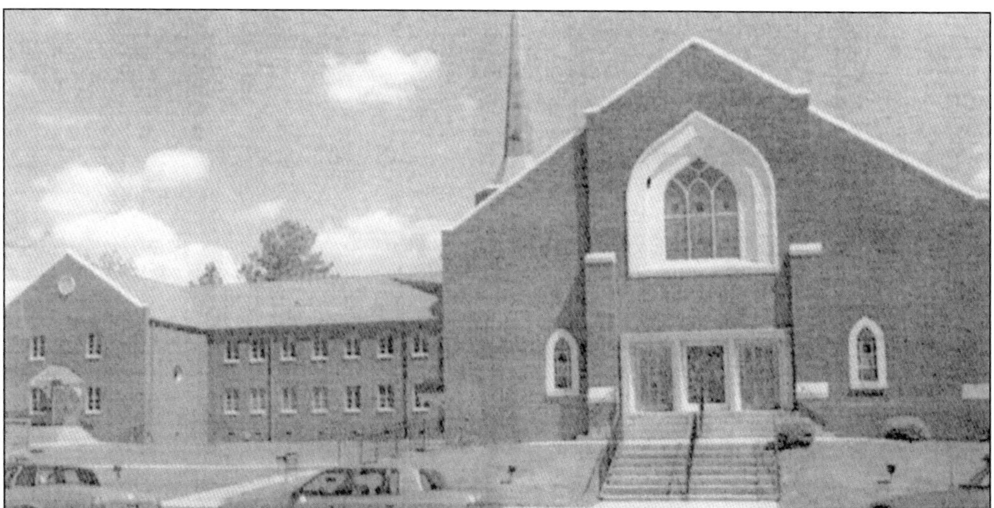

First Baptist Church.

Nine

Outstanding Citizens

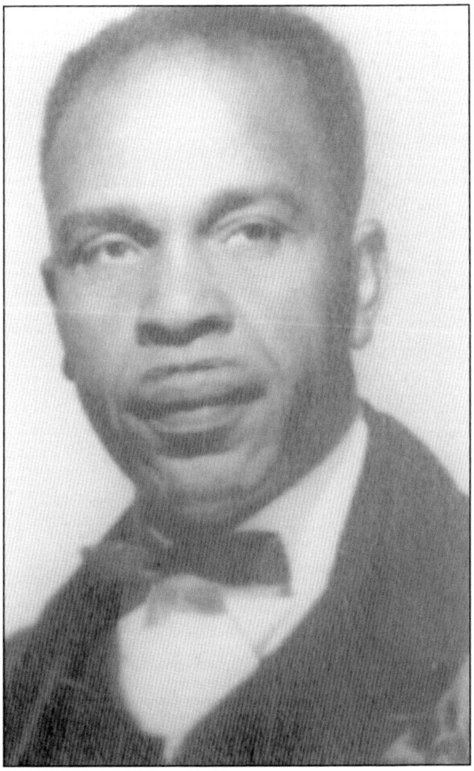

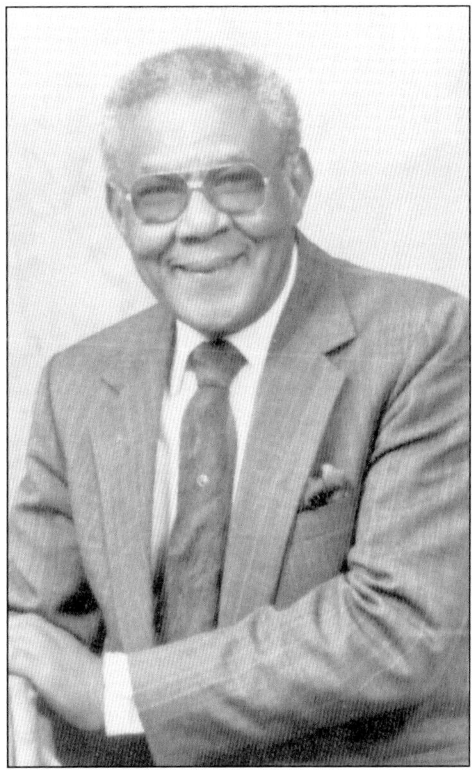

Left: **Dr. E.A. Armstrong**. A graduate of Fayetteville State Normal School and a local preacher, Dr. Armstrong worked as science teacher at E.E. Smith High School and rose to the level of school principal when he started the first high school for blacks in the county in 1936. The county's first black high school building, located in Eastover, was named in his honor. Dr. Armstrong was a member of several civic and religious groups and served as the president of the Fayetteville State Alumni Association for several years.
Right: **Thomas Bacote**. Thomas Bacote came to Fayetteville in September 1958 and joined the staff as director of the marching and stage bands. He served as director of the marching band until the late 1970s and taught music until the mid-1990s. In addition to his teaching duties, Mr. Bacote was active in the business and political communities, helping to establish the United National Bank and serving as the president of the Business League. In 1990, he ran successfully for the county commission and has held that position since that time.

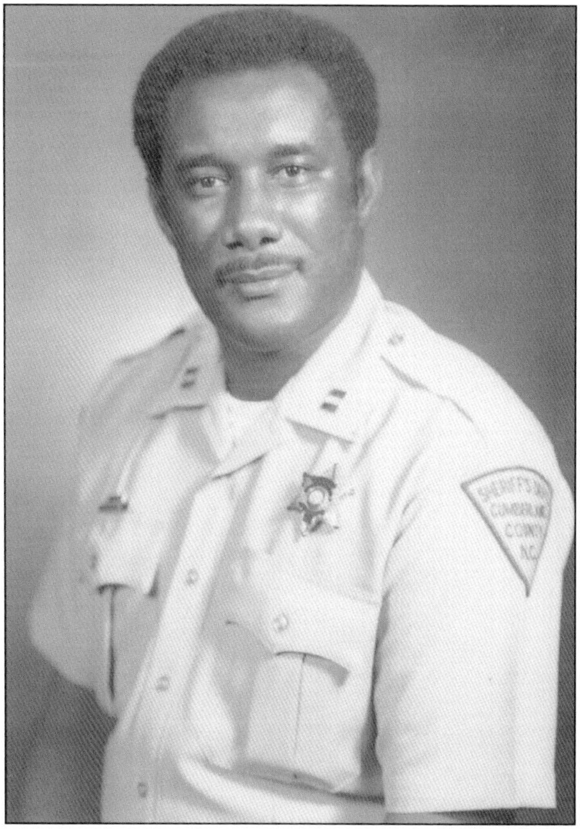

James Bowser. James Bowser became a deputy in 1976 and stayed with the police department until 1994, rising to the rank of major. He was promoted to major in 1991, making him the highest ranking black in the history of that department. He ran for the office of sheriff in 1994, finishing second in the general primary and losing to the man who was eventually elected sheriff in the run-off election. In an interesting twist of fate, Bowser was fired from the sheriff's department by the new sheriff, who then hired his Republican opponent. Among his awards are the Chaplain's Outstanding Service Award, NAACP Service Award (Cumberland County School System), Fayetteville Urban Ministry Find-A-Friend Program, and the Cumberland County Mental Health Department.

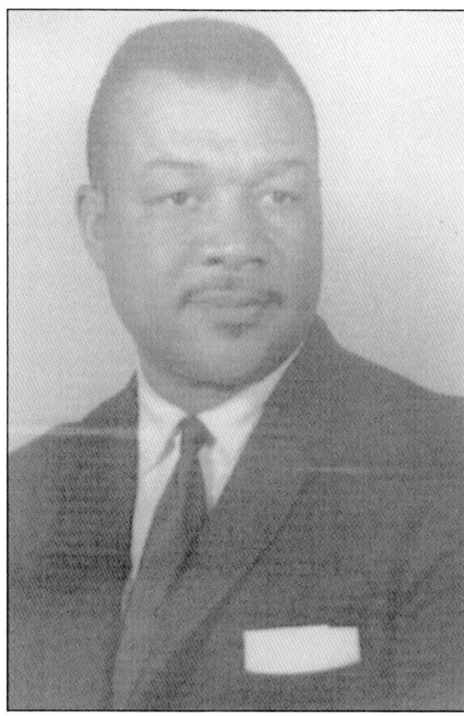

Bill Bowser. Bill Bowser was an icon in Cumberland County history. As the first black in the county to have his own radio show, he used his position to connect and empower people. His show was a great source of information during the Civil Rights Movement. A natural leader, he could rally people effortlessly and was at the forefront of the movement, working tirelessly to bring justice for blacks. His efforts led to the integration of theaters and other businesses in the downtown area. Even people who opposed him respected him because it was apparent that he was looking out for others instead of himself. Bowser was a leader and businessman. There has not been a leader of his measure since his death in 1979.

Dr. William T. Brown. Dr. Brown began his teaching career in Summerville, South Carolina, before returning to North Carolina. He worked at E.E. Smith before being named assistant principal at Ferguson-Easley. He served as principal at Washington Drive for 12 years and at E.E. Smith before being named assistant superintendent of city schools in 1973. In 1985, he was named associate superintendent for Cumberland County schools. Dr. Brown held seats on numerous boards and has served as a member of the board of trustees at Fayetteville State. Presently, he is a member of the University of North Carolina Board of Governors. In 1993, the county named its first year-round elementary school in his honor.

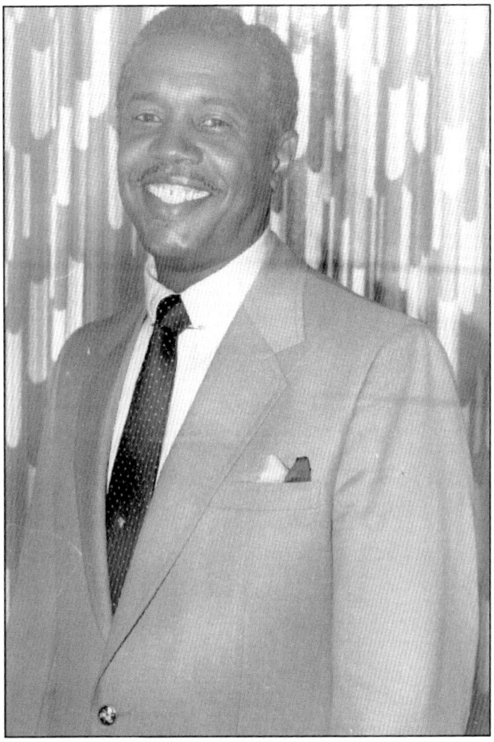

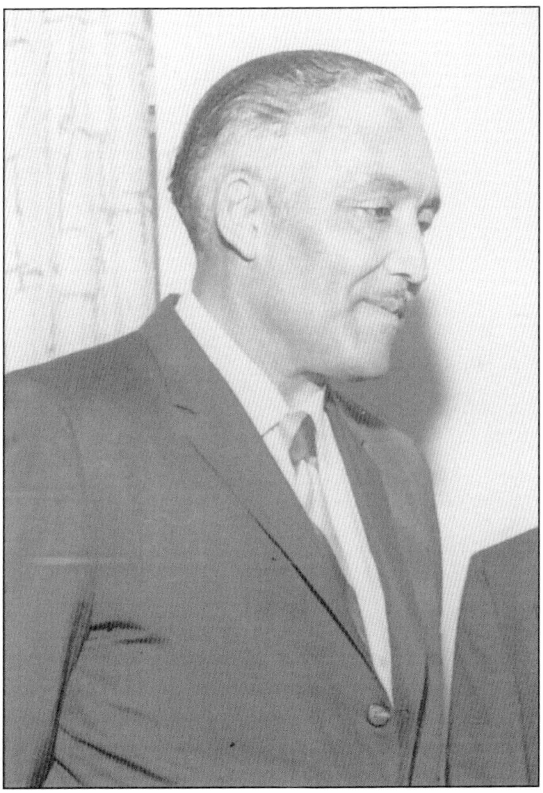

Dr. George Butler. A Fayetteville native and graduate of E.E. Smith High School, Butler attended Howard University School of Dentistry, graduating in 1955. He was a member of the Old North State Dental Society and a driving force during the Civil Rights Movement. He was selected to serve on the mayor's Biracial Committee, which negotiated the desegregation of downtown Fayetteville. Dr. George Butler was appointed to the Fayetteville State Board of Trustees by Governor Terry Sanford. A 1940 graduate of Fayetteville State, he became the first black to chair the board of trustees in 1971. He was a member and a trustee of First Baptist Church and vice chairman of the Fuller School for Exceptional Children.

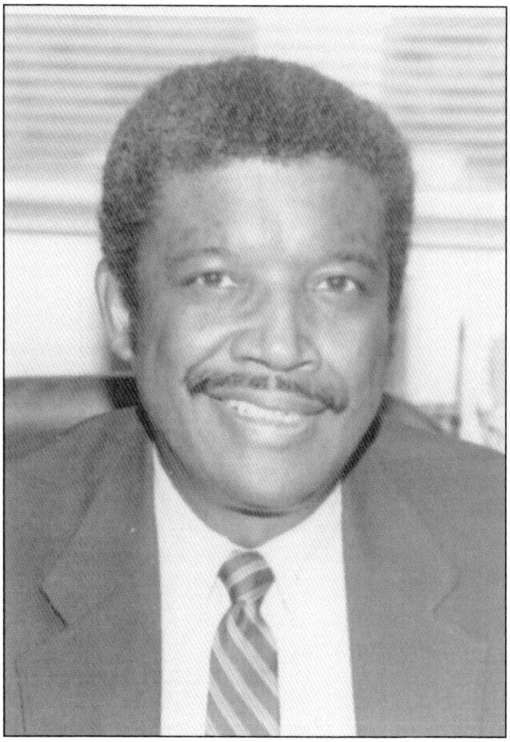

Dr. James Carson. Dr. James Carson came to Fayetteville as an administrator for Fayetteville State and served the university until 1988. After leaving the field of education, he entered the business arena, beginning a professional cleaning service. For a number of years, Dr. Carson had a dream of owning his own radio station. He went through the long and tedious process of securing the proper licenses, along with securing the financing. In 1997, he realized his dream of owning a radio station by becoming the owner of Carson Communications, which owns WCCG. It is the only station in Fayetteville owned totally by blacks. The station has become a major player in the community.

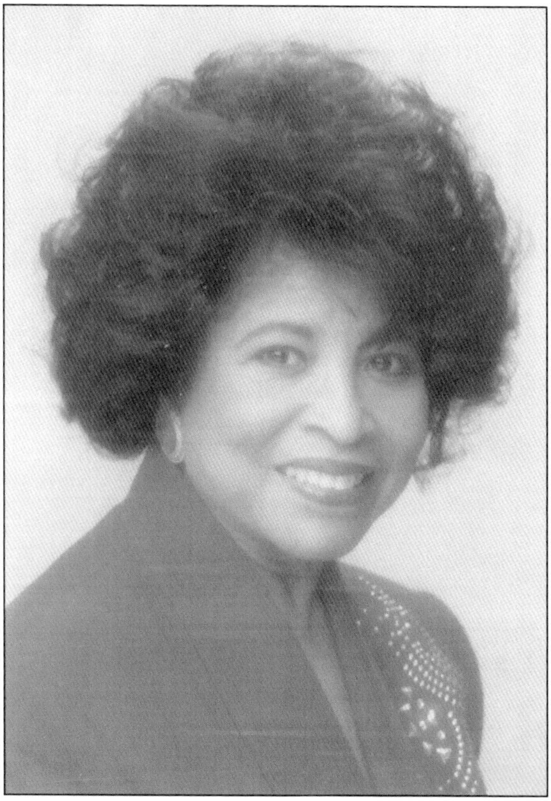

Mrs. Janie Chavis. Mrs. Janie Chavis retired as an educator in 1989 after serving as a teacher and counselor. Most of her life has been devoted to helping young people and participating in church and community activities. Mrs. Chavis is the founder and executive director of the Teen Involvement Projects (TIP), an organization that works with at-risk youth. Mrs. Chavis has been recognized for her tireless work for the good of the Fayetteville community. In 1983, she represented North Carolina as the NAACP Mother of the Year. More recently, she has been recognized as a Woman of Distinction by *Four-By-Four Magazine*, a Tower of Strength by Haymount Presbyterian Church, and was named as the Johnson C. Smith Alumnus of the Year 2000 by the Fayetteville Area Chapter.

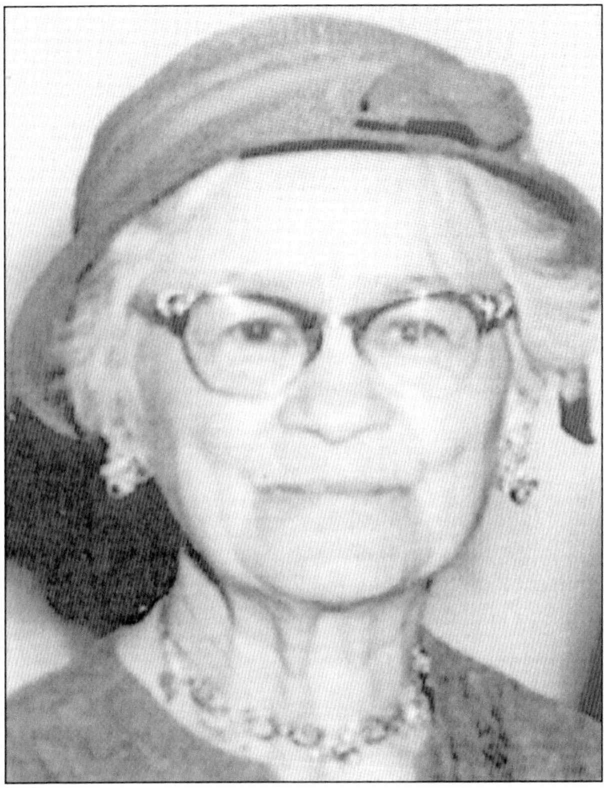

Sara Chesnutt. Born on September 8, 1877, Sara Chesnutt distinguished herself as an educator in Fayetteville. She was a graduate of Fayetteville State Normal School and served as a teacher for more than three decades. She was the sister of Charles and Anne Chesnutt.

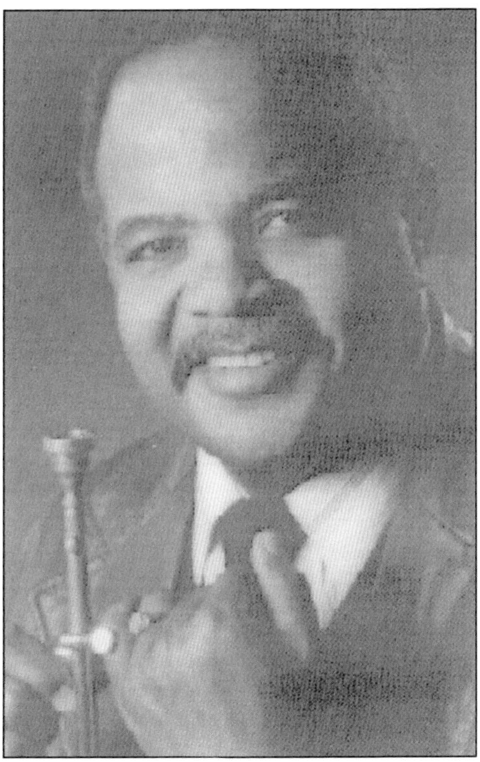

Raymond Codrington. Raymond Codrington began playing the trumpet in his high school band. He then went to college at Howard University, where he continued to excel in music. His talent was not restricted to the trumpet, for he won talent contests as a singer, accompanied by singer Roberta Flack. He returned to his hometown and formed a band, the Ray Codrington Quartet. He toured the East Coast for three years. A staunch family man, he chose not to move to a larger city as his permanent base but is a regular on the North Carolina jazz circuit. He has groomed his son, Reggie, to be a nationally known musician. A housing manager with the Fayetteville Housing Authority, he continues to be a star on the local scene, playing regularly with Malachi Sharpe, Reggie Codrington, and others.

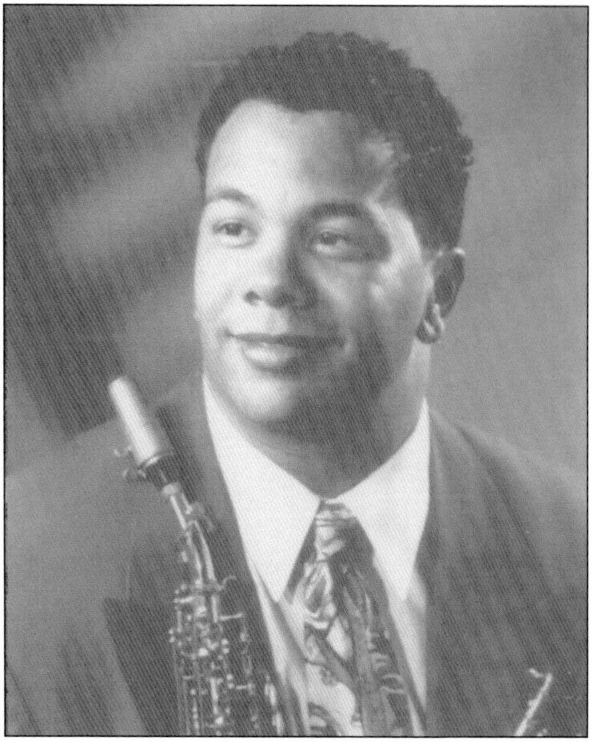

Reggie Codrington. The son of trumpeter Ray Codrington and one of Fayetteville's top young artists, Reggie Codrington is a rising star in the world of jazz. He started out with his father's instrument—the trumpet—but moved to the clarinet in the fifth grade. Reggie developed his taste in music early in his life and had access to his father's collection of classic jazz. He developed a love for genuine blues and be-bop that was inspired by his father and his friends. Reggie marched to a different tune, playing Charlie Parker tunes flawlessly. His real training was a combination of his father's instruction and and listening to John Coltrane, Hank Mobley, and others. He has worked with the likes of Harold Vick, Lonnie Plaxio, and Lewis Nash.

Renee Corders. The principal at E.E. Smith High School, Corders is the first woman to hold that position and has served with distinction since taking over in the fall of 1999, having been selected the Cumberland County Principal of the Year for 2000. She is the second E.E. Smith principal to be so honored, and this is her second selection as Principal of the Year. In 1992, she was named Principal of the Year while at Spring Lake Junior High. In 1991, she earned the School Improvement Award and received the Golden Key Award in 1994. The standard that Mrs. Corders has set has penetrated the school in just one year. E.E. Smith swept the Assistant Principal of the Year honors, along with Teacher of the Year, and the Outstanding Secondary Educator Award. This is the first time that a school has swept all of these awards.

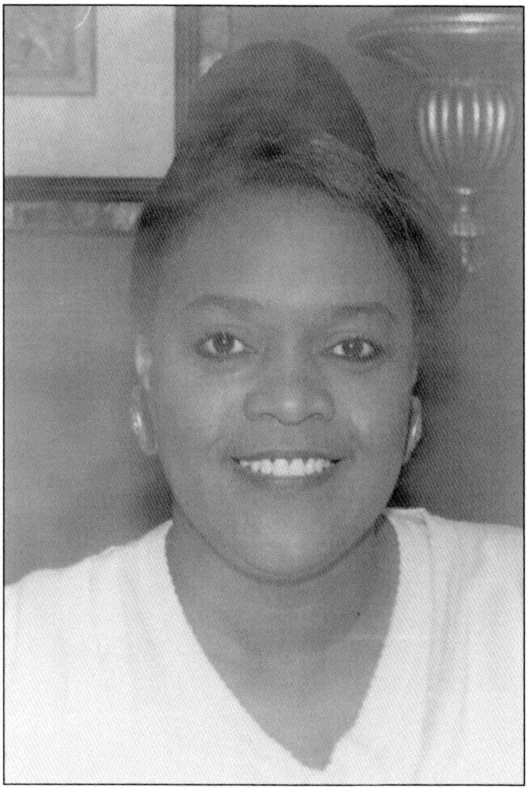

Jessica Daniels. Earning a B.S. degree in psychology from Fayetteville State in 1964, Daniels went on to earn her Ph.D. from Harvard School of Medicine in 1969. In 1976, Dr. Daniels was hired by Harvard School of Medicine as a psychology instructor and was a teaching fellow at Harvard Law School. She also worked at the Judge Baker Children Center as a psychologist. Dr. Daniels is a member of the following groups: the Board of Registration of Psychologists, St. James AME Church, American Psychological Association, and the Massachusetts Psychological Association. She has been honored as a Black Achiever of Boston, Distinguished Alumni Citizen of the Year by the National Association for Educational Opportunity (NAFEO), a Resource of Harvard Negotiation Project (Harvard School of Law).

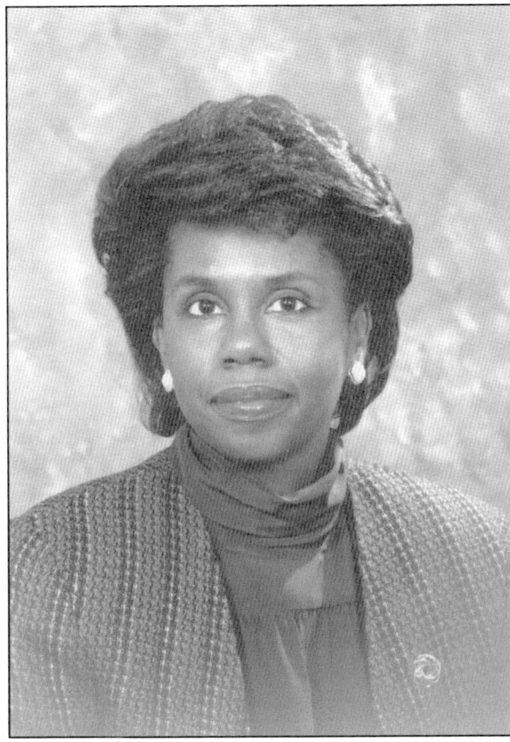

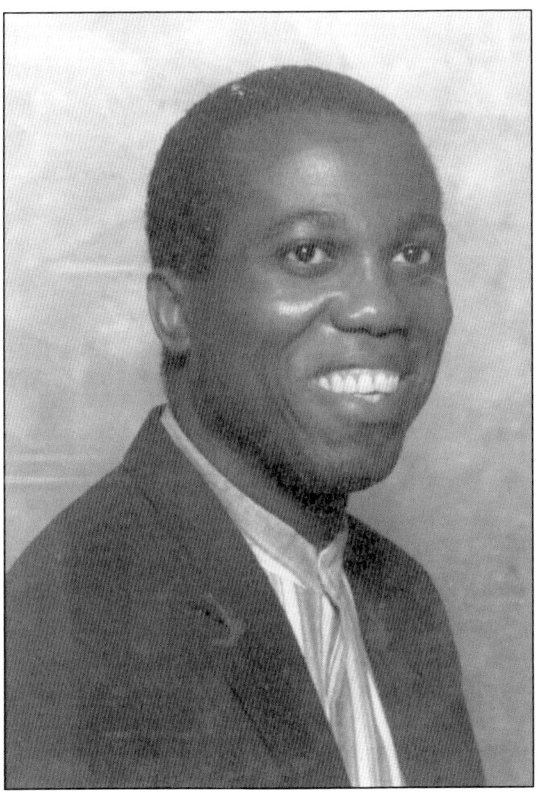

Paul Andrew Dawkins. A native of Jamaica and a graduate of Western Carolina University, Dawkins also attended the North Carolina School of Journalism. Having spent the last decade in the Fayetteville area, he began publishing newsletters and other printed materials dealing with the welfare of children. Dawkins established the Paul Andrew Dawkins Children's Project, a non-profit organization that promotes health and safety issues for youth, and in 1996, he established Paul Andrew Dawkins Television. These shows are produced with the help of young people, who carry out most of the production duties, from pre-production to camera operation to hosting. In many cases, this provides them with valuable on-the-job training.

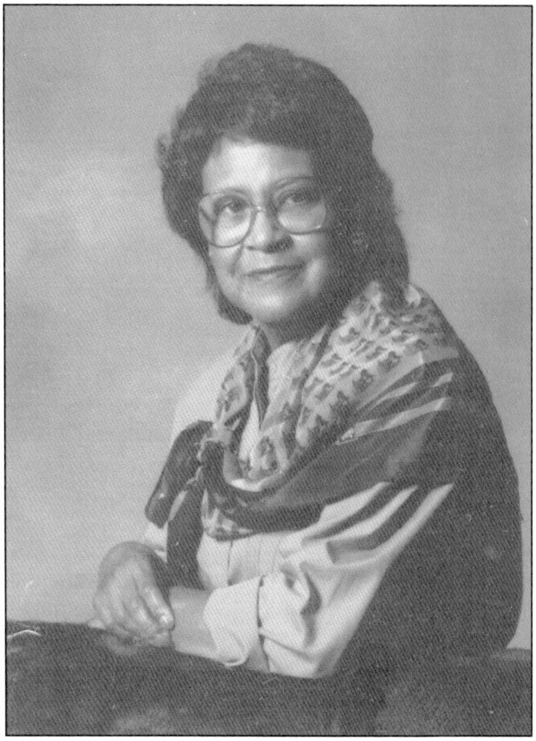

Jessie M. DeVane. A graduate of Winston-Salem State and Kate B. Reynolds School of Nursing, DeVane was a member of the first staff of Cape Fear Valley Hospital and worked as a staff supervisor. She was the second black to be hired as a public health nurse for Cumberland County, where she served for 19 years. She has more than 40 years of experience in the area of nursing. Presently, she serves as a nurse for Operation Sickle Cell. She was part of an experimental program in 1981 that screened black babies for sickle cell and because of her efforts, all black babies are now screened. Each summer, Ms. DeVane takes a group of children with sickle cell to summer camp, and she refuses to allow them to be left out because of their disease.

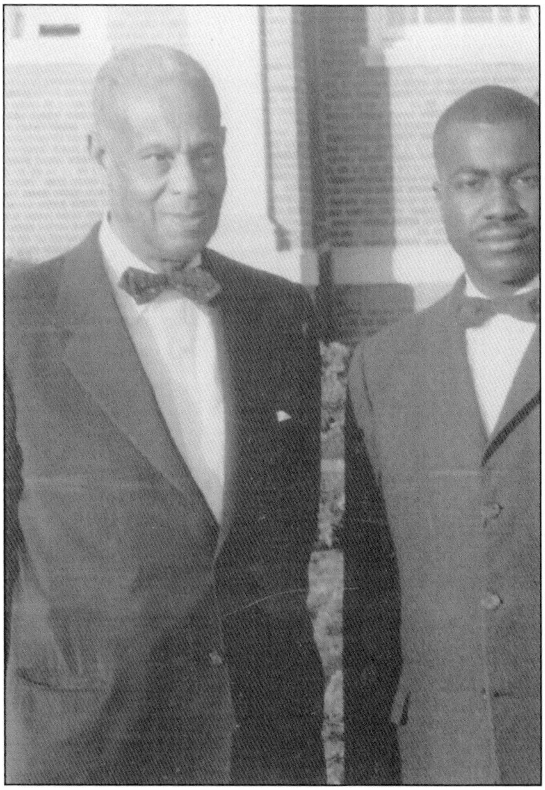

Dr. William P. DeVane. Dr. DeVane, pictured on the left, was history personified. A man who believed that it was not enough to be good, but to be good for something, he was a graduate of Shaw University, served in the United States Army, and then studied medicine at MeHarry Medical College. While there, he helped to established Community Hospital. When Dr. Devane moved to Fayetteville in 1924, there was a rising tide of political action among the black community. Because there were no black elected officials in the South at that time, Dr. DeVane offered himself to the citizens of Fayetteville to fill that void. The effect of his presence was immediately apparent. Streets were paved, water and sewer lines were laid, and streetlights were installed. This occurred in black as well as white neighborhoods.

ARTHENIUS DEW. Earning his B.S. degree from Fayetteville State and his master's degree from the University of North Carolina in Chapel Hill, Dew taught the seventh grade at Ashley Elementary School for several years and was promoted to principal of Manchester Elementary School in 1966. He retired in 1990 from Westarea Elementary School and is presently active in the Cumberland County Participatory Education Program. He has been a member of the Fayetteville Technical Community College Boarch of Trustees.

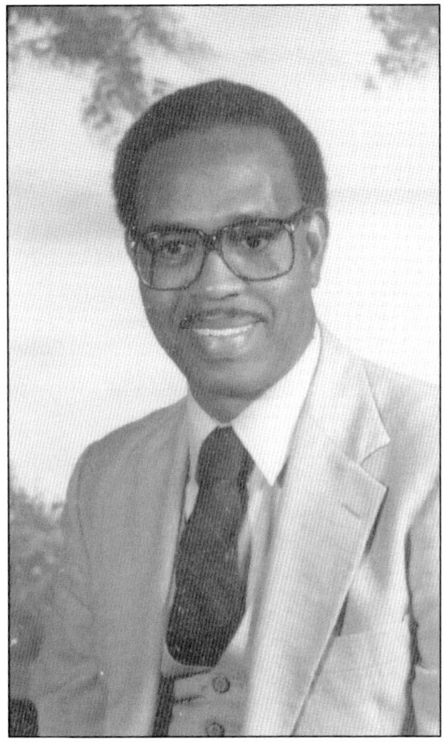

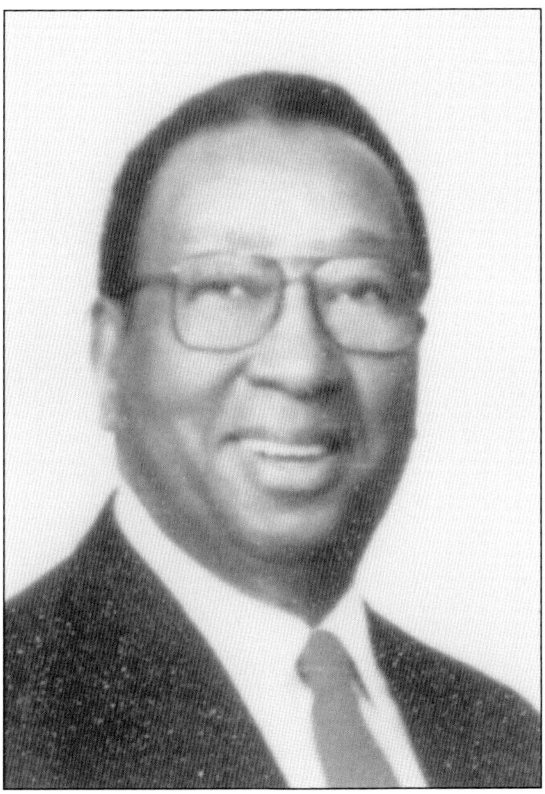

REVEREND C.R. EDWARDS. Reverend Edwards arrived in Fayetteville on Easter Sunday in 1953, and for the past 40 years, he has served the Fayetteville community tirelessly. He was pastor of First Baptist Church for 37 years, retiring in 1990. In recent years, he opened the first black-owned senior citizens housing complex in Fayetteville, located across the street from the church. It was named Edwards' Place in his honor. His first venture into politics came when he was named to the board of education. In 1982, he was elected to the State House of Representatives, representing House District 17. He demonstrated a lot of savvy while fighting for his constituents; he was not one to duck controversy. In 1989, he was the only black legislator to attend a session of the legislature held in Fayetteville. He retired in 1996.

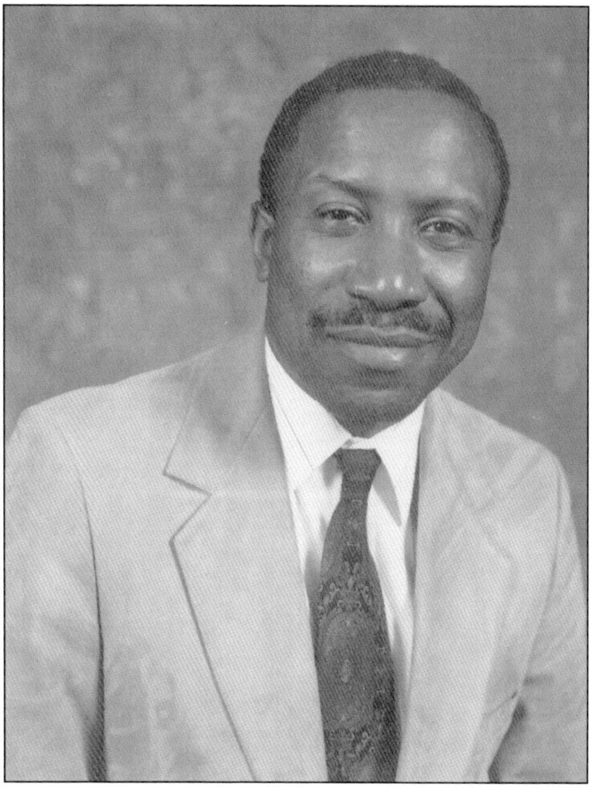

Dr. Leo Edwards. Earning his B.S. degree in mathematics from Fayetteville State in 1966, Edwards returned to his alma mater in 1974 as a mathematics instructor and supervisor of student teaching. He also served as advisor for freshman and sophomore mathematics majors. Upon returning to Fayetteville State, Dr. Edwards was promoted to associate professor of mathematics and was named director of the Mathematics and Science Education Center. Dr. Edwards is a member of the North Carolina and National Council of Teachers of Mathematics, Phi Delta Kappa, Phi Kappa Phi Honor Society, and Beta Kappa Chi Scientific Honor Society. He has been selected as one of the Outstanding Young Men in America and an Outstanding Alumnus.

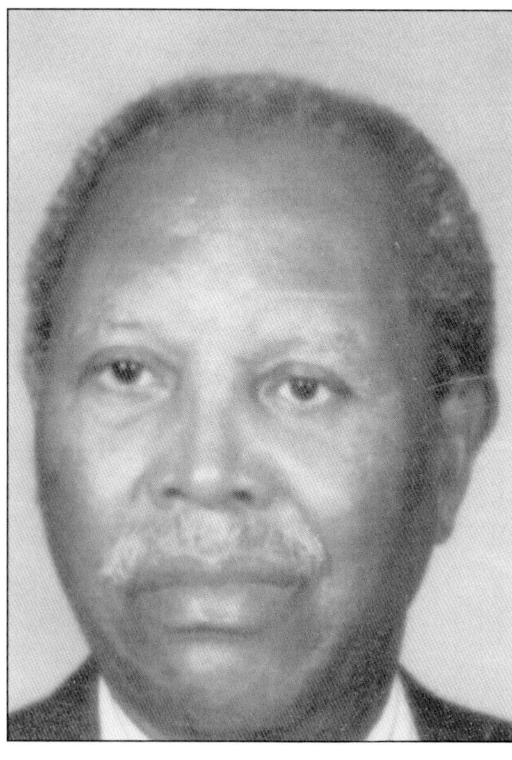

Dr. Eldridge. Dr. Eldridge joined the Fayetteville State staff in 1950 and was chairman of the Department of Math and Science. He gained valuable experience while serving as a field researcher for Stanford University and as a consultant to the North Carolina Teachers Association. He established and taught a special math class for sixth graders at Newbold School and conducted workshops on teaching math. He authored the book *Self-Help Basic General Mathematics*. Dr. Eldridge was a member of: the National Education Association (NEA), North Carolina Teachers Association, Beta Kappa Chi, National Institute of Science, Omega Psi Phi, and College Heights Presbyterian Church, where he was a deacon. His interest in education gave him the opportunity to be the chairman of the United Negro College Fund Drive. He is also listed in Leaders in Education.

Dr. Valeria P. Fleming. Coming to Fayetteville State in 1960 as a biology teacher, Dr. Fleming has served the university well in a number of capacities, including dean of women, director of general studies, acting head of the division of arts, director of arts and science, director of summer school, evening program, and weekend college, and head of the division of physical and life science .In 1985, she was promoted to the position of university provost and vice chancellor for academic affairs. She is the first black woman to be provost in the history of the UNC System. At the time she was approved by the board of trustees, she had served on an interim basis for five months and then served officially for four years. Returning to the classroom, she is one of Fayetteville State's most tenured instructors.

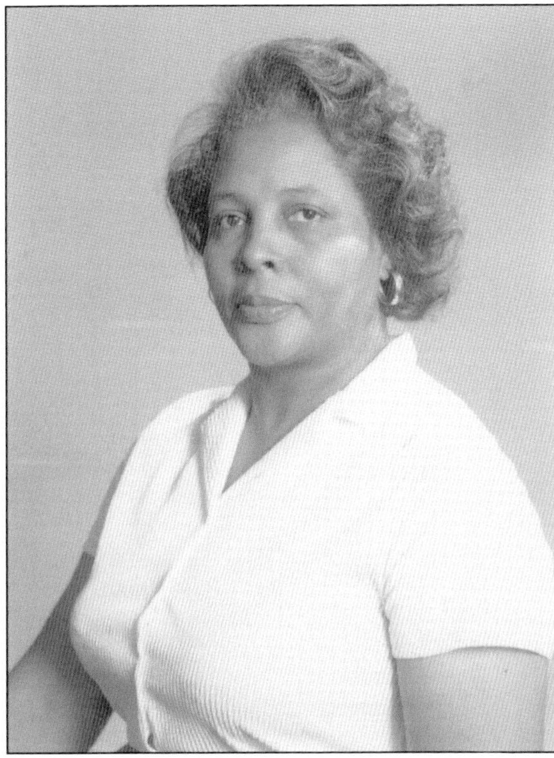

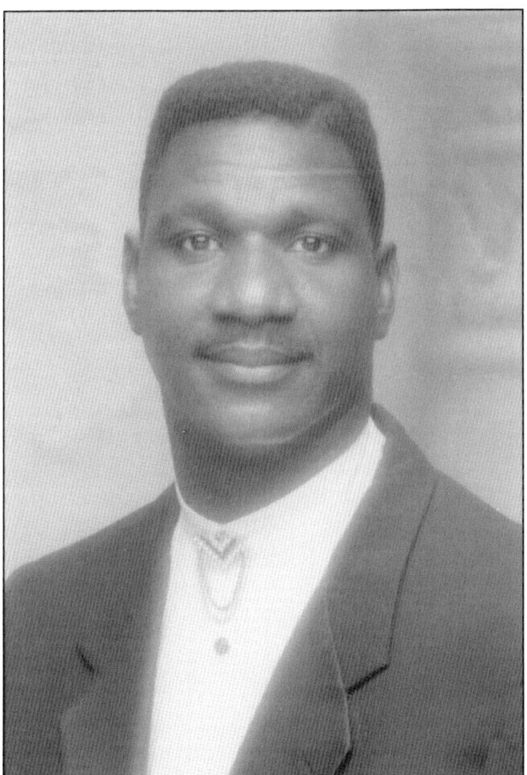

Elder William Thomas Ford Sr. Elder Ford accepted the call of God in his life to spread the gospel of Jesus Christ at age 12. He evangelized at Park's Chapel in 1973 and was soon preaching in other churches. Before long his ministry had spread to New York, Washington, Connecticut, Virginia, and Georgia. Young Elder Ford had to wrap his ministry around his education., for he graduated from Westover High School in 1979. His life took a major turn in 1982, when he moved from the role of evangelist to pastor of Piney Grove Freewill Baptist Church. In 1990, he returned to his roots and assumed his present position of pastor at Park's Chapel Freewill Baptist Church. Under his leadership, Park's Chapel has continued to grow and prosper to the point that the church is bursting at the seams. In 1997, the church purchased land for a new sanctuary and other services that will benefit the membership and the community.

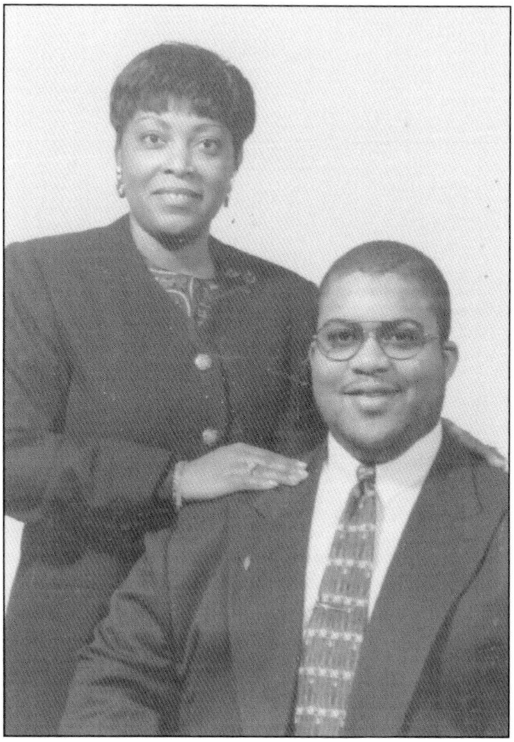

Reverend Sheridan A. Knight. One of five ministers in the Knight family, Sheridan Knight (right) followed the call to preach the gospel that was also answered by his parents, Reverends Irvin and Martha Knight—plus a brother and a sister who are also ministers. Reverend Knight was educated at North Carolina A&T State University, where he earned his bachelor's degree in political science in 1980. He furthered his education at the International Theological Center. Answering the call to preach on August 20, 1977, Reverend Knight was licensed to preach later that year and was was ordained itinerant deacon in 1978 and itinerant elder in 1981. Previously serving as pastor for St. Paul AME Church in Danville, Virginia, and St. James AME Church in Durham, North Carolina, Reverend Knight came to St. Luke in 1990. In addition to his pastoral duties, Reverend Knight is a member of the Fayetteville/Cumberland County Martin Luther King Committee.

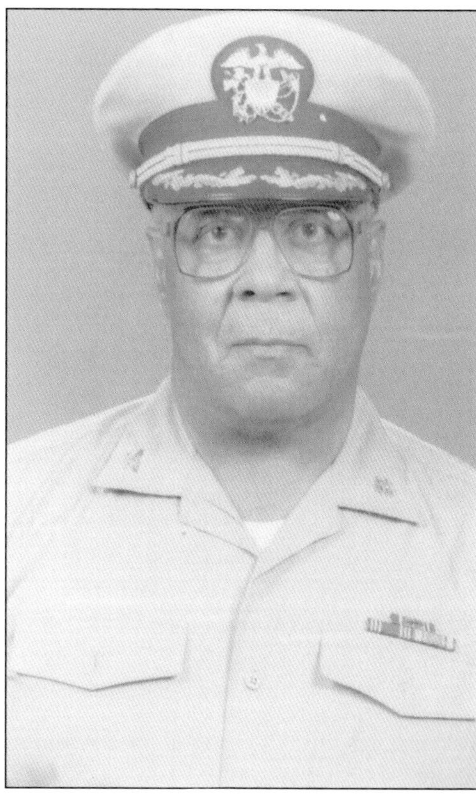

Dr. Joseph L. Knuckles. Truly a scientist's scientist, Dr. Knuckles was an intricate part of FSU for 44 years, teaching biology and other science courses. Much of his life has been devoted to the cultivation and training of young scientists. He helped to build the science program at the university and pushed his students to go beyond the ordinary teaching careers and to pursue research. A number of his former students went on to earn terminal degrees. An inventor of a number of research tools that have been used internationally, Dr. Knuckles was the first person from Robeson County to earn a Ph.D. In 1999, Dr. Knuckles died on his way to class.

ANNETTE LANIER. A graduate of North Carolina A&T State University, Lanier has spent her career in nursing and health education. She has worked at O'Berry Center and Wayne Memorial Hospital in Goldsboro, North Carolina. Locally, she has worked at the Veterans Hospital and Highsmith-Rainey Memorial Hospital. In 1982, she joined the staff of the Cape Fear Valley Hospital as a health nurse. After only eight months, Lanier was promoted to Infection Control coordinator, and in 1992, she was promoted to assistant administrator for general services. The Goldsboro native holds a master's degree from Central Michigan University.

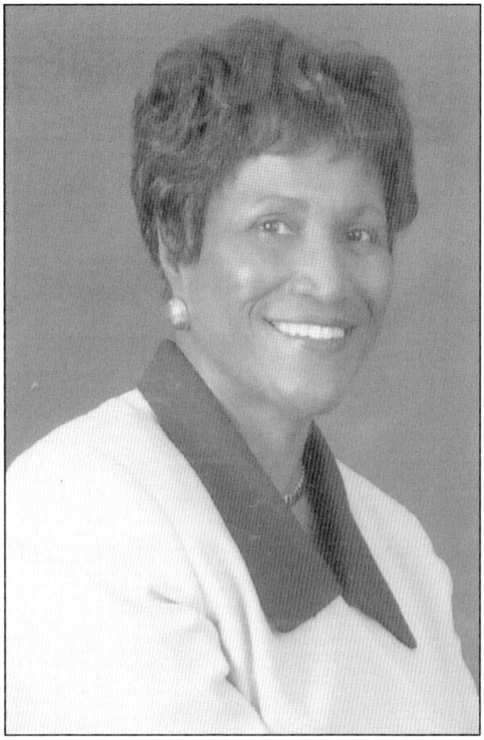

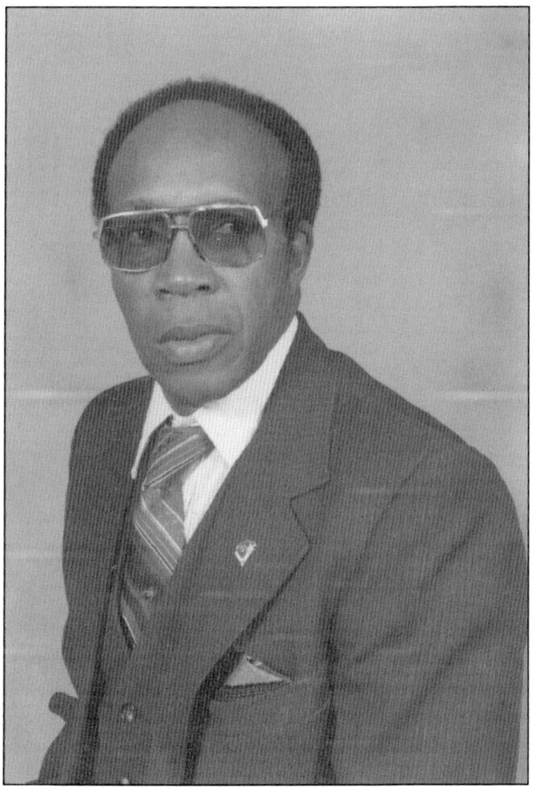

BILLY MANNING. A military policeman, Manning retired as a career soldier in 1970. He settled in Spring Lake and served the town as police chief for ten years. Manning was the first black to head a law enforcement department in Cumberland County. He later stepped down as police chief and took a position with the county sheriff's department. He retired from law enforcement in 1995. Manning entered politics when he was elected to the Spring Lake Board of Aldermen in 1985. He was a part of history, in that he helped to form a black majority on the board. This was the first time blacks had been a majority on any elected board since 1870. In 1993, Manning successfully ran for mayor. He was reelected in 1995 and has announced that he would not seek reelection.

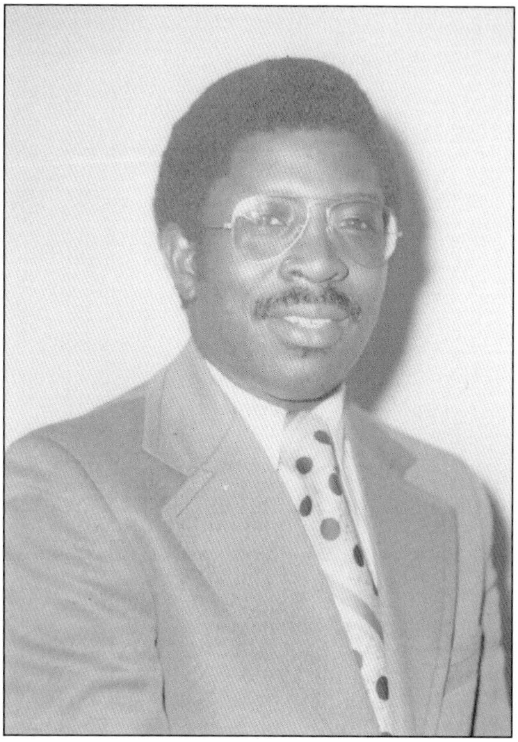

LONNIE J. MCALLISTER. A native of Fayetteville, he earned his bachelor's degree from Fayetteville State in 1965, earned his master's degree in administration from A&T State University in 1976, and did post-graduate work at East Carolina and North Carolina State. He has spent his career in the Fayetteville City School System and in 1978 was promoted to principal at Pauline Jones Elementary School. In 1993, he returned to his alma mater, E.E. Smith, as the school's principal. McAllister is an active member of First Baptist Church and a facilitator for the Lift Every Voice Youth Enhancement Program. He retired after the 1999 school year.

METTARENE MCLEAN. Known as a caring and elegant lady in the Fayetteville community, Miss McLean influenced a number of her students to pursue library science as a career. Following graduation from college, she went to work in Plymouth, North Carolina, for six years and was then contacted by her former principal at E.E. Smith about a vacancy in their library. A devoted librarian, she would leave her job after school and go to the public library to help students find information for school work. She was an active member of First Baptist Church, the North Carolina Central University (NCCU) School of Library Science Alumni Association, La Madrinna Toastmistress Club, Zeta Phi Beta, and the Association for the Study of Afro-American Life and History. Miss McLean spent 44 years as a librarian believing that we are all here to serve God and mankind.

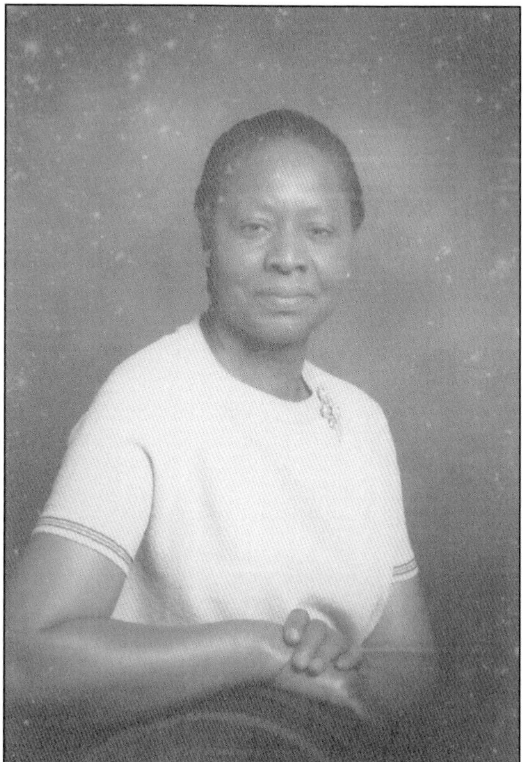

ARCHIE "DOO-DOO" MCMILLAN. Recognizing that shining shoes could be a lucrative hustle, McMillan began with a wooden shoe-shine box as a teenager and worked areas frequented by soldiers. He spent 20 years at Fort Bragg before opening his own shop in downtown Fayetteville. His shop, the Esquire Sports Center, is one of the most successful businesses in the downtown area. A graduate of E.E. Smith, McMillan is deeply rooted in Fayetteville. Outspoken, but always a gentleman, he is constantly sharing pointers with young people. His wisdom, along with his faith in God, makes him a strong voice in the community. In addition to operating a successful business, McMillan presently serves as sergeant at arms for the North Carolina Senate.

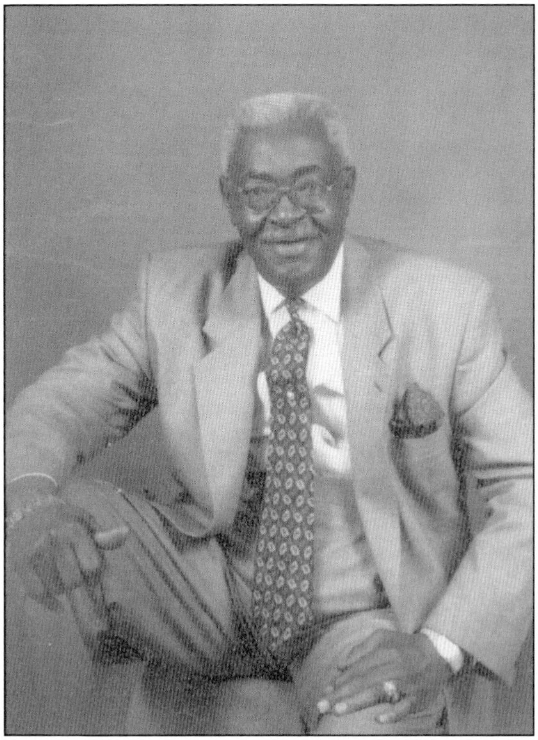

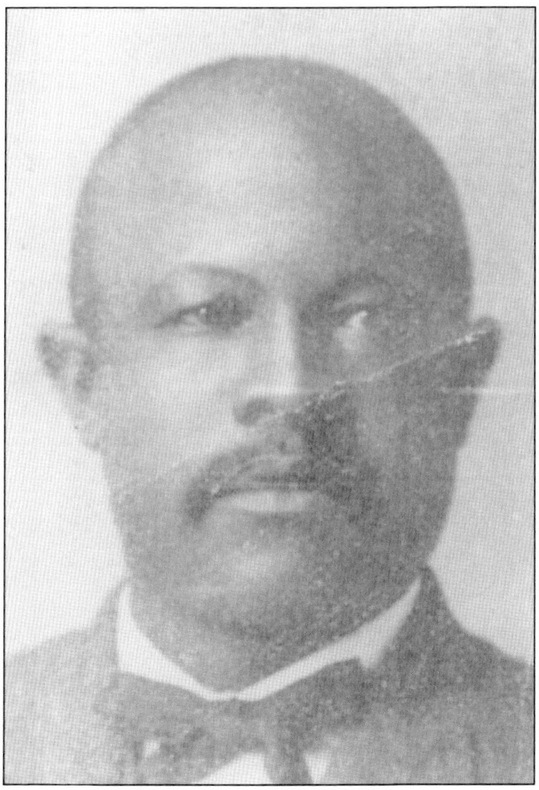

DR. PAUL NEWTON MELCHOR. One of the five signers of the note to purchase the Murchison Road site, where Fayetteville State is now located, Dr. Melchor was the son of German immigrants of African decent and was born in Concord, North Carolina, on December 28, 1865. He was educated in local schools before enrolling in Shaw University, where he was an honor graduate in the Leonard Medical School. Dr. Melchor set up his practice in Fayetteville, but did extensive traveling in the surrounding area taking care of the sick. He cured many illnesses that baffled the science of his day. Dr. Melchor married women from two prominent Fayetteville families. He died in 1928. His son, Warren, is a Fayetteville State graduate.

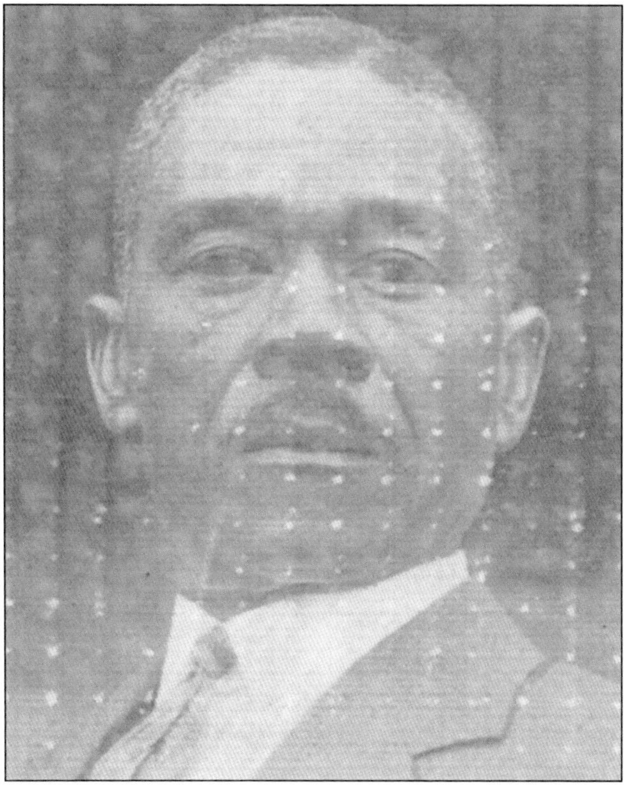

Samuel Murchison. A distinguished builder and contractor in Fayetteville, Murchison was an active member in both church and fraternal organizations. His work can be seen around Fayetteville in some of the older churches and homes.

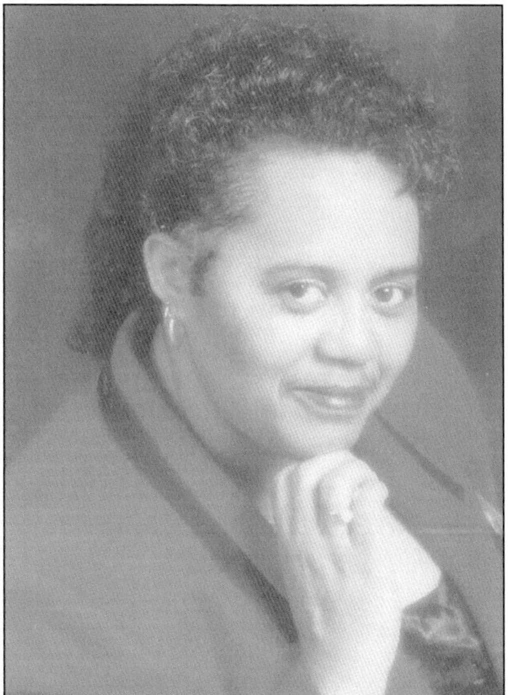

Lieutenant Jackie M. Paul. A Fayetteville native and a graduate of Cape Fear High School and Fayetteville State, Paul started her career in law enforcement as a bailiff in 1980 and has risen steadily through the ranks. In 1982, she was promoted to deputy and worked as a detective on white-collar crimes from 1982 until 1998. During this time, she was promoted to sergeant in 1986 and lieutenant in 1993. At each level after sergeant, she made history as the first black female at any of these ranks and positions. In 1998, Lieutenant Paul became the highest-ranking black female in North Carolina when she was promoted to road commander, a position that oversees all the road patrols for the sheriff's department. Lieutenant Paul owes her success to hard work and a strong faith.

Ambrose Pemberton. One of the first blacks in the Fayetteville area to become an agent with a major insurance company, Pemberton, an A&T graduate, began working with Allstate in the early 1970s. Later, he opened his own Allstate agency. Pemberton has built a strong business and is giving back to the community. He has been a major supporter of Fayetteville State and community organizations. He is a founding member of the Cape Fear 100 Black Men and is a member of the Cumberland County Board of Elections.

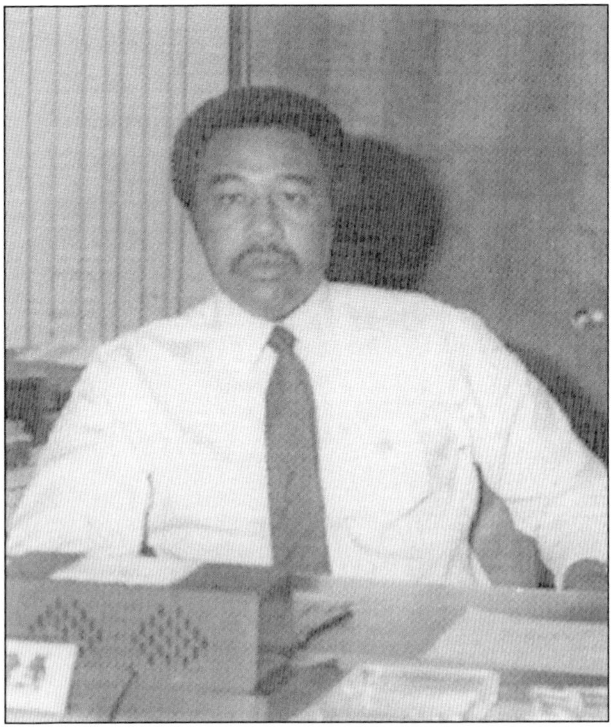

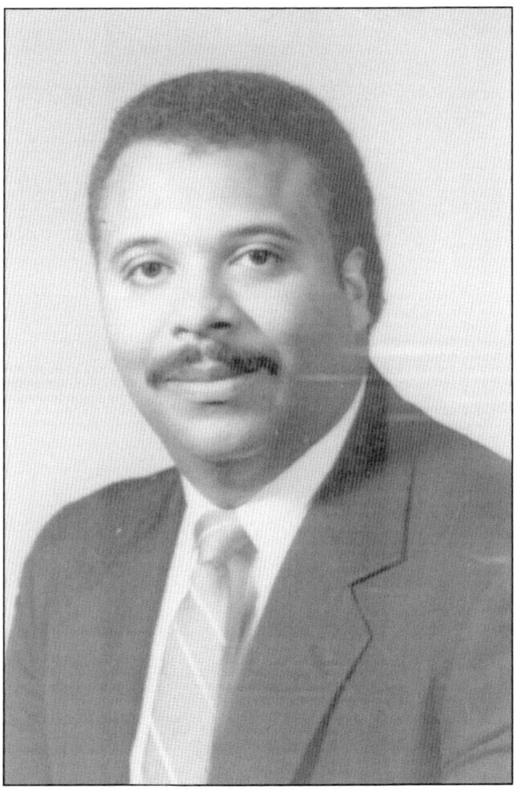

Judge Ed Pone. A native of Cumberland County, Judge Pone grew up in the Gray's Creek area. He graduated from North Carolina Central University and earned his law degree from the University of North Carolina. Pone served for a number of years in the public defender's office before joining the firm of Rand and Gregory. He then worked with that firm for many years before venturing into politics. He was unsuccessful in his first run for office. However, in 1996, Pone was appointed a district court judge, one of two black judges on the bench in the Fayetteville area.

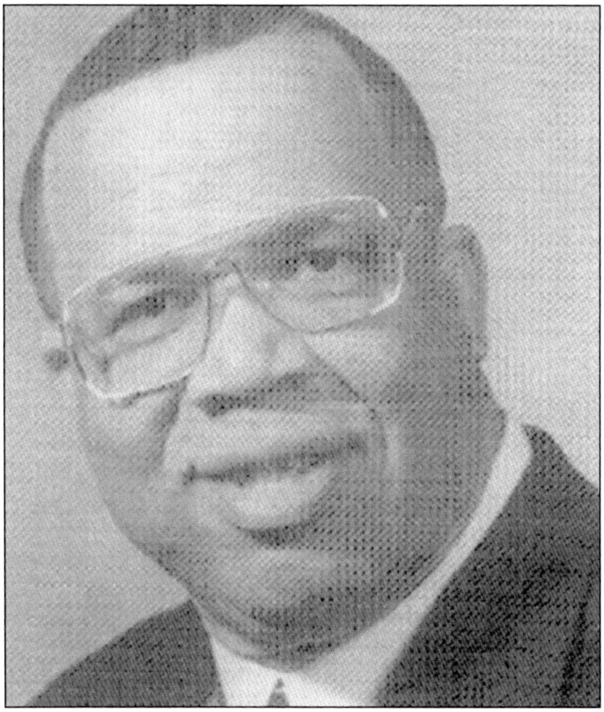

Bishop J. Venturio Porter. A graduate of Fayetteville State, Porter returned to Fayetteville after a stint in the military and founded the United Gospel Fellowship in 1980. From a small building and only a few members, he has built a thriving and dynamic ministry. In addition to the main sanctuary, Christ Cathedral, on Deep Creek Road, there is an annex, Christ Cathedral (North), on Murchison Road, and Christ Village, on the old Green Valley Country Club property. A Christian academy and daycare center are also part of the ministry. Bishop Porter's ministry reaches around the world; his ministry is the first to originate from Fayetteville to have such a reach.

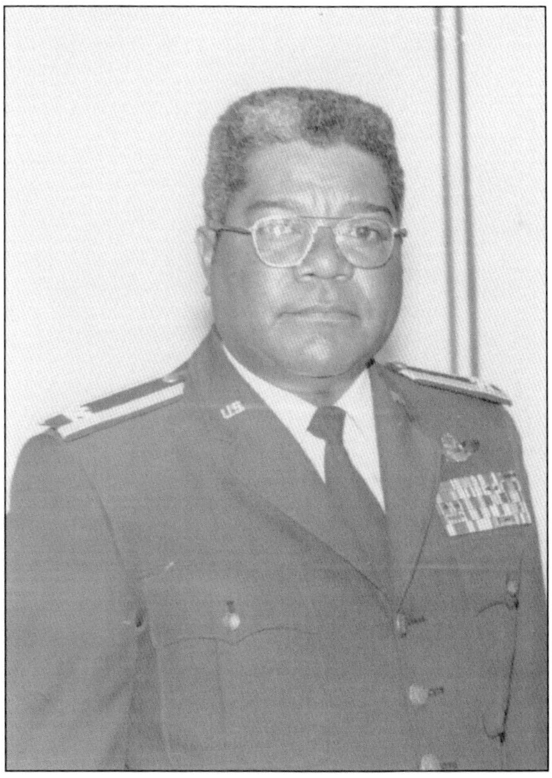

Colonel Ronnie Peoples. A trailblazer for black military officers in all branches of the services, Colonel Peoples was named, in 1986, commander of the Pope Air Force Base, which provides air support to activities at Fort Bragg. He is the first black person to command an Air Force base in North Carolina. Peoples came to Pope from Rhein-Mein in Germany. He had logged more than 5,000 flight hours, and his honors include the Distinguished Flying Cross for flights in Vietnam. He was equally capable of flying the C-130 and the smaller jets such as the C-9, which he flew for Nightingale flights in Germany. As a graduate of Tennessee State, Peoples was a distinguished member of their ROTC program.

Mary F. Ray. A native of Bladen County, North Carolina, Mrs. Ray earned a B.S. degree from Fayetteville State in 1974. She furthered her education at North Carolina Central University, Vance-Granville Community College, UNC-Chapel Hill, and Louisburg College. She has work as an elementary school teacher at South Granville Elementary School. Mrs. Ray is also active in her church, St. Joseph AME Zion Church. She is a member of the church's trustee board, a teacher in its adult Sunday school, and also serves as Sunday school treasurer. She has twice served as a counselor for the Youth Leadership Camp.

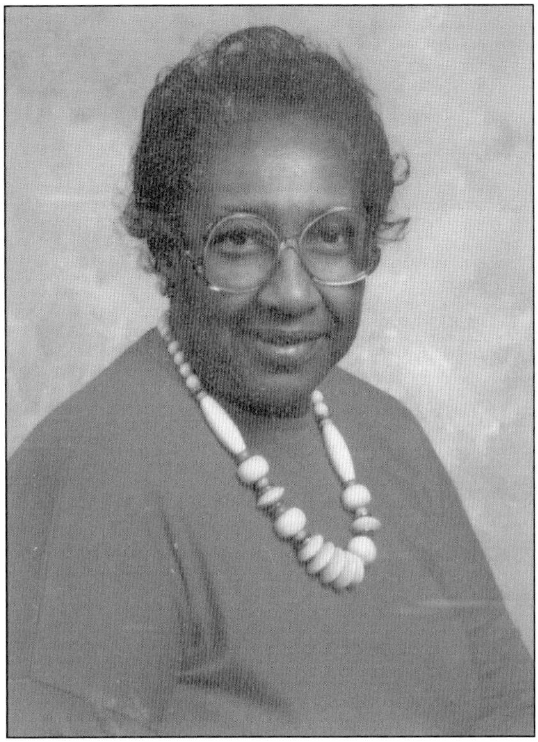

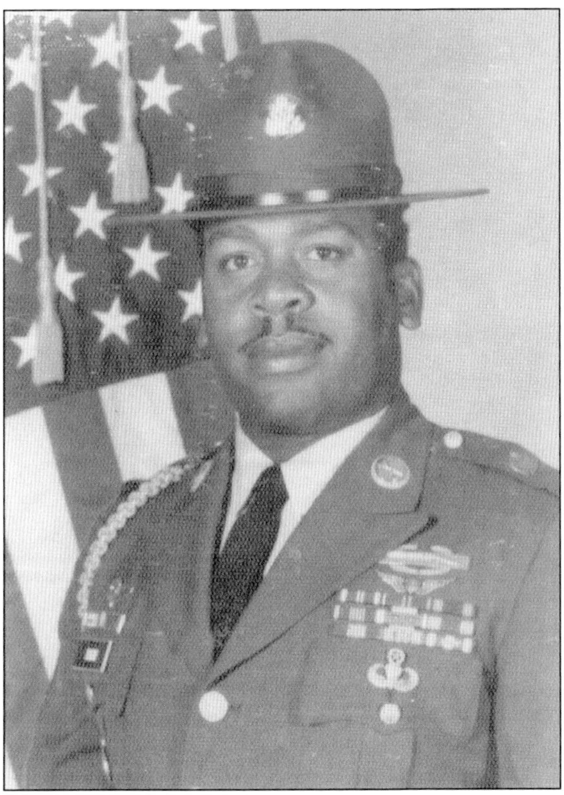

Sergeant Roger Redd. Sergeant Redd is a 22-year veteran of the 82nd Airborne Division, from which he retired as a sergeant major. He did three tours in Vietnam and won five Purple Hearts and a Bronze Star. A retired drill sergeant, Sergeant Redd applies the skills that he once used to mold airborne troops to now shape young men who have gone astray. At 6 a.m., he is in the courthouse parking lot working with young men who lack direction and other social skills, helping them to take the first steps toward self-improvement. His program is a form of boot camp aimed at first-time and low-risk offenders. Redd was one of 12,500 nominees for the prestigious Jefferson Award and became a national winner in July 1996. Since 1992, Sergeant Redd has been working to make young men into winners.

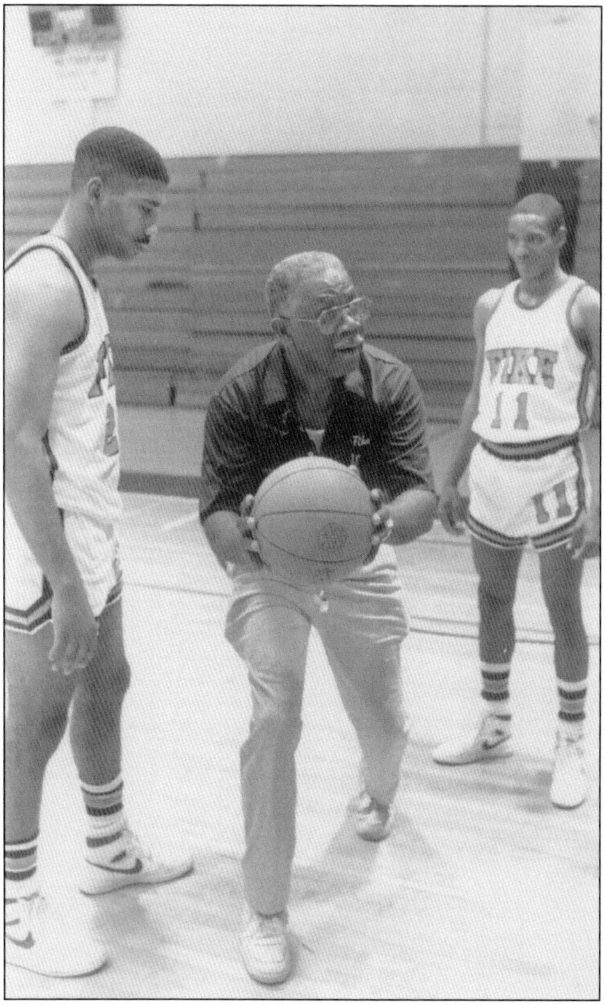

Harvey Reid Jr. Frederick Douglass High School in Elm City became a basketball powerhouse under the guidance of Harvey Reid Jr. In 1989, Reid coached Fike to a 28-1 record before taking a bow in the state finals despite losing seven key players from the 1988 team. Reid's call to coaching came early when, as a six year old, he snuck into the locker room at Fayetteville State. This adventure has turned into 20 conference, 14 district, and 7 state championships. He has receive nearly every possible coaching honor, including National Coach of the Year in 1975. He has served as a coach in the East-West All Star game. Coach Harvey Reid Jr. died doing one of his favorite things in life: helping young men to be their best. Coach Reid compiled a record of 818 victories.

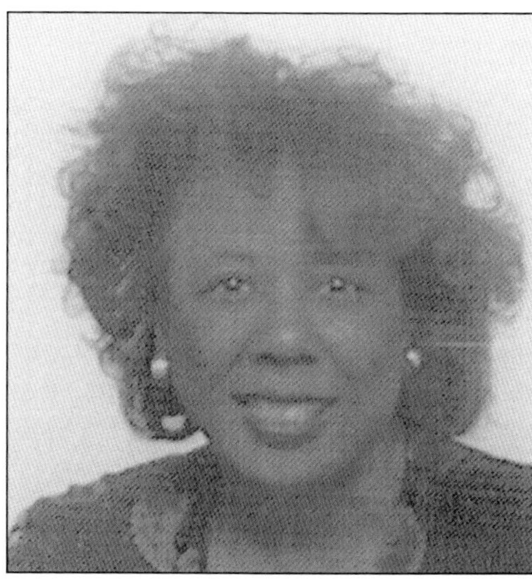

Bernadette M. Ross. Coming to Fayetteville as a librarian at Reid Ross High School, she later moved to Terry Sanford as its librarian. Ross has sought to expand learning opportunities for her students and has created the Charles Chesnutt Film Festival and the Terry Sanford Book Endowment Program. Ross has written and received grants to assist student educational opportunities and to enhance student achievement. Among her honors are Teacher of the Year in 1987 and 1997 and Who's Who in Education in 1992–1993 and 2000.

Malachi Sharpe. One of Fayetteville's most qualified musicians and possibly the area's best music teacher, Sharpe has spent 30 years in the public school system teaching music and directing bands. He still works hard to pass on his knowledge to the next generation and owns a music school, Play Rite Music, on Gillespie Street. Working with beginners and polished professionals, Sharpe helps to cultivate many talented musicians. About six times each year, he showcases their skills to the public, usually at the Radison-Prince Charles Ballroom. Sharpe has built several local bands, and some of his mentored musicians have gone on to play for the likes of James Brown and the SOS Band. He remains an icon in the music world as a gifted teacher.

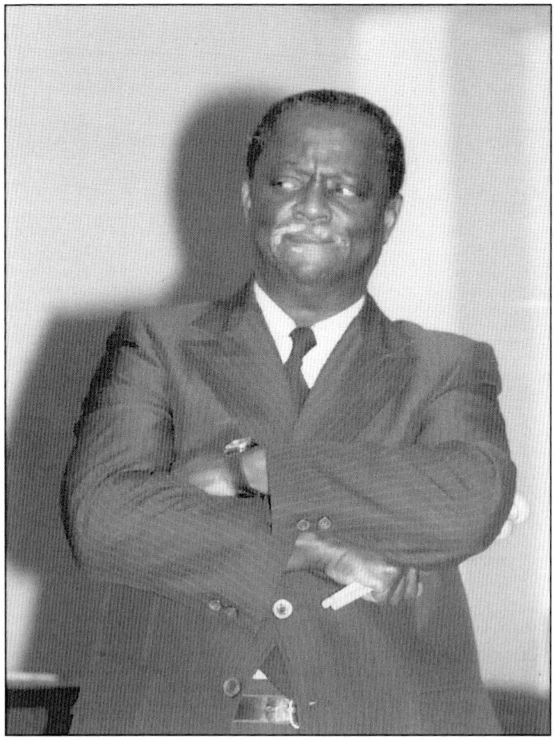

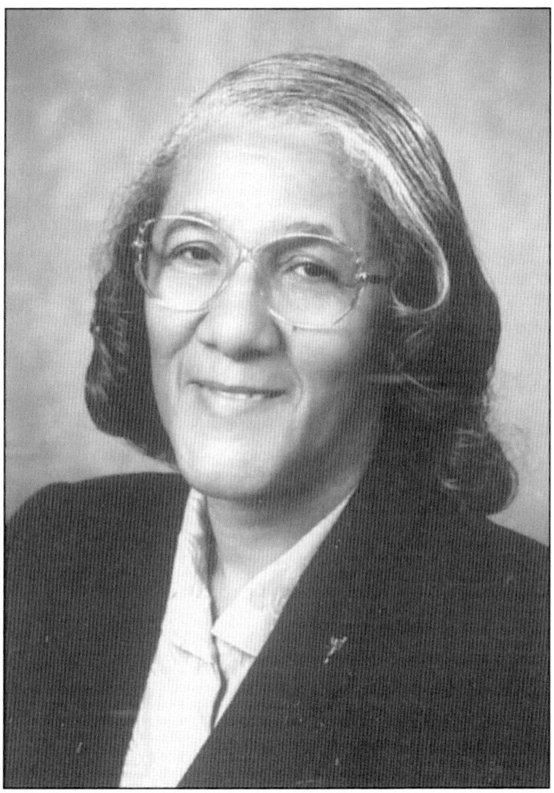

Mrs. Mable Smith. A Fayetteville native, she was a fighter for civil rights during the 1960s and has been a major figure in local politics since that time. During the 1960s, she was an organizer and marched for desegregation. Working at the precinct level, she helped to register blacks to vote at a time when few were registered or voting. For many years, Mrs. Smith worked in the office of the register of deeds. She was helpful, especially to senior citizens. Smith offered herself as a candidate for the city council seat representing District 2 after it lost its longtime advocate, Ida Ross. She won the seat in 1999.

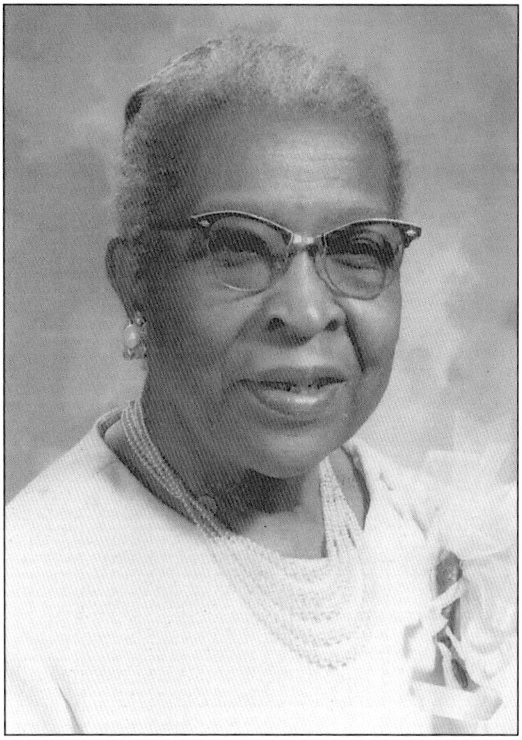

MARY ELIZABETH MCMILLAN THOMPSON. She was a public health promoter for the black population of Cumberland County. Hired in the 1930s, she served with dedication for 38 years and was the only link to medical care for many. She organized a midwife team, pushed for immunizations, and took part in broadening health-screening efforts in the school in the 1950s. "Nurse Mac," as she was known, was totally responsible for the health of all blacks in the county. She also organized the health program at Fayetteville State. Operating from a room on the third floor of the courthouse, she taught health, birth control, personal hygiene, and nutrition to her constituents. After her retirement, she had a hand in the development of Operation Sickle Cell. Nurse Mac died in 1982 at age 79.

THELBERT TORREY. A life-long resident of Fayetteville and the grandson of a slave, Torrey graduated from E.E. Smith High School, where he was a member of Golden Bulls' Negro High School basketball national championship team in 1939. He began his college education at Fayetteville State, where he was a member of the 1941 EIAC championship team coached by former E.E. Smith coach H.A. Black. Following World War II, Torrey transferred to South Carolina State College, where he earned a degree in vocational agriculture. He taught in the Fayetteville and Cumberland County school systems. In 1985, Mr. Torrey ran for the city council, winning the seat to represent the 4th District. He served seven terms.

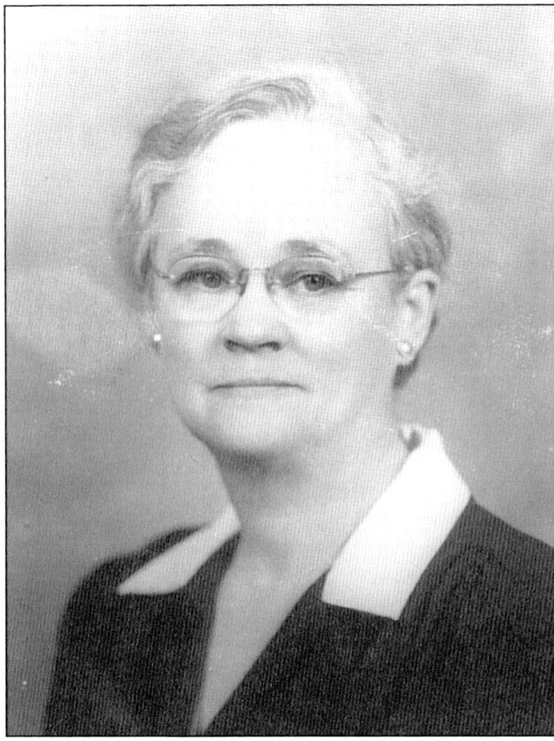

Anne Chesnutt Waddell. A native of Fayetteville and the sister of Charles Chesnutt, Waddell worked as a classroom teacher for 12 years. In 1912, she was appointed Cumberland County supervisor of school and served in that capacity for 22 years; she retired in 1936. Anne Chesnutt Junior High School is a former all-black high school that was named in her honor. She was a member of Evans Metropolitan AME Zion Church. She died on November 1, 1966.

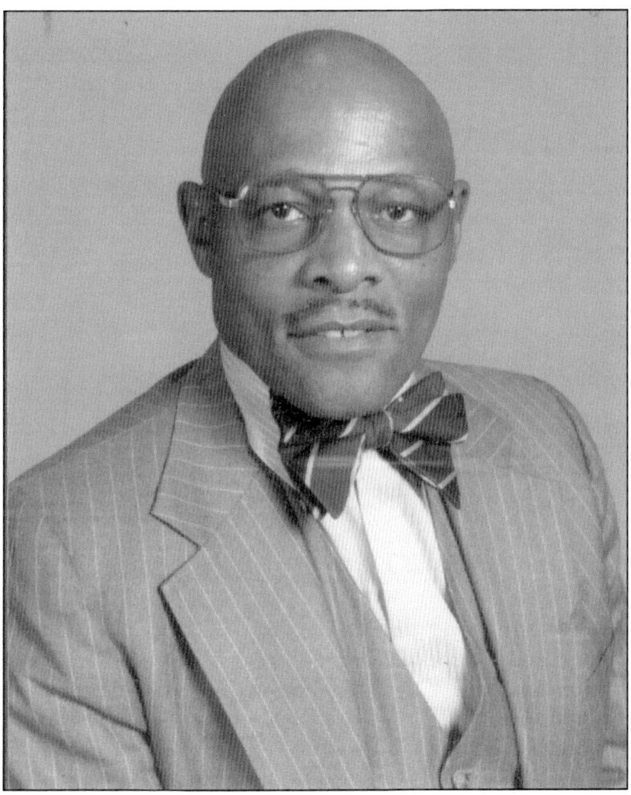

Dr. Jesse F. Williams. Dr. Williams earned his B.S. degree in biology at Fayetteville State and, in addition to excelling in the classroom, was the quarterback for the football team. He was also a part of the first Bronco tennis team and a member of the concert band. Dr. Williams furthered his education at Howard University School of Medicine and Freedmen's Hospital. In 1975, Dr. Williams was appointed Cumberland County's director of public health services. Under his leadership, the department has grown and serves the standard purposes for the county, as well as a teaching source for regional universities. He held the position until 1999.

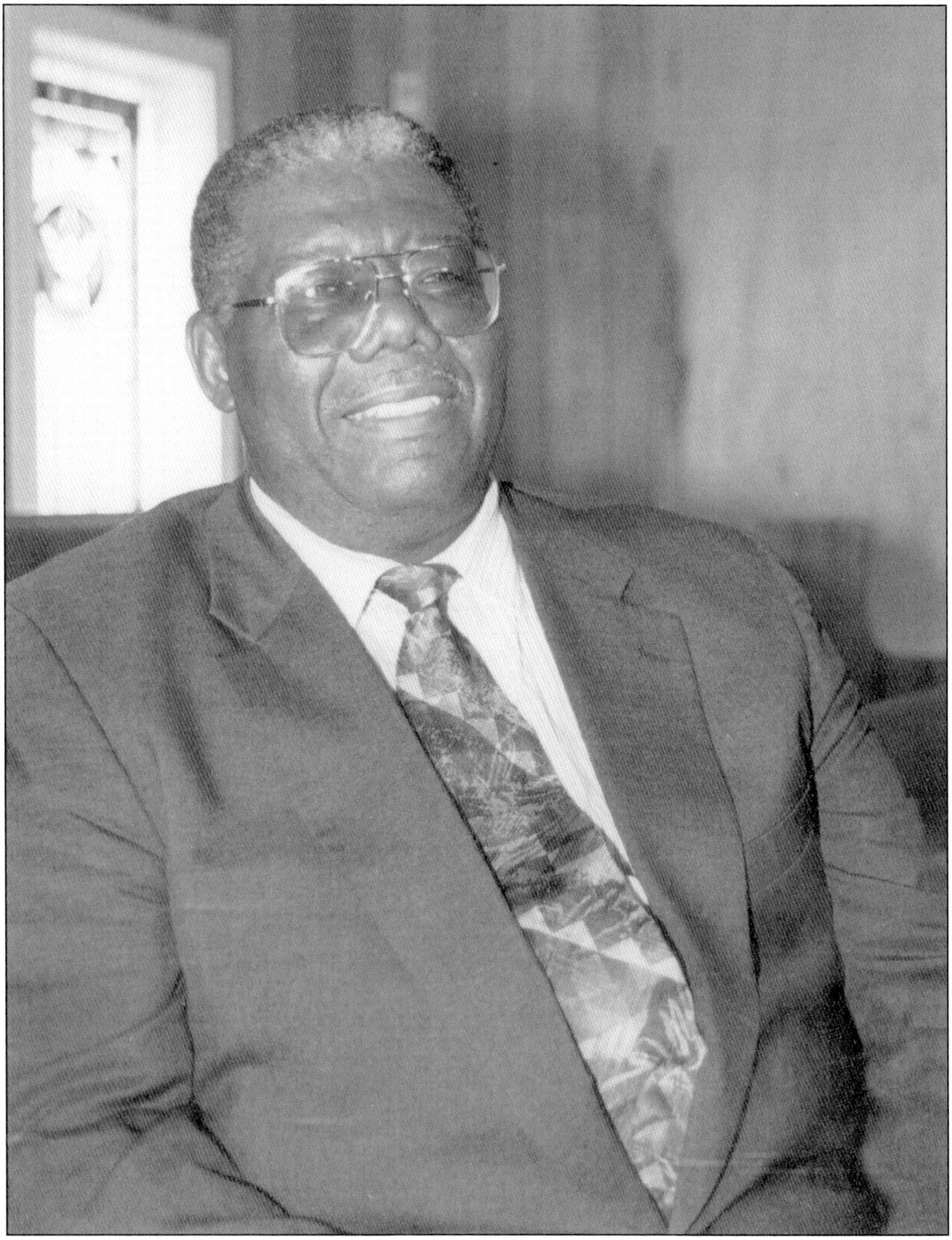

Bishop Jesse Williams. Born in Washington, North Carolina, Reverend Williams came to Fayetteville in 1967 and was named the pastor for Anderson Temple Church of God in Christ. He led the church in the building of their present sanctuary and has seen the congregation grow from a few faithful to hundreds. Presently, Reverend Williams pastors two churches. At his side through all of this has been his wife, Naomi. The couple has been married for 51 years. Under their leadership, both churches are thriving. Anderson Temple has made great strides in working with the young people from the impoverished areas in East Fayetteville.

Curtis Worthy. A native of Spring Lake and a graduate of Fayetteville State University, Worthy works as an auditor with the IRS. Worthy is active in Park's Chapel Church and was elected to the city council in 1997. He is currently in his second term representing District 9.

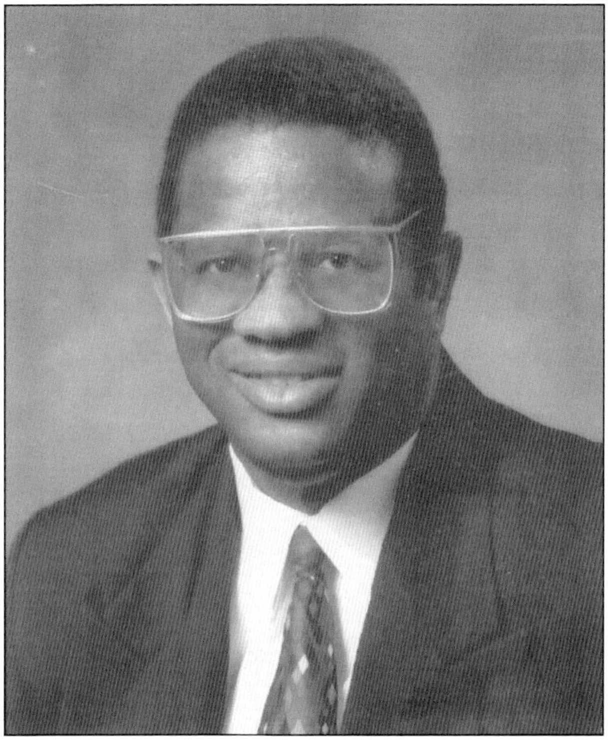

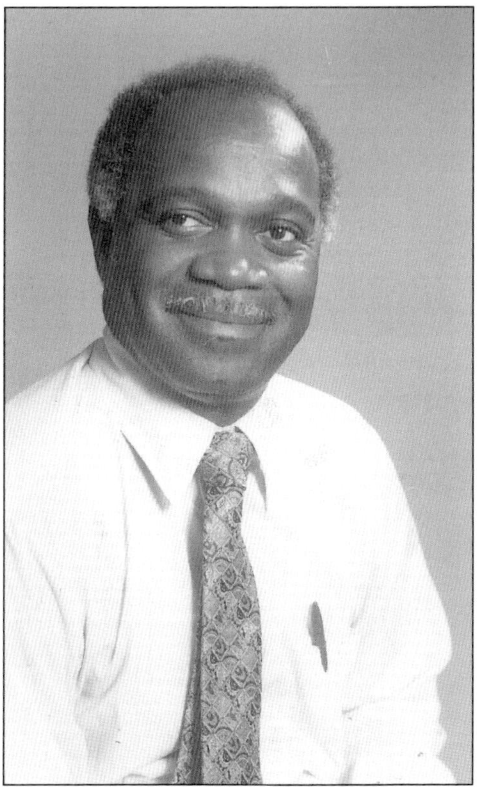

Milton Yarborough. A lifelong Fayetteville resident and a graduate of Fayetteville State, he worked in the field of education for many years, then went to work at his alma mater. Most of his career was spent in student services and general administration. He was a strong advocate of school spirit among the students and was a regular at most Broncos games. Yarborough has been active in local politics for more than four decades. He has worked in the precincts and with the Get Out the Vote efforts. He also ran successfully for a seat on the Cumberland County Board of Education and has been reelected twice. A former running back during the 1940s, Yarborough is still a fixture at Broncos games.

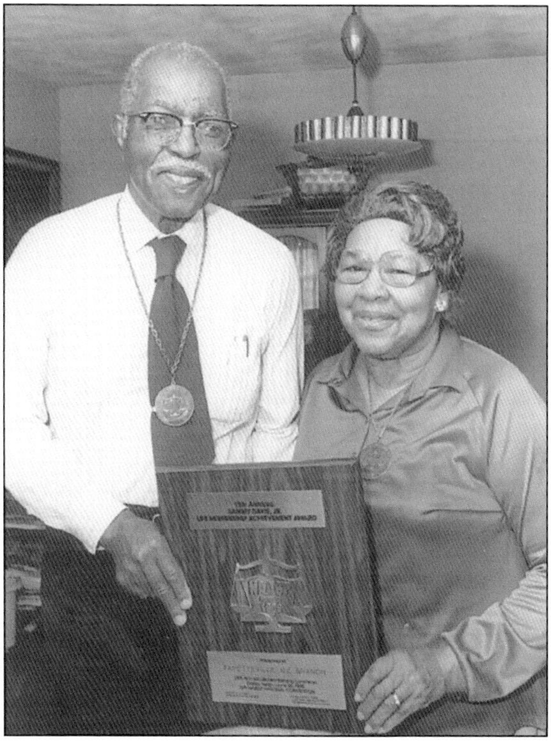

Sipio and Sadie Burton. One of the first couples of the Civil Rights Movement, they were a dedicated team who put their lives and property on the line for the cause. Both were giants. Mr. Burton served as NAACP president during the struggle of the 1960s. One of his best qualities was his ability to negotiate. He possessed skills that are not taught in colleges, and he got the results that he wanted. He took businesses to task for not hiring blacks but taking money from them. Sadie was his right hand. A wealth of wisdom, she melted her enemies with a smile but was always ready to fight if needed. Fayetteville is a better place because of the Burtons.

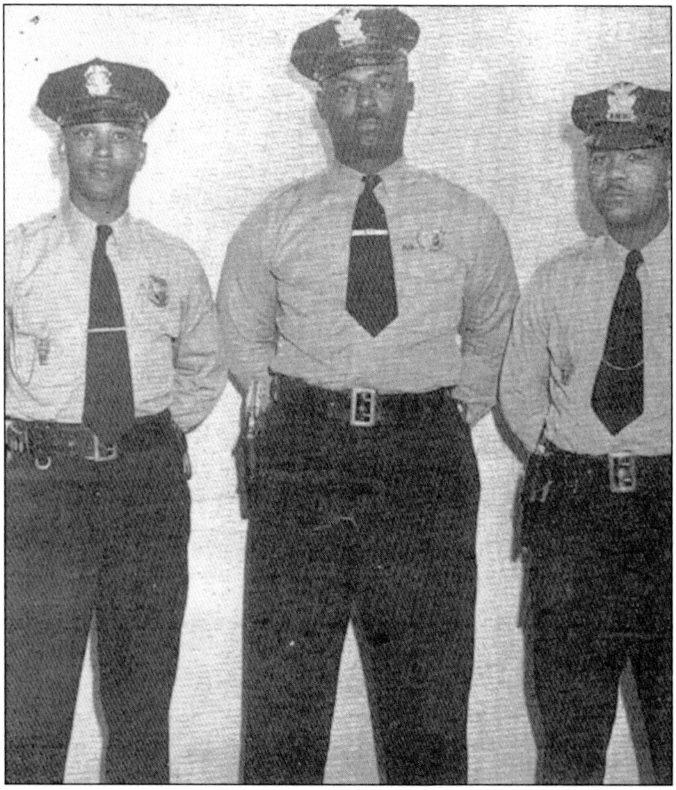

Three of Fayetteville's Finest. Edward N. Taylor, Al Banks, and Fred Truett were three of Fayetteville's first black police officers. Banks retired as a sergeant with over 20 years on the force. Truett retired with more than 30 years on the force and rose to the rank of major, the highest rank to be reached by a black. After the retirement of the police chief, Truett served as interim chief until the present chief took over.

Pearl J. Marshall. A graduate of the Precola De Vore School of Charm and Modeling, Ms. Marshall has a talent for recognizing and cultivating talent. She served as fashion coordinator for *Together with Evangeline* (WNCT-TV) and *Out of the Depths* (WUNC-TV) and was a career day consultant of modeling. Marshall owned and directed a charm school in Halifax and Northhampton Counties and in Chapel Hill. She is the director of the Pearl Jackson School of Charm and Modeling Agency of Scotland Neck and Fayetteville. Since 1987, she has been state director of Hal Jackson Talented Teens International of North Carolina. In ten years, she has produced seven top-ten finishers in the international competition. In recent years she has begun pageants for younger girls to develop future talented teens.

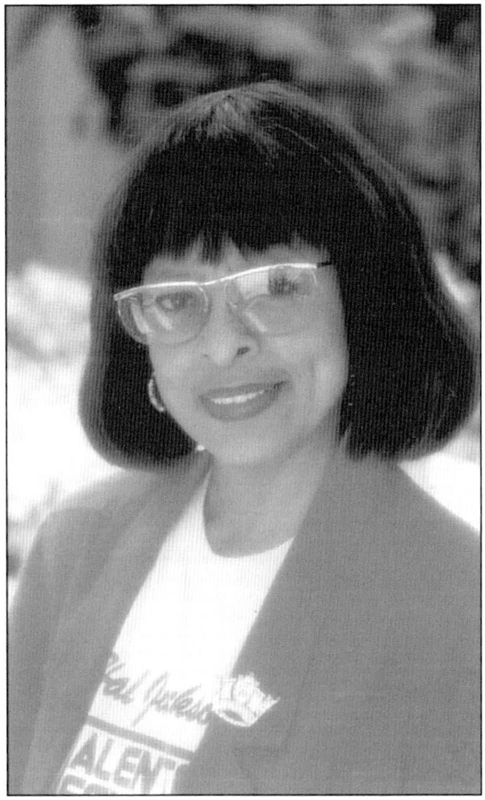

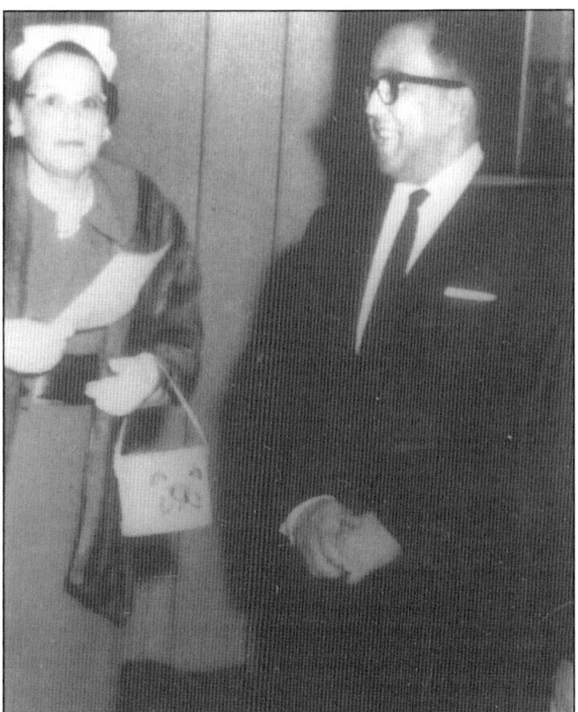

Langston Hughes. Hughes, right, made a visit to his roots in the late 1950s. Fayetteville is the hometown of his grandmother, Mary Patterson Learry, who lived until her late teens in the area near the present location of First Baptist Church. She left during the migration of the 1850s and settled in Ohio. She married Lewis Learry, who was killed at Harpers Ferry, West Virginia. Later, she helped to raise Langston Hughes. Although she was not totally supportive of his writing, she made sure he had a good education. An important figure in the Harlem Renaissance, Hughes authored more than a dozen books of poetry and many of his works are considered classics.

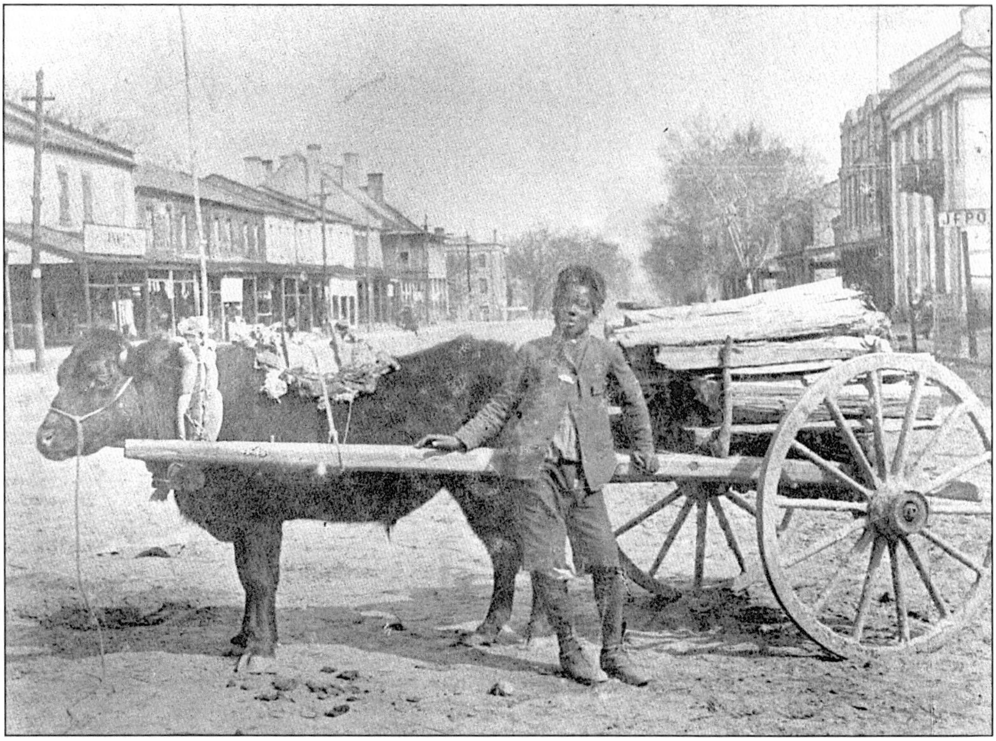

Early Black in Fayetteville. This is one of the best-known images of a black person in Fayetteville. This young, unidentified boy is selling wood from an oxcart around 1898.

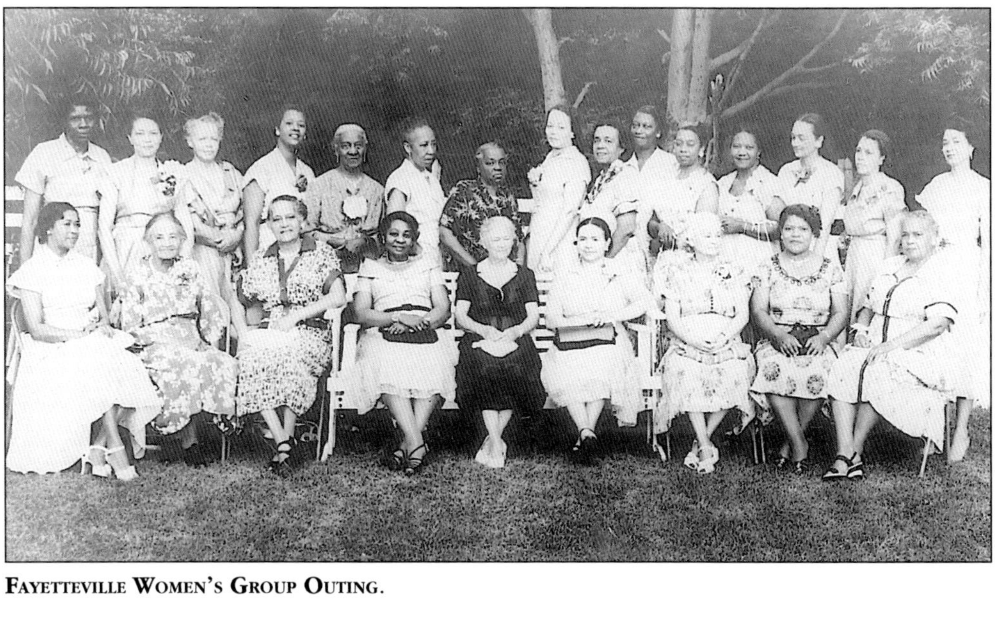

Fayetteville Women's Group Outing.

LATANYA DEE MAJOR HARDY. One of the greatest athletes in the history of Cumberland County high school sports, Hardy starred, at E.E. Smith, in volleyball, basketball, and track and was all-conference in each sport. Hardy attended Pembroke State, where she participated in volleyball and basketball, earning All-Carolina's Conference, All-District, and All-NAIA honors in basketball as a senior. She was also named the Lady Braves' most valuable player. She is third in career scoring for the Braves with 1,555 points and still holds the school record with 504 assists. Hardy was Carolina's Conference Female Athlete of the Year in 1986. In volleyball, Hardy was named All-State, All-Conference, All-District, Carolina's Conference Player of the Year as a senior, and the team's player of the year. Hardy is now the volleyball and basketball coach at E.E. Smith. She was inducted into the Pembroke State University Athletic Hall of Fame in 1995.

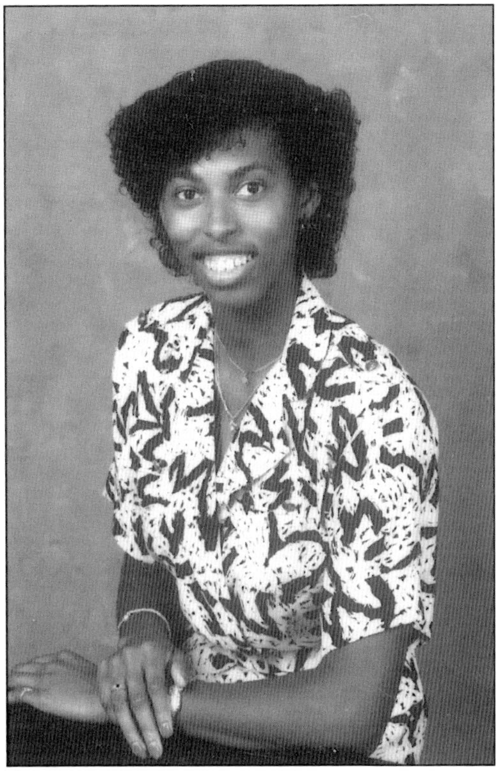

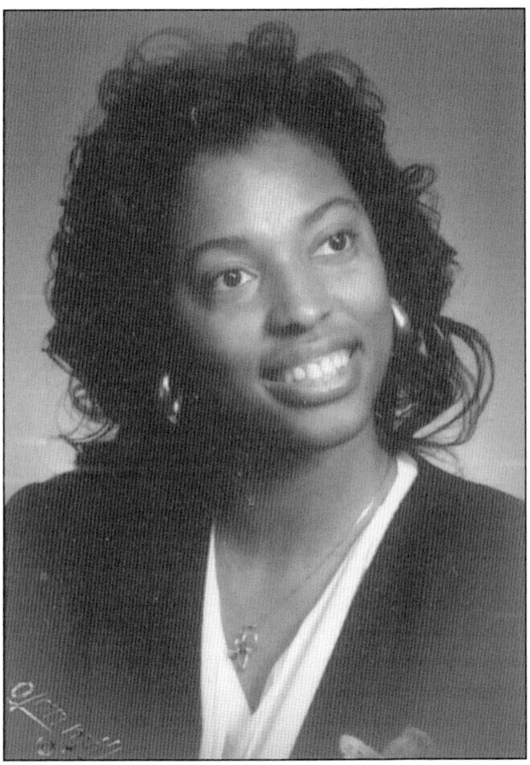

ROSZELLA A. MAJOR-WILLIAMS. She was the Mid-South Athlete of the Year in 1978, earning All-Conference honors in volleyball, basketball, and track. She still holds the record for the triple jump in the regionals. In addition to excelling as an athlete, she was also a member of the National Honor Society. In college, at East Carolina, Major-Williams starred in volleyball and track and lettered in field hockey. Though hampered by injuries, she still lettered each year. After college, Major-Williams entered coaching, achieving coach-of-the-year honors in 1990, 1991, and 1995. She was also teacher of the year in 1990 and named Who's Who among High School Teachers. She is now assistant principal at Terry Sanford High School.

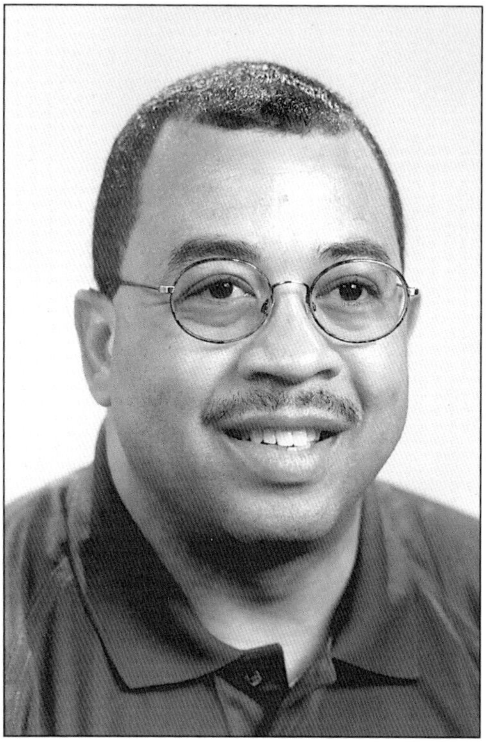

Charles Baggett. When people talk about quarterbacks in Cumberland County schools, the name Charles Baggett invariably comes up. He was the premier quarterback for E.E. Smith High School's legendary D.T. Carter in the late 1960s. Baggett's football career began in midget league at Seabrook Park under "Monk" Smith. He moved into the starting role as a sophomore, and during his first year, the Golden Bulls posted a record of 8-1-1. They faced cross-town Terry Sanford for the first time, and they lost, 29-0, in their only loss of the year. E.E. Smith was the black state co-champions. Baggett earned a scholarship to UNC, but they were not ready for a quarterback and asked Baggett to change. He refused and transferred to Michigan State, where another former Golden Bull, Jimmy Raye, was coaching. He starred at quarterback for the Spartans for three years. After graduation, Baggett went into coaching at his alma mater. In 1994, he moved up to the professional level and is now with the Minnesota Vikings.

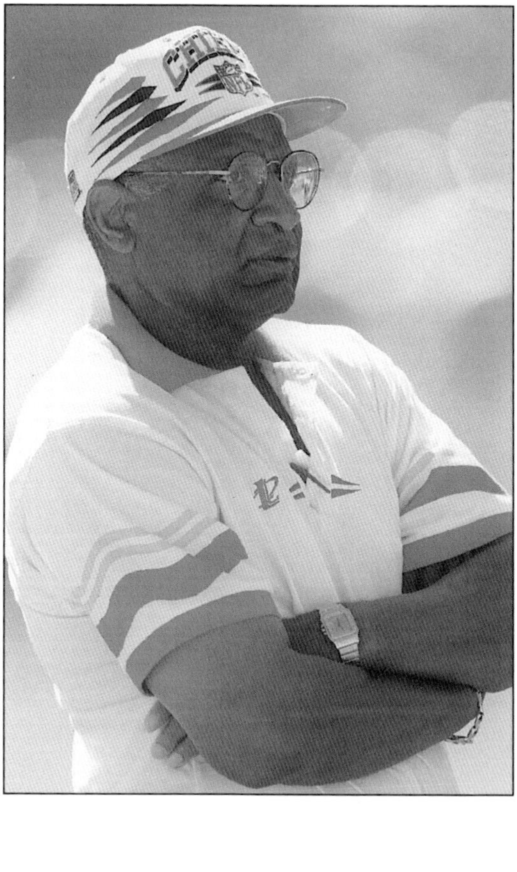

Jimmy Raye. The first great quarterback to play under D.T. Carter, Raye, as a senior, led the Golden Bulls to their first conference title. Raye had every skill that any college program could want, but he was black. No Southern school would take him, so Raye went to Michigan State. There, he established himself as a great quarterback. In 1966, he had a banner year with the Spartans, leading them to the Rose Bowl Championship. The only blemish on their record was a 10-10 tie with Notre Dame. After graduation, Raye made a name for himself as a coach. A student of the game, he has served as an assistant and offensive coordinator for several professional teams. His name is mentioned prominently among those who are likely to become head coaches in the NFL.

CARL GALBREATH. At 5 foot, 8 inches and 168 pounds, Galbreath was the most dominant back in the CIAA. He led the North Carolina Central Eagles in rushing yardage for four years and was a three-time All-CIAA selection and a member of the 1948 *Pittsburgh Courier* All-American team. But his skills were not restricted to football. He was also a member of the Eagles basketball team and played for the legendary John McLendon. In 1946, Galbreath was a member of the team that won the first CIAA Tournament. Galbreath returned to Fayetteville as a teacher and coach. He worked at Anne Chesnutt and later at Seventy-First. He served as an assistant principal until his retirement.

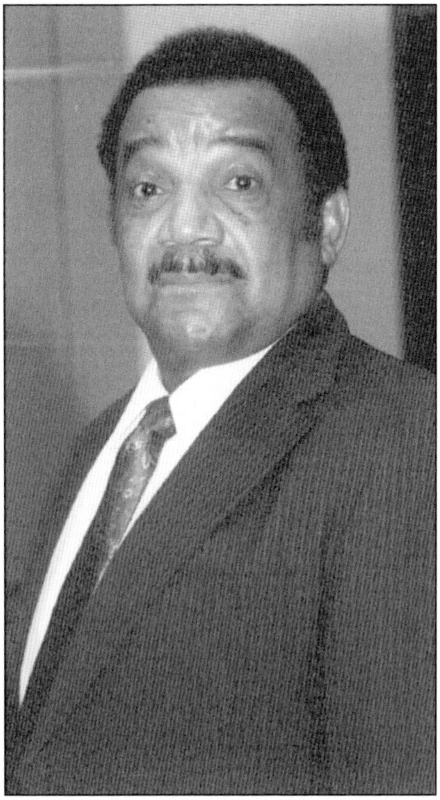

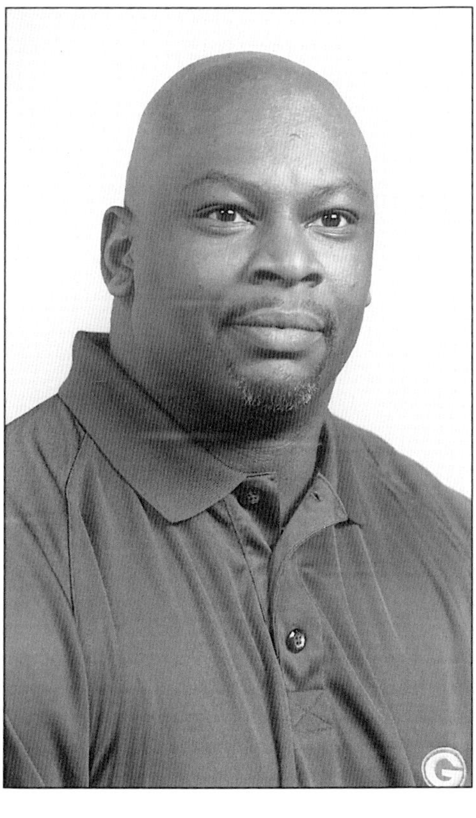

HARRY SYDNEY. A local star in football and basketball at Seventy-First High School, Sydney was the quarterback of the powerful Falcons and played on the tennis team. He earned a scholarship to the University of Kansas, where he was an All–Big Eight running back. Like many young men, Sydney aspired to play football professionally. In 1987, he signed with the San Francisco 49ers and made the team as one of five running backs out of ten in the pre-season camp. Sydney played backup fullback and distinguished himself as a special teams player. He was a member of two Super Bowl teams. After retirement in the early 1990s, Sydney went into coaching. In 1997, he earned his third Super Bowl ring as a running back coach for the Green Bay Packers.

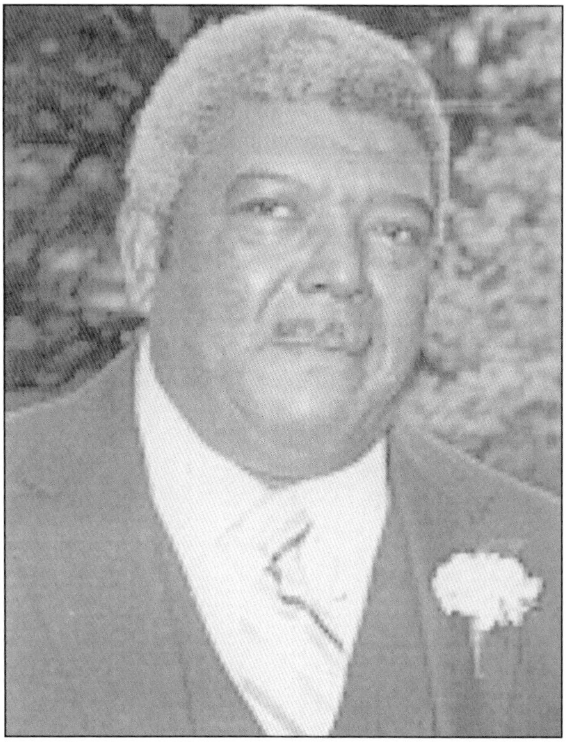

Charles Fuller. One of the most successful men to be born in Fayetteville, Fuller built his company from scratch into one of the Black Enterprise 100 Black Businesses. Mr. Fuller spent his childhood in the Wilmington Road area and graduated from E.E. Smith. After three years in the Army, he started a company with a used oil truck and worked out of his home on the kitchen table. He built it into a business with $10 million in sales. He understood the need for blacks to have access to finances, so he helped to establish United National Bank. He kept the bank solvent by continually putting his own money in it. Mr. Fuller was recognized in 1987 as North Carolina Minority Business Person of the Year.

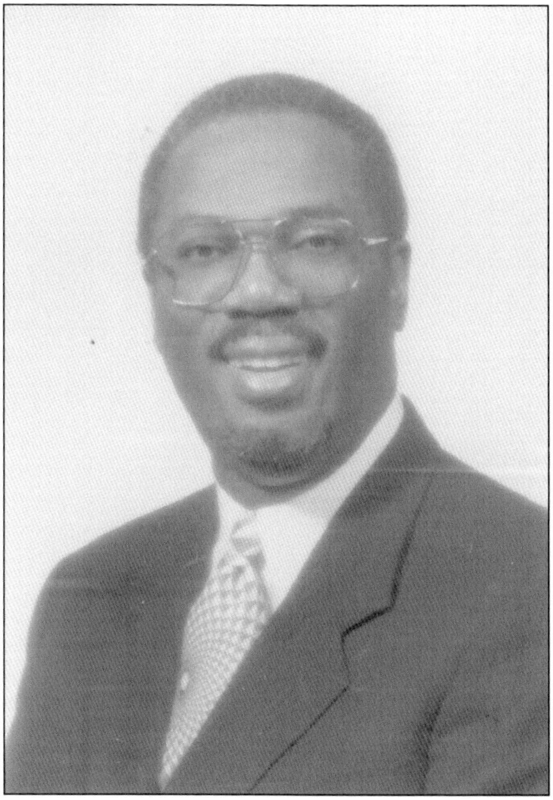

Dr. John D. Fuller. Dr. Fuller has been pastor of Lewis Chapel Baptist Church since 1973. Under his leadership, Lewis Chapel is the one of the fastest-growing congregations in the area. Fuller has worked tirelessly in the community and the church. He has served as the president of the Union Baptist Association, fourth vice-president of the General Baptist State Convention of North Carolina, chairman of the Human Relations Committee (Union Baptist Association), co-chairman of the Joint Relations Committee (Union South River Associations), a member of the executive board of the Lott Carey Foreign Missionary Convention, and a member of the Shaw School of Divinity Board of Visitors. He presently serves as the president of the General Baptist Convention.

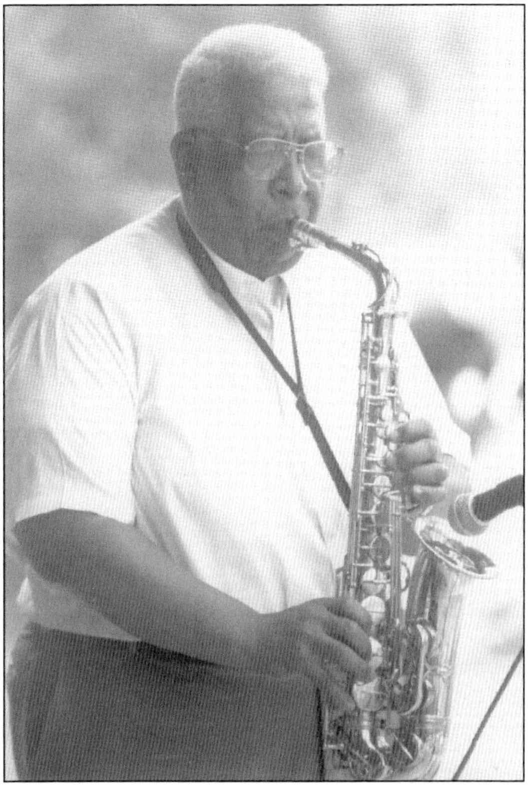

Thomas Gavin. An auto mechanics teacher at Fayetteville State and an accomplished saxophonist, Gavin helped to organize the concert band for Fine Arts Week in 1958. This band was the foundation for the Fayetteville State Band, which was founded by Thomas Bacote that same year. Gavin had a distinguished career in music. He had played in a military band during World War II and was a member of the Rhythm Vets, who performed on the soundtrack for the movie *Pitch a Boogie Woogie*. After retiring from teaching, Gavin continued to play jazz with Malachi Sharpe.

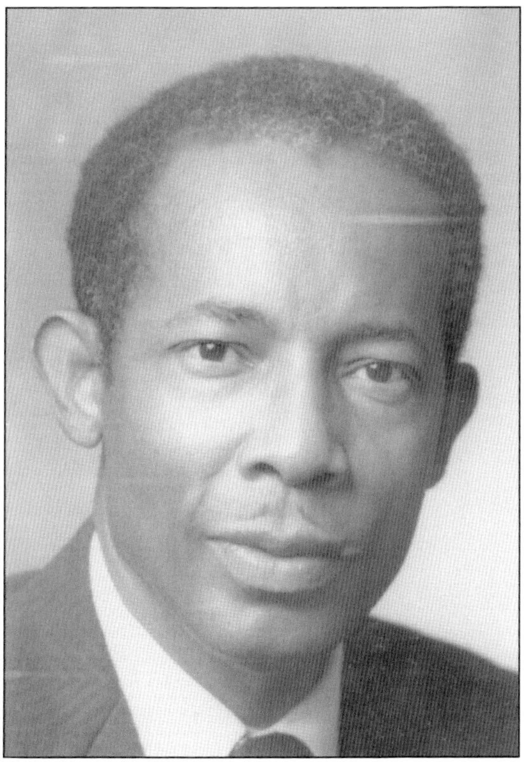

Dr. Marion George. Dr. George entered North Carolina A&T State University (NCA&T), but his education was interrupted by a military duty—he served as a combat soldier in World War II. George was severely injured in combat and lost his arm. He later earned a B.S. degree from NCA&T. Dr. George made history when he completed his doctoral work, becoming the first veteran to earn three degrees under the Veterans Rehabilitation Bill. A member of Evans Metropolitan AME Zion Church, Dr. George has served as a district director of Christian education. One of his most notable achievements was his election to the Fayetteville City Council in 1969. He was only the second black to be elected to the council since Reconstruction. He served for ten years—two as mayor-pro-tem.

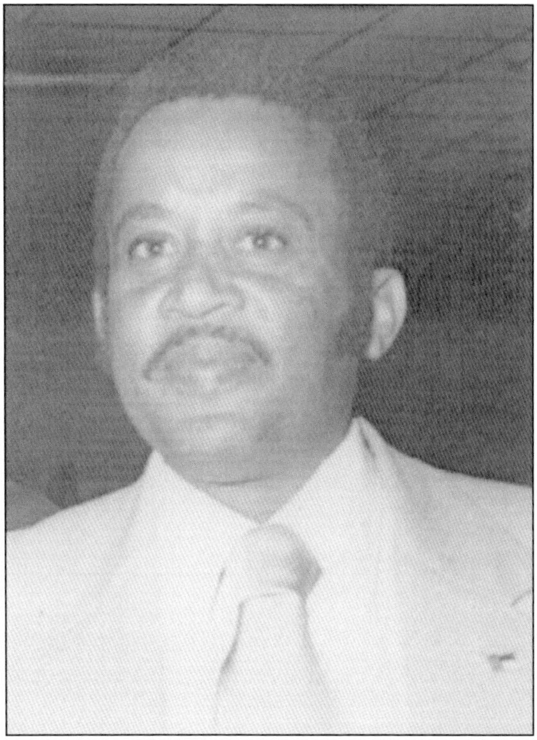

Marion "Rex" Harris. In 1966, Harris bought A & H Cleaners, which was nearly bankrupt and in a previously all-white section of Bragg Boulevard. Over the next few years, Harris was constantly harassed—a cross was burned in front of his store and bullets were fired into his car. Finally, in 1968, A & H Cleaners was burned to the ground. This fire came just after he was awarded a five-year contract with Fort Bragg. By 1970, Harris had rebuilt and expanded A & H Cleaners, and in 1981, he ventured into another area with Rexon Coal Company, a business that brokers coal to such companies as DuPont, Cannon Mills, Camp LeJeune, CP & L, and Detroit Edison. Throwing his hat in the political arena, Harris was appointed to the state board of transportation under Governor Holshouser. Harris is a driven man and one of America's prize entrepreneurs.

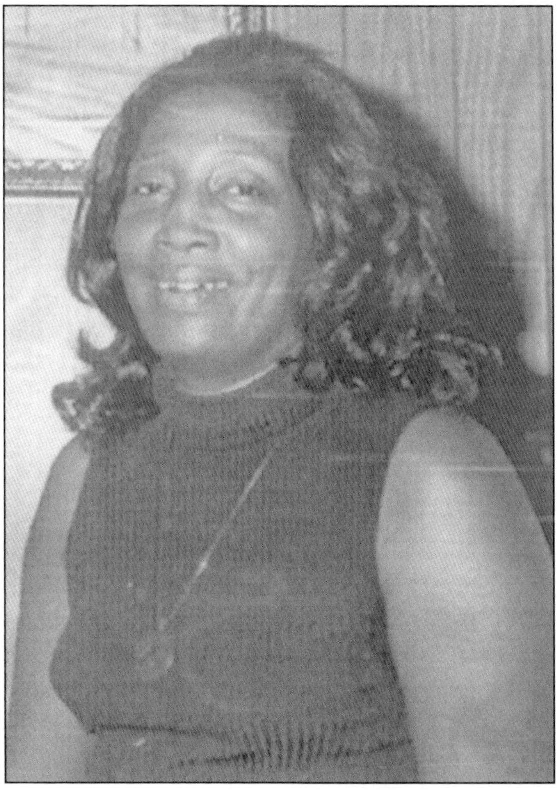

Martha Hayes. Hayes was a cosmetologist, with a specialty in hair weaving. She was known for her flamboyant styles and her ability to help those with extreme hair problems. An interest that she pursued diligently was the creation of clothes fashioned from hair. She created several dresses from human hair, including one that was placed in Ripley's Believe It or Not Museum in 1989. The dress was also featured on television. A woman of generosity, Mrs. Hayes was a licensed Pentecostal minister and the pastor of Matchem Chapel Pentecostal Church in Eureka Springs until her death.

Dr. Maurice B. Hayes. Earning his B.A. at Fayetteville State, Dr. Hayes was the first black to earn a degree in elementary education. He worked as a teacher and a principal in Hoke County and later became dean of Continuing Education at Sampson Technical Community College in Clinton. He joined the staff of Fayetteville State as the director of Institutional Development and served until his retirement. Active in the community, he was one of the founders and driving forces of the Gospel Singing Union and the Youth Singing Union. An ordained minister, he presently serves as the pastor of Beauty Spot Baptist Church.

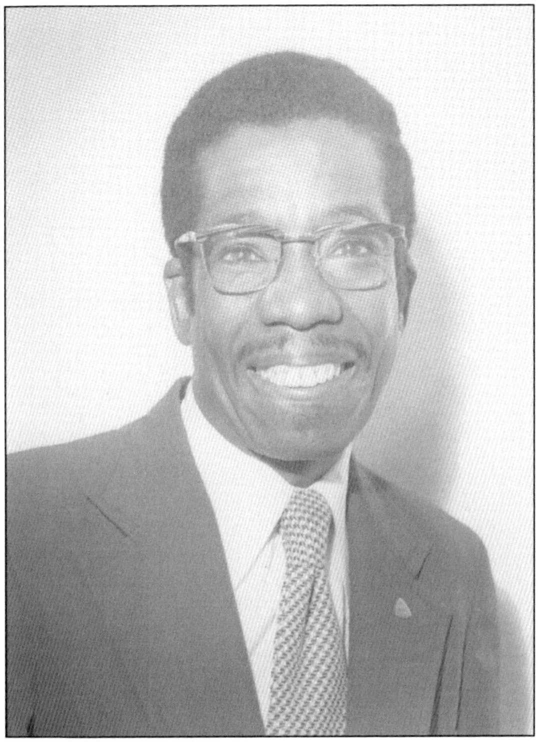

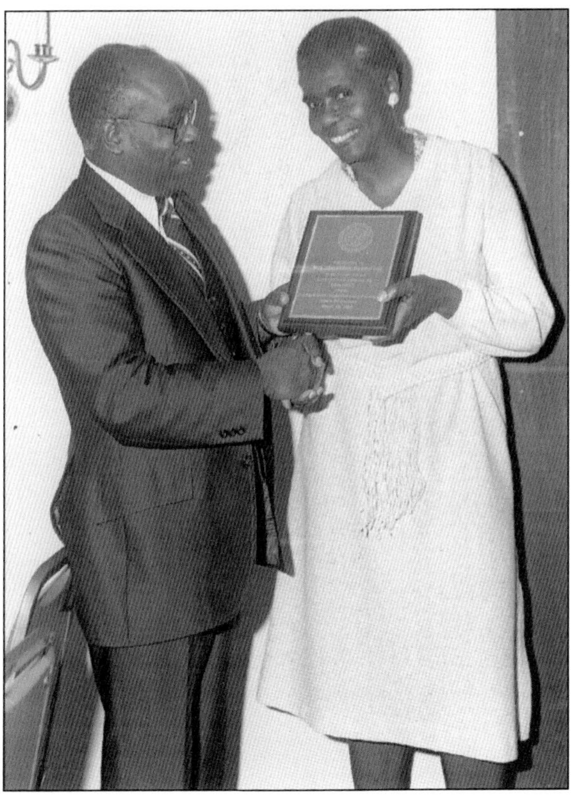

Geraldine T. Henderson. Mrs. Henderson entered Fayetteville State at the age of 40 and graduated magna cum laude. She did a brief stint in the classroom in the Fayetteville School System, but then left the classroom and spent 20 years working with the Social Security Administration. Mrs. Henderson serves as the president of the Afro-American Heritage Group and has served on the board of the Cumberland County Mental Health Department, the Personnel Review Board for the City of Fayetteville, the Mayor's Bond Issue Task Force, and the Jefferson Awards Screening Committee. She has long been a life member of the NAACP and has served for several years as its branch president.

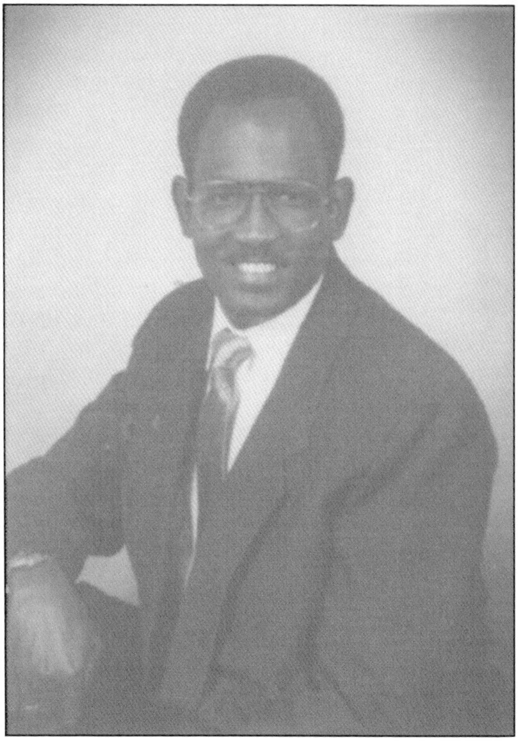

Bishop Kenneth L. Hill. A retired soldier, Bishop Hill spent time in the Army's Special Operations Command, and while on active duty, he organized two churches. A pastor of the North Ramsey Street Church of God, Hill was elected president of the Southeastern Regional Fellowship in 1944. This organization oversees churches in eight Southeastern states and involves 75 churches. Hill s a member of the Church of God Eastern North Carolina State Evangelism and Home Mission Board. He also serves on the State Ministerial Examining Board and is district overseer of the Sandhills District of Eastern North Carolina. Bishop Hill provides a platform for the training of pastors and has a full understanding of the need for being prepared.

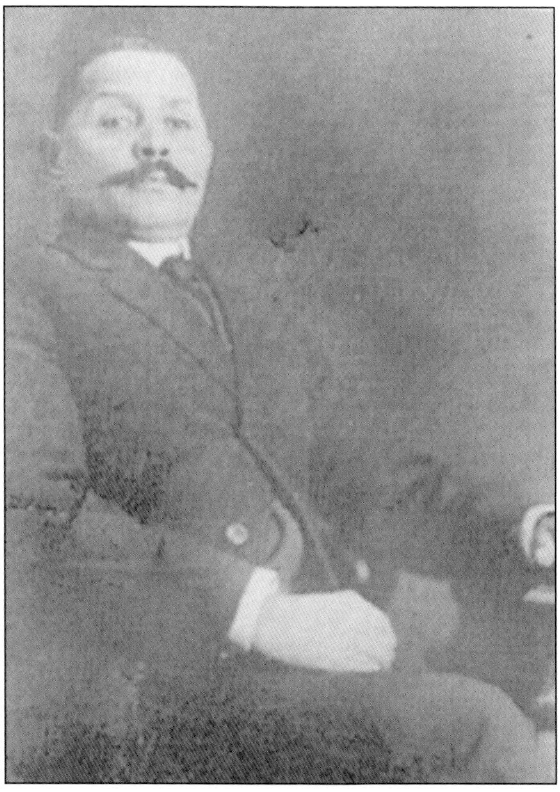

Samuel Hodges. Born in the Manchester area of the county and the oldest of nine children, Hodges was forced to work at an early age in the wood industries. When the cotton mill opened, the company called it Hope Mill. Hodges was the company's jack-of-all trades, playing the role of the blacksmith, carpenter, chauffeur, cook, horse trainer, medicine man, mill watchman, and payroll carrier. His work ethic showed that he believed in his motto: "It is better to wear out than rust out." The company had a need for lots of wood, and to meet that need, the company offered Hodges land in return for the wood he cut and hauled to the mill. Taking advantage of the offer, by 1887, he owned 300 acres of land, making him one of the major landowners in Cumberland County. Hodges would eventually triple his holdings.

Dr. William Taft Holland Sr. Born in Holly Springs, North Carolina, Dr. Holland received his degrees from Shaw University. He began his ministry as a circuit pastor and, in 1955, was appointed pastor of St. Luke AME Church, where he served for 14 years. In 1969, Dr. Holland was appointed presiding elder of the North Carolina Conference, holding that position for 22 years before retiring. Active in the community, Holland served on the board of directors of Kittrell College, was a commissioner of the Fayetteville Metropolitan Housing Authority, and was a life member of the NAACP. Most notably, Dr. Holland was awarded the Connectional Lay Organization of the African Methodist Episcopal Church.

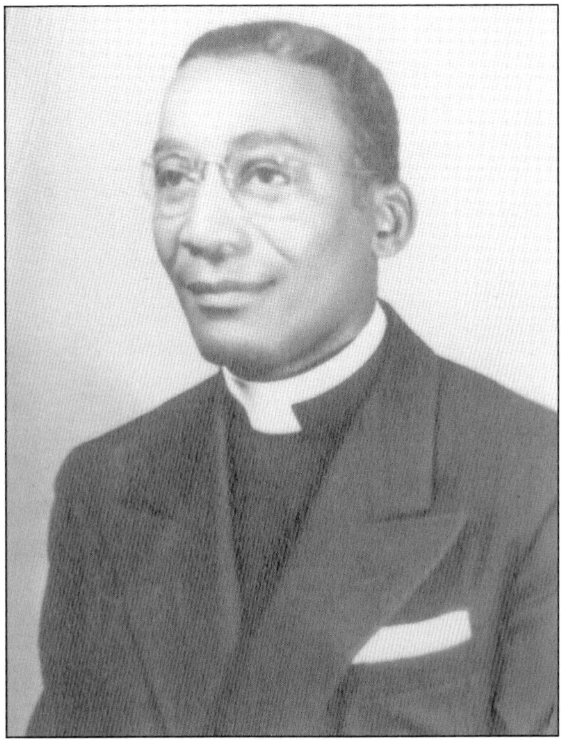

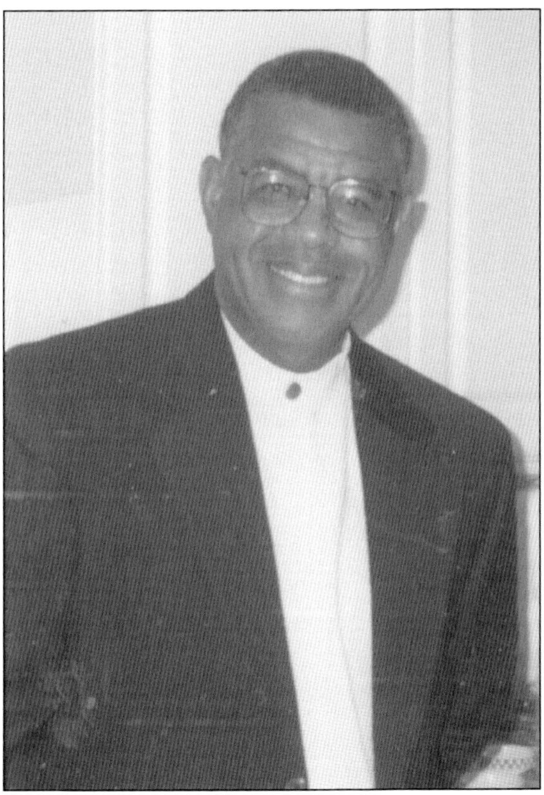

Dr. Carey Hughley. A native of Fayetteville, Hughley graduated from E.E. Smith High School, where he played football for D.T. Carter. He also played quarterback for Hampton Institute and was the team's most valuable player in 1964–1965, leading the team in passing, total offense, and punting. With a minor in biology, he graduated with honors in 1966 with a degree in health, physical education, and recreation. He earned a master's degree from the University of Massachusetts and a Ph.D. from Ohio State. He has done extensive study in the area of cardiac risk reduction through supervised exercise programs. Dr. Hughley is presently an administrator at North Carolina Central University, having served as the athletic director and a member on the Faculty Athletic Committee.

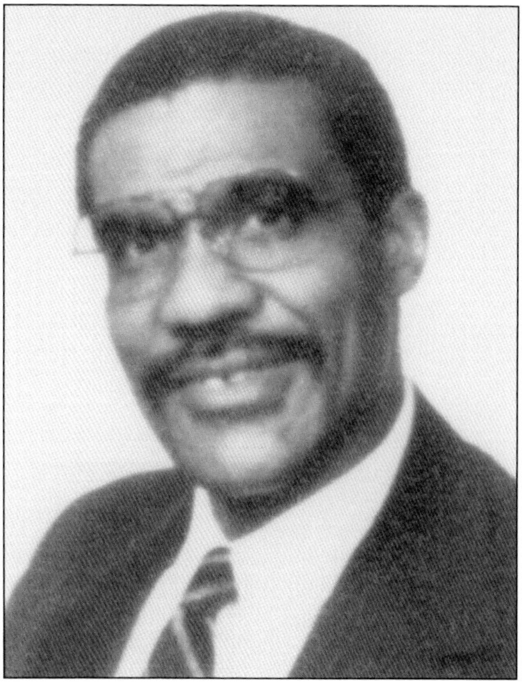

Luther "Nick" Jeralds. A graduate of E.E. Smith and North Carolina Central University, Jeralds returned to Fayetteville to enter business after a brief tenure in professional football. He was also active in local politics, holding a number of board and committee memberships. In 1982, he was elected to the 17th District House seat and held the seat for ten years. He died in 1993. Nick Jeralds Middle School and the football stadium at Fayetteville State are named in his honor.

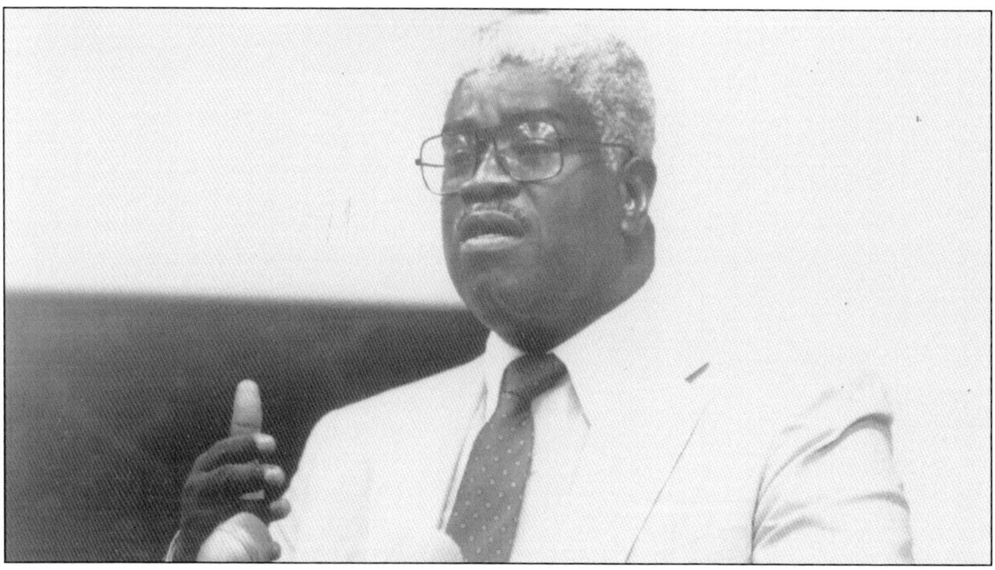

Dr. Aaron J. Johnson. A pastor Mt. Sinai Baptist Church, Johnson worked as a community relations consultant for the North Carolina Human Relations Commission in the early 1970s. In 1981, Johnson successfully ran for city council and served two terms. During his second term, he served as mayor pro-tem, was a delegate to the Republican National Convention in 1980, and was chosen to deliver the opening invocation. He served as a member of the North Carolina Committee to elect Ronald Reagan in 1980 and 1984. In 1984, he was chairman of the Minority Affairs Committee for Jim Martin. On January 7, 1985, Johnson was sworn in as the sixth secretary of corrections for the State of North Carolina. He was the first black member of the governor's cabinet in the twentieth century.

REVEREND CURETON L. JOHNSON. Reverend Johnson was called into the ministry in 1976 and was ordained by the Martin Street Baptist Church in Raleigh, his home church. His first pastoral position was New Red Mountain Baptist Church in Durham County. Under his leadership, the church constructed a new sanctuary and fellowship hall. Prior to coming to Fayetteville, Reverend Johnson was a pastor of the Baptist Grove Baptist Church in northwest Raleigh. In 1991, he assumed the pastorate of First Baptist Church in Fayetteville. During his tenure, the church has added 36 units of senior citizens housing to their inventory of low-income housing. The development is called Edwards Place in honor of the previous pastor, Dr. C.R. Edwards. In addition to his pastoral duties, Reverend Johnson has taken an active role in the community and is poised to lead First Baptist into the twenty-first century.

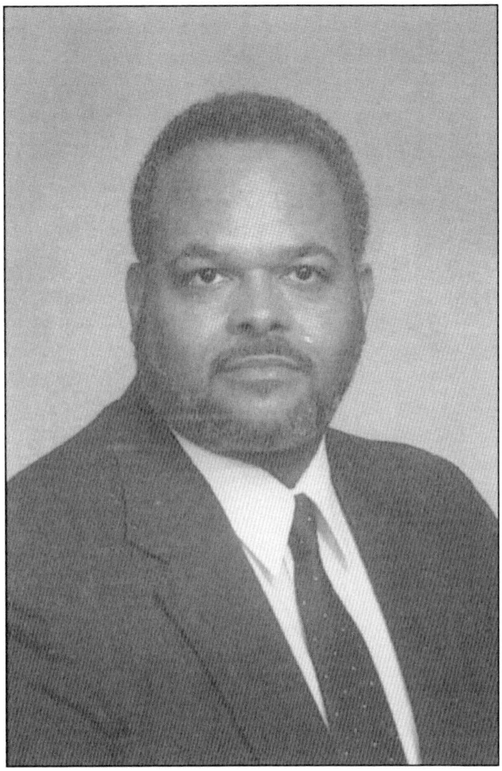

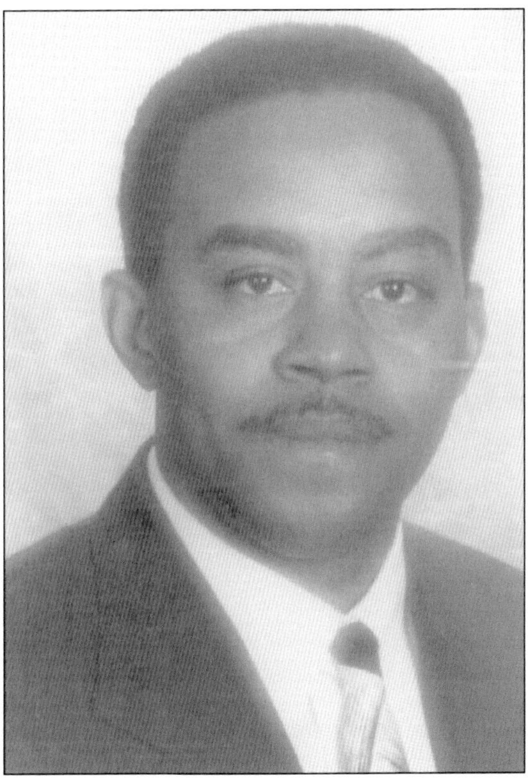

J.J. JONES. Jones founded the *Fayetteville Press* out of an idea that had been bounced around by two friends. The odds were against it from the beginning since neither man knew how to produce a newspaper, though both had been journalists in the military. Jones had spent some time working with the *Challenger* in 1987, but the paper was moved out of Fayetteville in 1989. Still, Jones parleyed his skills as a photographer into a winning newspaper. People around Fayetteville recognize and respect "JJ" for his veracity and confidence. His involvement in and dedication to the community has opened doors for Jones and his paper. Though it is only published monthly, the newspaper is possibly the best-composed paper to ever serve the black community.

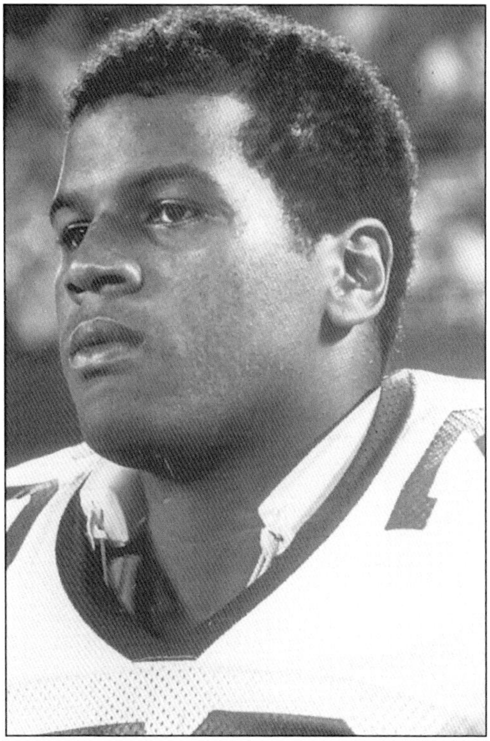

Marvin Powell. Born at Fort Bragg, Powell became one of the most dominant athletes ever to play in Cumberland County. At Seventy-First High School, he excelled in football, basketball, and track. and was named all-conference three times, as well as all-state and All-American in 1973. He earned a scholarship to the University of Southern California, where he was moved to offensive tackle and was named All-PAC 8 three times, and All-American twice. He played in three Rose Bowls and the Liberty Bowl. Powell was drafted by the New York Jets in 1977 and made an immediate impact on the National Football League. He was named to the All-Rookie team and would go on to a stellar career. He was named to the Pro Bowl five times, was the Jets' most valuable player in 1979, and won the 1982 Forrest Gregg Lineman of the Year Award. He also served as the team's union representative.

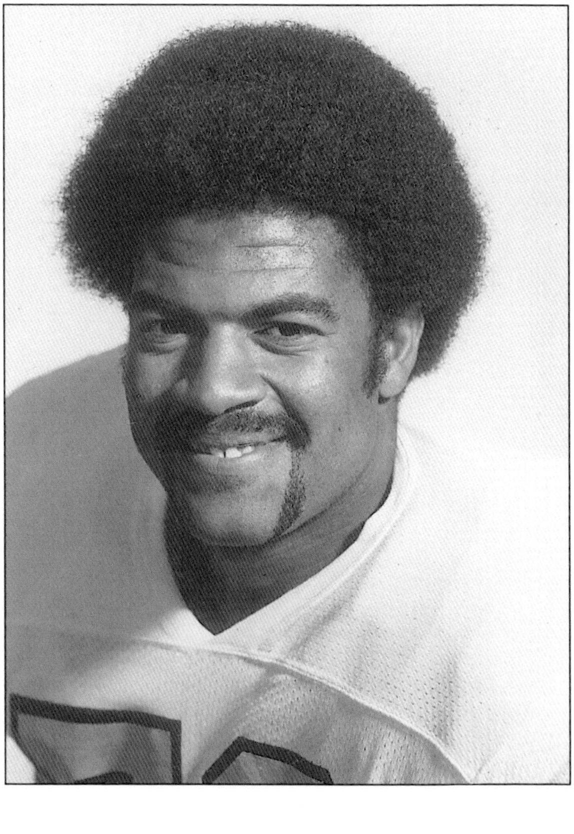

Larry Tearry. An All-American tackle for D.T. Carter, Tearry was recruited by Wake Forest and changed to center. At the time, he was the only black playing the position at a major college. He was named All-ACC and to the Kodak All-American team in 1977. Tearry was drafted by the Detroit Lions in 1978 and moved into the starting line-up as a rookie. He went on to earn All-Pro honors, though his career was cut short by injuries. Returning home, Tearry became a teacher and has coached at the junior high/middle school, high school, and college levels. He is currently teaching and coaching at Terry Sanford High School.

JAMES HAWKINS. Hawkins graduated from Fayetteville State Normal School in 1936 and earned his bachelor's degree in 1942 and later his master's degree from Iowa. He worked with Coaches Armstrong and Black at Fayetteville State. In 1947, Hawkins joined the staff of the Xavier University as the head basketball coach, and in 1960, he became the athletic director, head basketball coach, and assistant football coach at Fort Valley State College. In 1980, he retired as the athletic director and went on to serve as the commissioner of the Southern Intercollegiate Athletic Conference (SIAC) until 1990. One of the earliest black members, Hawkins served as a member of the NCAA Council from 1971 to 1973 and also on the basketball and track and field committees for Division III. Throughout the years, Mr. Hawkins has remained close to Fayetteville State, for he helped to establish the Fayetteville State Athletic Hall of Fame.

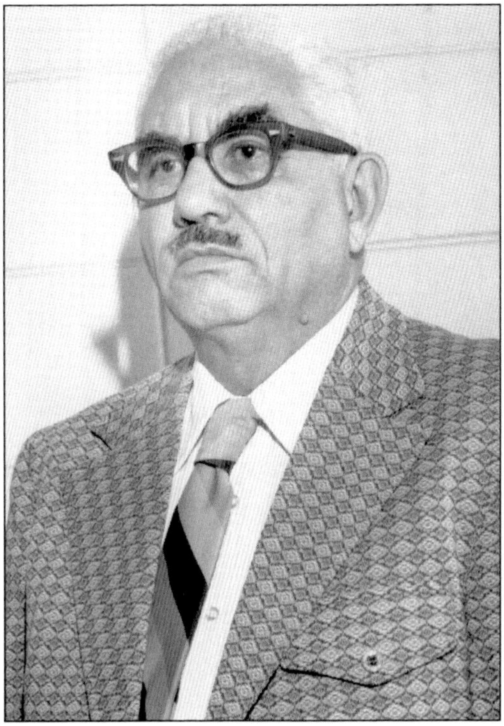

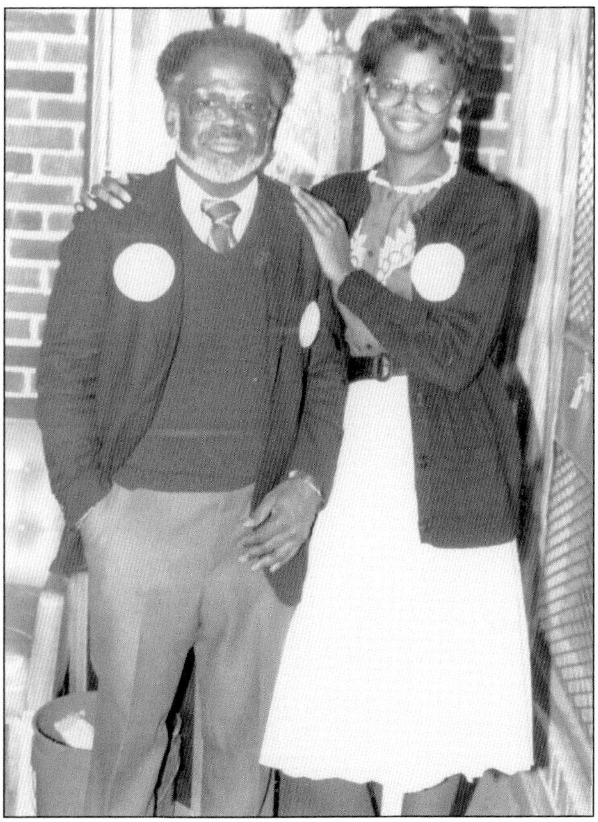

MARION AND WRENN CROWE. Both father and daughter graduated from Fayetteville State in 1985. A retired sergeant major, Marion Crowe was active in student government and was a statistician for the football team. While he was working with the recreation department, he trained several Double-Dutch national champions. He is now a sports information director. His daughter, Wrenn, was Miss FSU and is now a business executive.

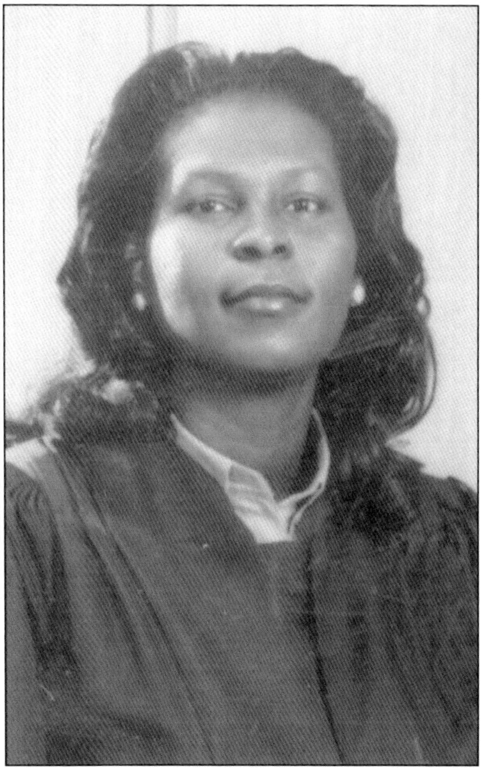

Judge Patricia Timmons-Goodson. Her first cases were fought on the basketball courts around Cumberland County, where Timmons-Goodson proved that she was a winner. After earning her undergraduate and law degrees from the University of North Carolina, she continued her winning ways in the courts of law. First, she served as a staff lawyer for the Lumber River Legal Services. Then, she moved to the district attorney's office. In 1984, she was appointed district court judge in the 12th Judicial District and was later re-elected to three consecutive terms. During her years on the bench, she was known for her fairness, compassion, and firmness. In addition to her day duties, she served on the North Carolina Courts Commission and the North Carolina Supreme Court Dispute Resolution Committee. She is a member of the North Carolina Association of Black Lawyers and the Association of District Court Judges. In January 1997, she was appointed to the North Carolina Court of Appeals and was elected to that position in 1998.

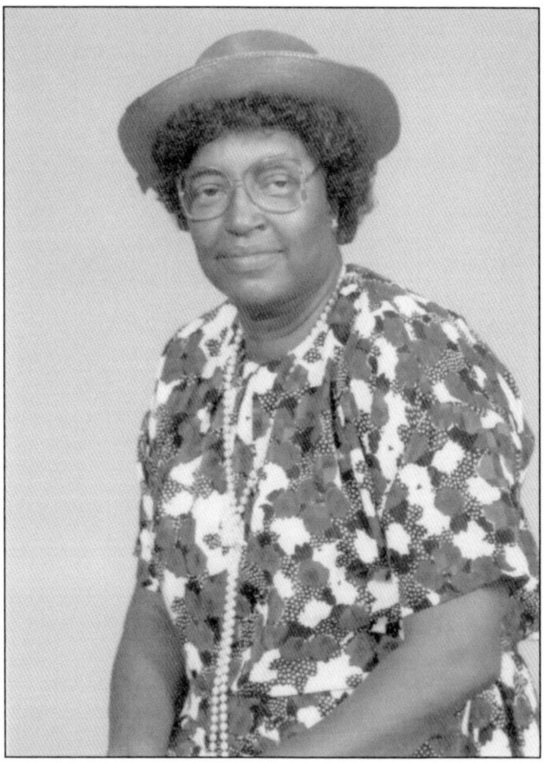

Lula B. Whitted White. Educated at Livingstone College and Fayetteville State, Lula worked in several professions, including teaching adult veterans' classes in Bladen County and teaching elementary and middle school classes in Harnett County. A longtime member of the Dove Chapel AME Zion Church, she has served as an usher, choir member, president of the Lay Council, chairman of the Home Missions Board, class leader, and treasurer. She served one year as assistant to the president of the Goldsboro District Women's Home and Overseas Missions Society and then held the presidency for 37 years. She also served two and a half years as a board member of the North Carolina Alliance for the Mentally Ill.